Enterprise Resource Planning

A Managerial Perspective

Veena Bansal

Department of Industrial and Management Engineering
Indian Institute of Technology Kanpur

Pearson

Associate Editor–Acquisitions: Neeraj Bhalla

ISBN 978-81-317-8703-8

First Impression

Published by Pearson India Education Services Pvt. Ltd, CIN: U72200TN2005PTC057128

Head Office: 1st Floor, Berger Tower, Plot No. C-001A/2, Sector 16B, Noida – 201 301,Uttar Pradesh, India.

Registered Office: Featherlite, 'The Address' 5th Floor, Survey No 203/10B, 200 Ft MMRD Road,Zamin Pallavaram, Chennai - 600044
Website: in.pearson.com; Email:companysecretary.india@pearson.com

Digitally printed in India by Trinity Academy for Corporate Training Ltd, New Delhi in the year of 2025.

Dedicated to Manu, Gita and Devika

Contents

Preface

This book provides a managerial perspective to ERP projects. An ERP system is a software solution that integrates all facets of a business. When an ERP system is implemented and deployed in an organization, it impacts the culture of the organization, its processes, structure and everyone in the organization. Careful planning is required to handle an information technology project that involves people as well as organizational issues. In 2004, I, along with three of my students at Indian Institute of Technology Kanpur started exploring ERP systems and found it very interesting. We visited organizations of different sizes across the country to learn about the entire life cycle of ERP projects. The effort resulted into a graduate level course that I started teaching at IIT Kanpur to management students. I then started developing course notes which were augmented by the current research papers and my own consultancy work in the area of ERP and this has resulted in this book. It will serve as a textbook for a semester-long course on ERP as well as a reference book for practitioners.

A manager would be able to follow the book to manage an ERP project, whereas an uninitiated reader will gain a thorough understanding of an ERP project life cycle. The first chapter explains the role that an ERP system plays in an organization and its evolution. The stages theory that has been included in the first chapter is, very interestingly, applicable to an individual's evolution as well with different names of stages . Chapter 2 describes the life cycle of an ERP project. Each phase of the life cycle is covered in detail and in depth, supported by theoretical framework and examples in subsequent chapters. The exercises at the end of each chapter are divided into two parts with an objective of testing and applying the knowledge gained. I urge the readers to attempt exercises to get the best out of their reading effort. The references at the end of each chapter provide a rich source of knowledge that can be used for identifying research problems. Appendix B provides a list of cases that should be discussed in the class to help students identify with the issues involved. Chapter 9 covers management of ERP project. I have deliberately not included the technological aspect in this book. This is because the readers should get a clear idea that ERP is not an information technology project even though technology is involved and constitutes an important part. I hope reading the book will be an enriching and fulfilling experience for the readers.

VEENA BANSAL

Acknowledgements

I would like to acknowledge the contribution of Kishore, Pallavi and Deepak Bakshi, who travelled with me. TCS, Lucknow; and Siemens, Gurgaon; supported and guided us in the initial phases. ERP companies in Kanpur contributed in their own ways. I would like to thank Tripti Negi for contributing a new modeling technique, and Deepak Saxena for carrying out experimental work at later stages. RetailS provided me the opportunity to work with them and study their ERP project that forms the case study present in the book. I led the ERP project at IIIT Delhi that provided an environment to me for using my knowledge of the subject. The contents of the book have been used by MBA students at IIT Kanpur for two semesters. I thank my reviewers for providing very valuable feedback—slightly negative but largely positive—that has enhanced my confidence in my book. I would like to thank IIT Kanpur for providing a conducive environment for working on the book. My family and my friends provided the support that I needed when I used to sit for long hours with the emerging book. I would like to thank Pearson Education for undertaking this project. It has been a pleasure working with the young squad at Pearson.

VEENA BANSAL

About the Author

Dr Veena Bansal received her MS from the University of Connecticut, USA, and Ph.D. from the Indian Institute of Technology Kanpur in 1999. She has been a faculty member of industrial and management engineering at IIT Kanpur since. Her research interests include large information systems and optical character recognition (OCR). She has pioneered ERP education at IIT Kanpur. She has also led ERP implementation at various government and private organizations. She has conducted multiple faculty workshops for university alliance programme for SAP. She has also conducted courses on ERP systems for faculty members from various colleges and universities. She is very passionate about teaching and considers it her duty to share knowledge. This book is the culmination of this very thinking of hers. She has published over 20 research papers in national and international journals and proceedings. She, along with her Ph.D. student, has identified gap in requirements engineering for ERP systems and created a model to fill this gap. This work has been included in this book. Her work on Devanagari OCR is widely cited by researchers working on Indian as well as other scripts from across the world. She has travelled widely to present her research work. She has guided many M.Tech. and Ph.D. students. She has taught at the University of Connecticut, USA; HBTI, Kanpur; IIM Lucknow and Tribhuvan University, Nepal.

VEENA BANSAL

chapter 1

Introduction to Enterprise Resource Planning Systems

LEARNING OBJECTIVES

After reading this chapter, you will be able to understand:

- Value chain framework
- The problems with disintegrated data in an organization
- Evolution of enterprise resource planning (ERP) system and what ERP systems are?
- The role of ERP systems in an organization
- Three-tier architecture and its benefits
- Stages theory and its application to the evolution of ERP
- Differences between custom-built systems and ERP systems
- Scope of ERP systems
- Different business models and support of ERP systems
- Major ERP companies

1.1 INTRODUCTION

In 1979, Information Technology Serving Society, USA defined Information Technology (IT) as a mean for the collection, storage, processing, dissemination and use of information. Information technology is not confined to hardware and software but acknowledges the importance of man and the goals they sets for this technology, the values employed in making these choices, the assessment criteria used to decide whether they are controlling the technology and is being enriched by it. Figure 1.1 shows components of an information system. At the core, there is hardware that stores the data and the software that implements the standard operating procedures of the organization to reflect organizational goals. The users access the system through Intranet or Internet using one of the many technologies (shown in paranthesis in Figure 1.1).

Information technology systems have evolved in the last 50 years and an Enterprise Resource Planning (ERP) system is also an evolved IT system. The objective of an ERP system is to provide an integrated view of the business. In this chapter, we will see how a business functions, and the problems faced in the absence of an integrated view of the business. But everyone in an organization would not be interested in knowing everything about the business due to lack of time and domain knowledge. The management

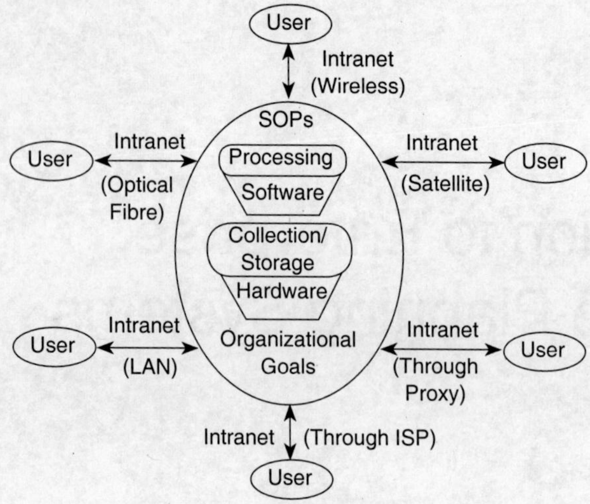

FIGURE 1.1 Information System and Its Components

cannot reveal everything about the business to everyone in the organization. An ERP system has an integrated database at the backend and provides different levels of access to data to different users. It virtually supports all types of businesses and their processes. In this chapter, we will learn about a framework that describes a business and how ERP supports the business. Of course, certain characteristics of ERP systems will enhance our understanding. ERP systems are different from a custom built software. It is important to understand the difference as it makes deployment of ERP system a challenge. By the end of this chapter, we will have a clear understanding of what ERP systems are, what they can do, and their characteristics.

1.2 VALUE CHAIN FRAMEWORK

The Value Chain Framework (Figure 1.2) of Michael Porter explains an organization as a system that performs activities to add value to its input. The value chain consists of the following units:

- Inbound logistics that include receiving, storing, inventory control and transportation scheduling.
- Operations that include machining, packaging, assembly, equipment maintenance, testing and all other value-creating activities that transform inputs to the final product.
- Outbound logistics include activities to get the finished product to the customers such as warehouse management, order fulfillment, transportation and distribution management.
- Sales and marketing include activities that will make a customer buy the product including advertising, channel selection, promotion, selling, pricing and retail management.
- Service includes customer support, repair services, installation, training and spare parts management.

These value-adding activities are supported by the following activities:

- Procurement of raw materials, spare parts, building and machines.
- Technology development—required to improve the products and services.
- Human resource management includes recruiting, training, retention and compensation of employees and management.
- Firm infrastructure includes general management, planning, finance, accounting and quality management.

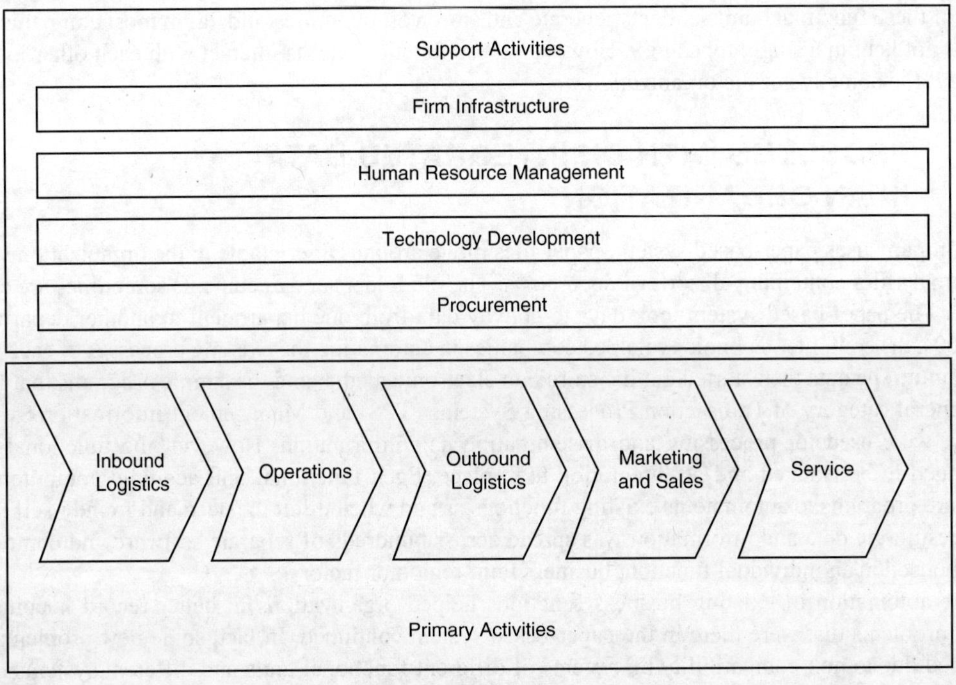

FIGURE 1.2 Michael Porter's Value Chain Framework

Organization can also be looked upon in terms of the following functional units (as shown in Figure 1.3):

- Sales and distribution
- Production planning
- Materials management
- Finance and accounting
- Human resource
- Procurement
- Infrastructure

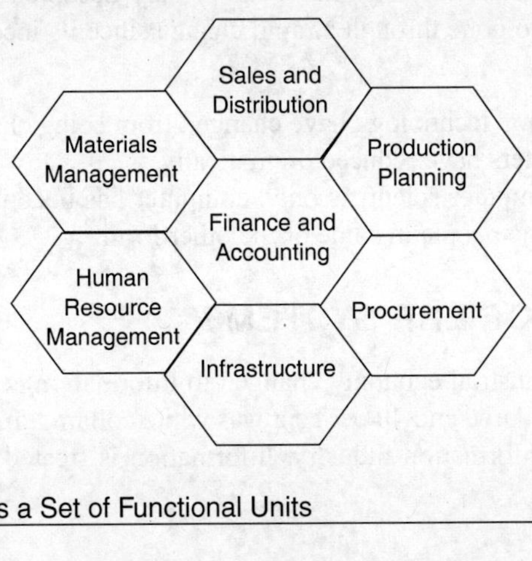

FIGURE 1.3 Organization as a Set of Functional Units

Each of these functional units collect, generate and store vast quantities of data. In most companies, the data is not kept in a single repository. However, these functional units interact with each other in order to fulfill the objective of the organization.

1.3 PROBLEMS WITH DISINTEGRATED DATA IN AN ORGANIZATION

If a company uses paper-based system, paper files move around. Every table in the organization would have many files containing all sorts of documents. The file folders and documents sometimes are colour coded. The paper-based system took days to convey data from one department to another department. In 1960s, the computer technology helped companies in automating the existing processes of each functional unit. The data then started getting stored on electronic media, and the simple programs that fall in the general category of Transaction Processing Systems (TPS) and Management Information Systems (MIS), were used for processing and disseminating data/information. However, the functional units continued to be isolated and no integration took place. Each functional unit acquired computers and software programs to automate its existing functions as and when it felt the need and found itself ready. As a result, the data and information was spread across hundreds of separate software and computers, each housed in an individual function, business unit, region or factory.[1]

The automation of existing business functions helped organizations in better record keeping but many problems that were there in the paper-based system continued. In fact, some new problems also surfaced due to non-compatibility of systems of different functional units and different systems of the same functional unit. Maintaining data on many different computers systems (hardware + software) lead to the following problems:

- A redundant, disorganized database structure.
- Inaccurate data.
- Difficulty in reporting and sharing information.
- Dependence on manual processes and human interventions.
- Problems in providing seamless customer service.
- Difficulty in complying with reporting requirements.
- Lack of capacity for process improvements.

Computer and information technology made an impact on every dimension of the business and its environment. The information technology has been widely accepted by the business community. Computer technology has also gone through a rapid change since its inception. The following are few of the examples.

- Computers and information technology have changed from being challenging to user friendly.
- The price tags on computers have reduced dramatically.
- From being useful to computer scientists only, computer has become an essential tool for everybody. It affects most of the people in some or the other form.

1.4 EVOLUTION OF ERP SYSTEMS

From 1960s to 1980s, the industrial economy changed to information economy. In 1960s, 60 per cent of the manpower was blue collared and 40 per cent was white collared. In 1980s, more than 50 per cent workforce was engaged in information industry. Information is treated as a resource in information economy. In the 1960s, the economy was based on manufacturing and the competitive strategy was to produce volumes at low cost (economies of scale). Companies could afford to maintain large quantities of inventories to meet production requirements and still stay competitive. In the 1970s, the companies could no longer afford to keep unlimited inventory. This led to the introduction of a system called Material Requirement Planning (MRP) followed by Manufacturing Resource Planning (MRP-II).[2] Main objective of MRP was to automate manual procedures for planning and controlling production schedules. MRP systems were designed to work back from the sales orders to determine the requirements for raw material for production. The objective was to integrate the functional units that had a direct impact on the competitive strategy such as sales and distribution, production, finance and accounting, and human resource. MRP is a complex system and consists of the following modules:

- Master production schedule
- Material requirements planning
- Bill of materials
- Inventory control
- Capacity requirements planning
- Rough cut capacity planning (high-level resource analysis)
- Routing/work centres
- Shop floor control
- Sales order processing
- Detailed operations scheduling
- Purchasing and receiving
- Forecasting
- Finance and accounting (MRP-II)
- Payroll/personnel (MRP-II)

MRP was a generic system that fell in general category of Commercial of the Shelf Systems (COTS). MRP represented a huge step forward in the material planning process. MRP system used sales order to work out a production schedule considering bill of materials (material needed to produce each finished product), available inventory and scheduled-to-arrive inventory. Once the requirements got calculated, it triggered events such as placing an order for procuring raw material. The system knew the time-to-procure and used this knowledge to modify the delivery dates if required or to cancel an order if it is clear that the supply date cannot be honoured. It used past sales data to forecast the demand for sales planning and customer order promising. Once the demand forecast became available, it is used to schedule procurements and production. MRP system also supported sales and operations planning to make use of the capacity of the manufacturing facility. MRP integrated main functional units of the organization through automatic data flow.

It is interesting to note that in 1970s, companies experienced difficulty in implementing MRP systems. Researchers studied the reasons for failure of MRP, and the consolidated reasons include organizational problems, technical problems and people problems. Managers did not believe in the capability of the system and did not spend enough effort to discover and use the potential of the system. MRP is an IBM mainframe system. The main objective of MRP was to manage inventory better, increase the efficiency of a manufacturing plant and hence serve the customer better by avoiding unnecessary delays. Organizations could justify purchasing MRP because they expected to reduce inventory cost and use their resources more efficiently. MRP was a generic system that IBM claimed would fit all businesses. However, not many business houses believed IBM as each of them thought their businesses to be considerably different from each others. Organizations who bought MRP also did not benefit from it as expected, because about 60 per cent of all MRP implementations failed. Failure could mean that return on investments (ROI) did not materialize as expected or the implementation overshot its budget or schedule or both. In the worst case, an organization had to halt its production. These failures are discussed in detail in further sections.

Let us look at the manner in which an organization evolves. Usually an organization is started by an individual or by a small group of people. The processes are all informally defined in an ad hoc manner. As the organization grows, more people are hired for performing different functions in the organization. Further growth is managed by adding more people to assist the existing staff. The data and information is shared only at the top level. Each department develops its own ad-hoc processes in isolation. There are no formal identified data flow paths. When these organizations implemented MRP to automate entry, storage, retrieval and flow of data, they did not know how it was all done. A leading consultant firm of US[3] reports that MRP requires 95 per cent accuracy in the bill of materials, 98 per cent accuracy in inventory balances, and a feedback to the planning process. In an informal environment, which was prevalent in most of the organization prior to micro-computer era, the required level of accuracy was difficult, if not impossible to achieve. MRP calculated Economic Order Quantity (EOQ) based on its own logic that was often times far from required quantity.

MRP and MRPII taught some important lessons and another big COTS solution ERP system came into the market Evolution of the information systems is shown in Figure 1.4. Gartner (claims to have) coined the term ERP in the early 1970s to describe the next generation of integrated manufacturing software. ERP is an information system that integrates data of all departments and functions across a company into one computer system. ERP runs off a single database, enabling various departments to share information with each other. It is a business management system that integrates all facets of the business including planning, manufacturing, sales and marketing. ERP automates finance and human resources departments, and helps manufacturers handle jobs such as order processing and production scheduling.

As an example, let us look at the sales process of a retailing organization. The process is shown in Figure 1.5. A sales order is received by a company for product X. The availability of the product is checked

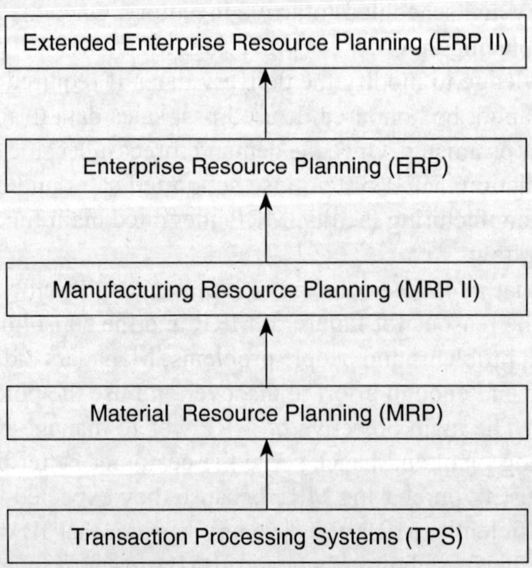

FIGURE 1.4 Evolution of Information Systems

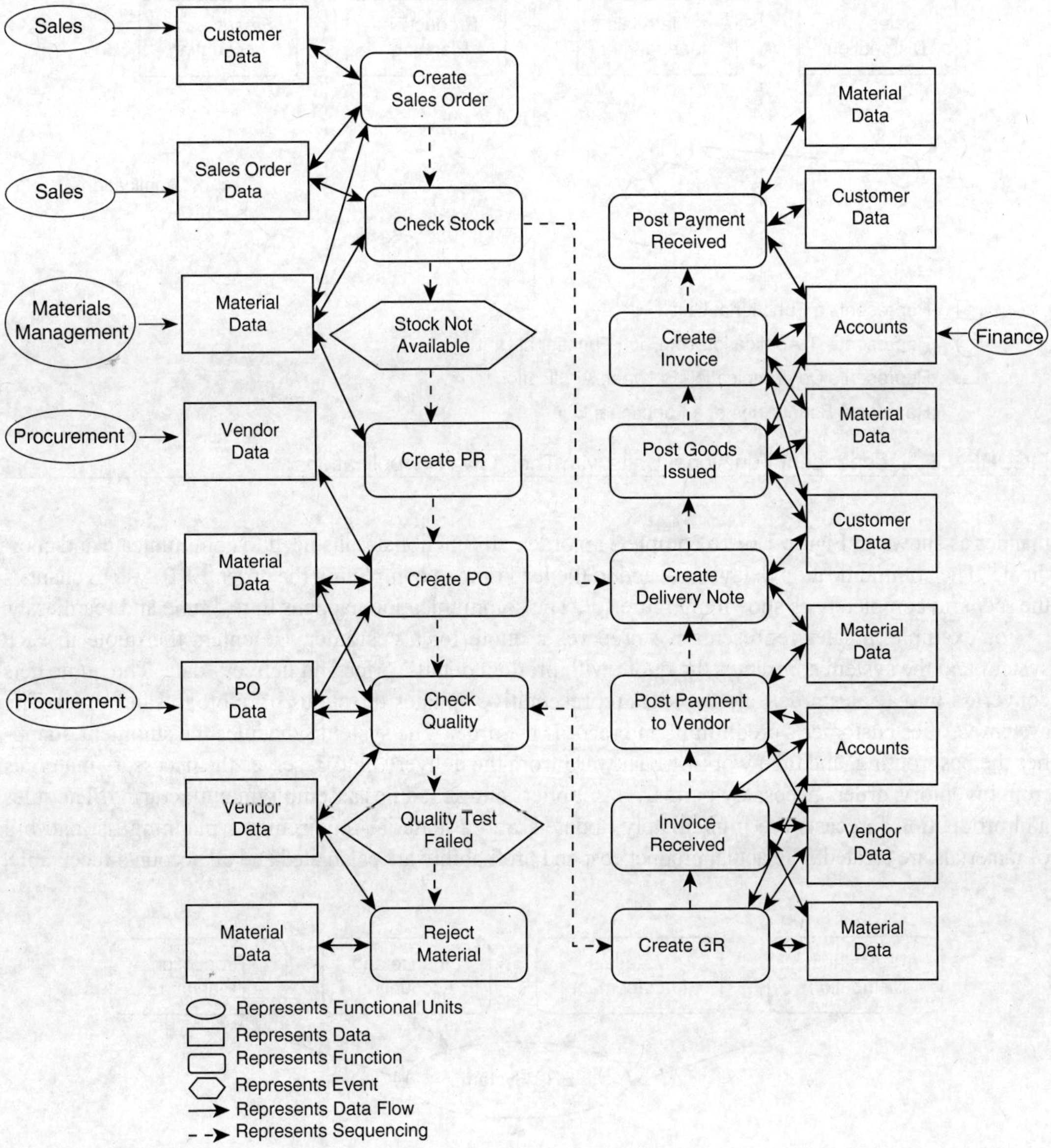

FIGURE 1.5 Sales Process of a Retailing Organization

and if it is available, product X is picked up, packed and shipped. The available inventory of product X is reduced appropriately. The customer is billed and the accounts receivable go up accordingly. The customer eventually pays that leads to accounts receivable to reduce and the bank account getting credited. In a simple scenario with only retailing and no manufacturing, if the product X is not available in sufficient quantity, the company would have to procure the product. Without an ERP system, individual functional units may have their own multiple applications that may not communicate with each other in a seamless

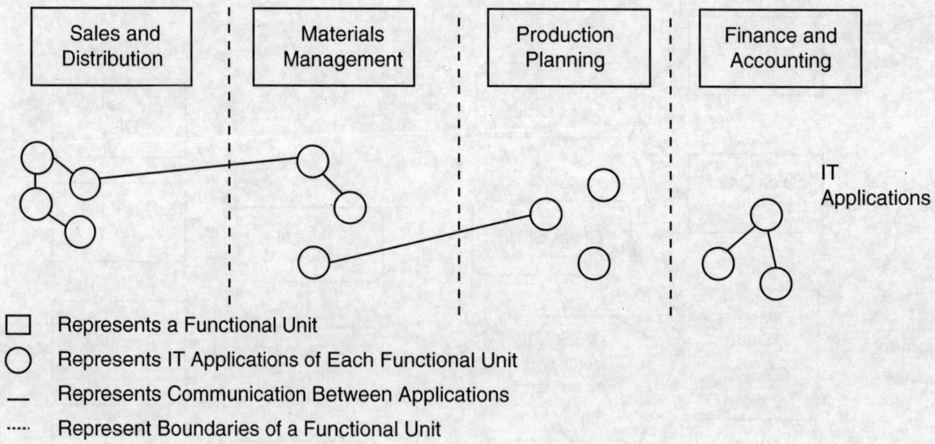

FIGURE 1.6 Independent Functional Units with Their Own IT Applications

manner as shown in Figure 1.6. To complete an order, all functional units need to communicate and coordinate. The communication delays may add to the lead time in completing the order. ERP system changes the scenario completely as shown in Figure 1.7. The communication happens in real time and seamlessly.

For example, a sales representative prepares a quote for a customer. He enters the quote in ERP system and the system completes the quote with product details, price and delivery date. The quote gets converted into a sales order and the sales representative updates the status of quote to sales order. The system verifies customer's credit limit and records the order. The system schedules the shipment, identifies the best routing, and then working backward from the delivery date, reserves the necessary materials from inventory, orders necessary parts from suppliers and schedules assembly/manufacturing. The sales and production forecasts are immediately updated, and a material-requirements-planning list and bill of materials are created. The actual product cost and profitability are calculated and all accounts-receivable,

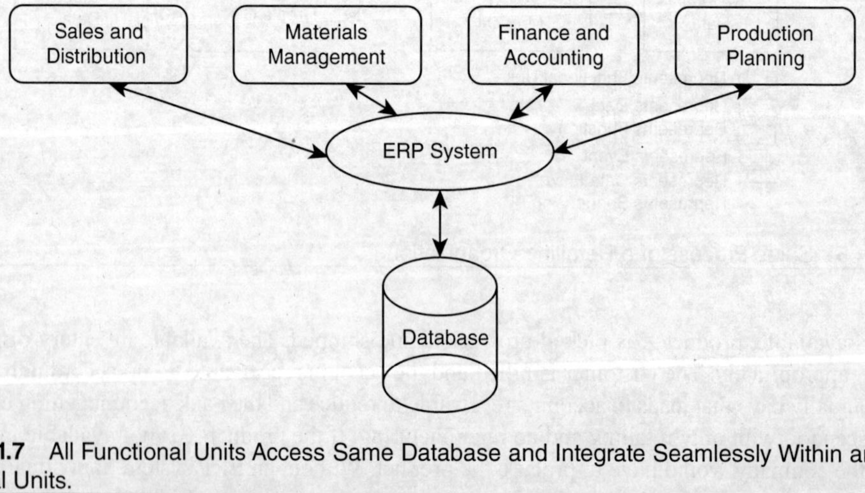

FIGURE 1.7 All Functional Units Access Same Database and Integrate Seamlessly Within and Across Functional Units.

payable, cost-centre and cash updated. The system performs nearly every informative transaction resulting from the sale (Figure 1.7).[4]

ERP began as a term to describe a sophisticated and integrated software system used for manufacturing. In its simplest sense, ERP systems create interactive environments designed to help companies manage and analyse the data associated with manufacturing, such as inventory, orders, accounting and so on. Although this basic definition still holds true for ERP systems, and is expanding. IT savvy users, increasing customer expectations, changes in manufacturing requirements and technology's relentless pursuit for innovation are just some of the forces reshaping the definition of ERP. In today's dynamic and turbulent business environment, there is a strong need for organizations to become globally competitive. The survival guide for competitiveness is to be closer to the customer and deliver value-added product and services in the shortest possible time. This, in turn, demands integration of the business processes of an enterprise, which is the stronghold of ERP. Economy has shifted from being based on manufacturing to service, and information has become the competitive advantage providing asset. ERP helps an organization obtain accurate and timely information. ERP has been defined in many different ways. The following is the functional definition of ERP software.

An ERP is a software-driven business management system which integrates all facets of the business, including planning, manufacturing, sales and marketing.

Put in simple words, *ERP systems comprise function-specific modules designed to interact with the other modules. ERP from an IT perspective is 'a comprehensive software package that stores, retrieves, modifies and processes the transactions of all the functions of an enterprise in an integrated fashion'.*

For an ERP project team, *ERP is a semi-finished product with tables and parameters that an organization and its implementation partner configure according to the business needs.*

1.5 ROLE OF ERP SYSTEMS IN AN ORGANIZATION

The Strategy, Technology, Organization-enterprise, People and Environment (STOPE) model[5] shown in Figure 1.8 helps in visualizing the role of ERP in an organization. This figure shows that the organization environment is the foundation on which company, technology and people rest. A company has internal business processes which are performed by functional units such as sales and distribution, production, finance and accounting, materials and human resource management. There are also some business processes to handle customers and vendors. The common thread that integrates the functional units is the information. If an organization uses information technology to run its business, then internal business processes are realized through an ERP system. An organization may use a Customer Relation Management (CRM) system for managing its customers and a Supply Chain Management (SCM) system to manage its vendors and suppliers. ERP, SCM and CRM together are termed as ERP-II. ERM, SCM and CRM together are termed as ERP-II (refer to Figure 1.9). We will learn about CRM and SCM in Chapter 10.

1.6 THREE-TIER ARCHITECTURE FOR ERP SYSTEMS

Major ERP systems run on three-tier client-server architecture. Components of three-tier architecture are a central database server, an application server and a presentation server. Three-tier architecture is shown in Figure 1.10. The database is generally a relational database management system and the organization data is stored in a relational database. Relational Database Management System (RDBMS) helps an organization in consolidating data and enforcing standards across the organization. Also, the data can

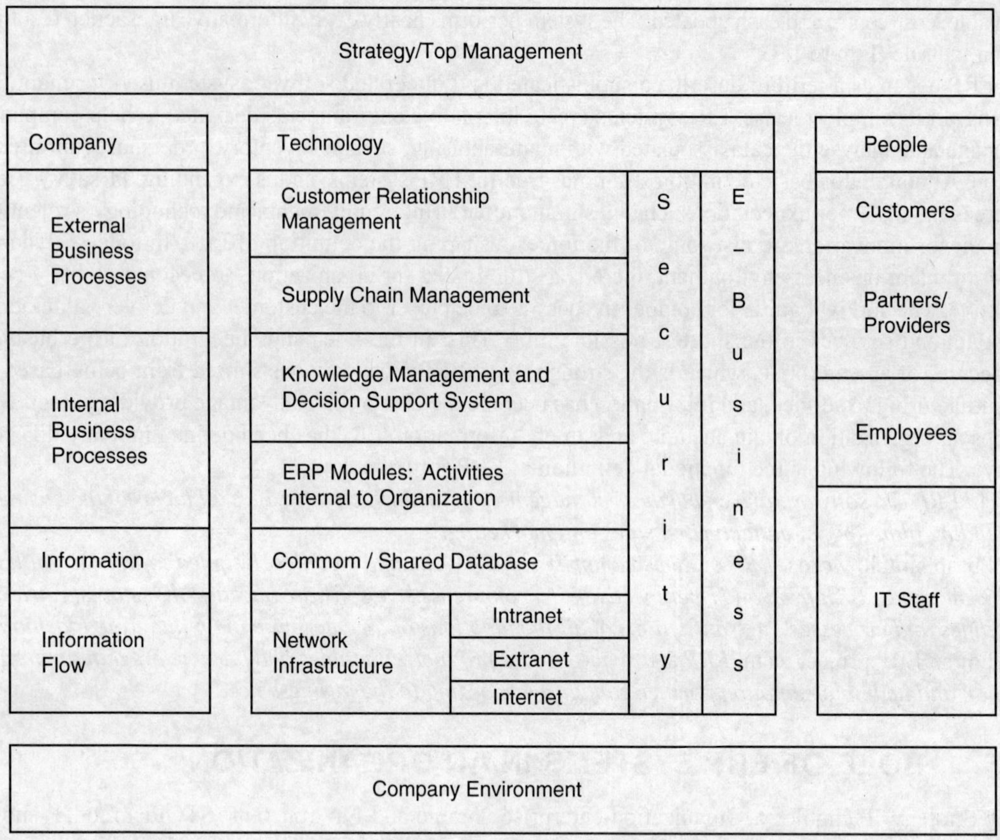

FIGURE 1.8 A STOPE Integrated View of ERP System

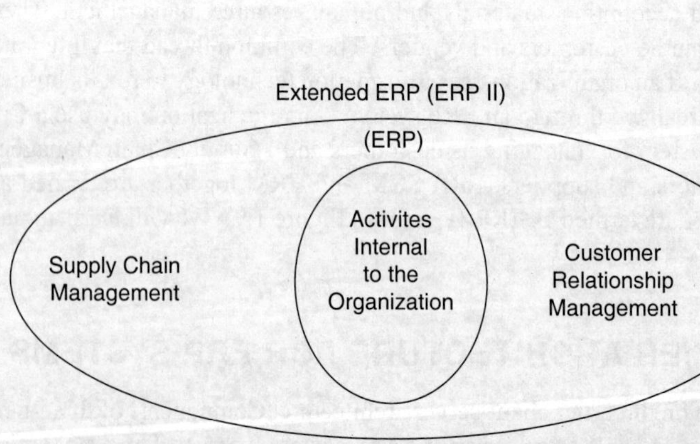

FIGURE 1.9 ERP-II or Extended ERP

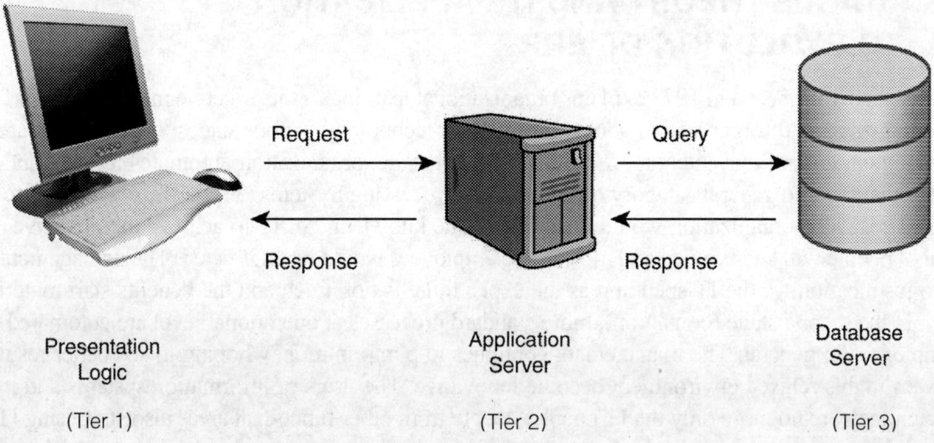

FIGURE 1.10 Three-tier Architecture of an ERP System

be distributed across many geographical locations as well as on many servers. The distribution remains transparent to the user. All major RDBMS such as IBM DB2, Oracle, Informix and Microsoft SQL Server can support most of ERP systems today. The ERP system is loaded onto the application server. All ERP packages provide Graphical User Interface (GUI) for its configuration and for its end users. The hardware requirements are modest from today's standards. A machine with couple of gigabytes of RAM and RAID-3 disks with a capacity of roughly 100 GB is sufficient. RAID architecture will ensure disk availability in spite of some disk failures. A server with two CPUs will help in 24 × 7 availability of the system. Most of the ERP systems require no special operating system. UNIX (its versions and cousins) and MS Windows operating systems are two major operating systems used by ERP software. Finally, presentation logic is loaded on user's desktop or laptop.

A small organization may use one server for database and application both. A large organization may have multiple application and database servers.

An ERP system supports many multi. For instance, it supports multi-currencies and multi-languages. It also supports multi-calendars, multi-time zones, multi-tax laws and multi-business rules (multi-environment). ERP supports multi-facility, multiple decisions and multi-companies under a corporate banner. It supports a multi-environment where business rules/tax rules may be different.

It supports multi-mode manufacturing which includes discrete process, continuous process, make-to-stock, highly repetitive, assemble to order (the final product is specified in terms of standard components), designed to order, and so on. Each of these manufacturing environments require different decision-making mechanism and all of these may be required under one single corporate banner. A mix of manufacturing modes help an organization fight severe market competition. The current business environment requires an organization to reduce total costs, maximize return on investment, shorten lead times and to be more responsive to customer demands, all at the same time. Highly dynamic markets call for effective enterprise information systems to enhance competitive advantage. An ERP is increasingly important in modern business because of its ability to integrate the flow of material, finance and information, and to support organizational strategies.[6]

1.7 STAGES THEORY AND ITS APPLICATION TO EVOLUTION OF ERP

The stages theory proposed in 1973 explains organizational learning of the effective management of IT within the organization. An organization adopts information technology in four stages.[7, 8] The stages are initiation, contagion, control and integration. In the initiation stage, organization automates its well-understood processes that fall into general category of Transaction Processing Systems (TPS). The objective is to reduce functional cost. The organization would need only some knowledge of IT to achieve the objective. Only a handful of people will be involved and most of the employees would be unaffected. The management would need no justification for the IT spending as the expenditure is not much and the benefits start materializing quickly. In the second stage (contagion), more standard processes at operational level are automated that affect employees in general. The management continues to pump in money hoping to see better results. The employees in this relaxed environment become innovative. The users of information systems and information technology are no more only the IT people. People from other functional areas also start using IT.

This relaxed environment does not continue forever. The management puts control mechanism in place to start the third stage which is control stage. The objective of the management is to achieve the better return on investments (ROI). By this time, however, the middle management realizes the potential of IT and starts using IT for decision-making activities. Employees either assume or are assigned responsibility for IT applications.

In the final stage, the organization starts integrating its IT applications that commences the integration stage. The organization develops a database that sits at the back end of all applications. Users start taking active interest in IT. The management starts treating IT investments like other investments which go through cost-benefit analysis. Each phase according to stages theory lasts about six to seven years The stages and their evolution is shown in Figure 1.11.

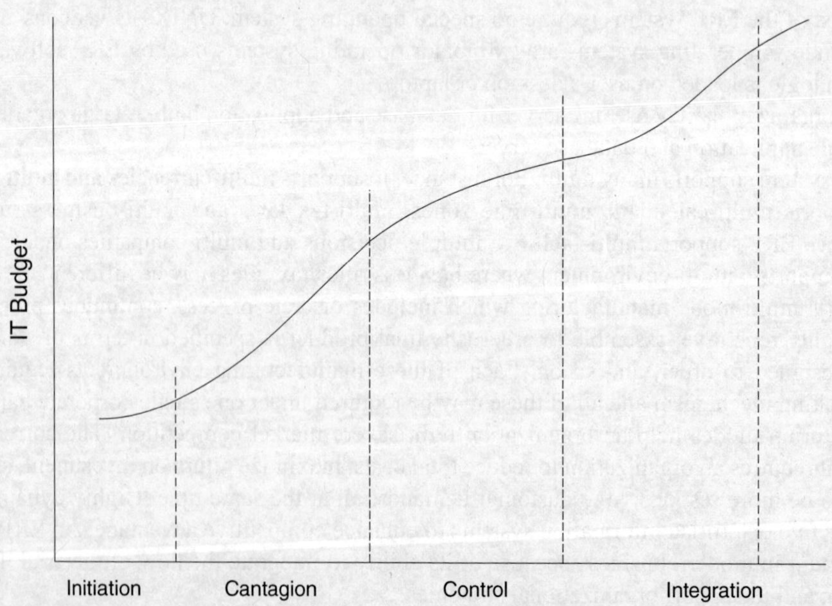

FIGURE 1.11 Stages of IT Evolution

The stages theory has been used[9] to explain ERP strategies across organizations. There are three sequential stages that are associated with ERP system use. In the first stage, an organization continues to use the legacy system to run the business and in parallel becomes aware of ERP system. It prepares itself for ERP implementation (we will learn the details in subsequent chapters). Stage one culminates with ERP implementation. ERP system aims at the automation of all processes with the goal of integrating information across the enterprise. ERP system replaces most of the legacy systems built over a period of time with a single-integrated information system. The integration process presents an opportunity to the organizations to uncover redundancies and inefficiencies. Second stage commences when ERP usage spreads throughout the organization, employees start exploring and exploiting the system. The management becomes interested in measuring the impact of the ERP system upon the business. The third stage commences when the organization starts feeling very comfortable with ERP and looks at it as a potential strategic tool.

An organization will have to start somewhere, learn and mature to the level where it will be able to use an ERP system as a strategic tool.

1.8 ARE ERP SYSTEMS DIFFERENT FROM TRADITIONAL INFORMATION SYSTEMS?

If an organization decides to implement an information system solution in the organization, they will first decide the scope of the project. Within the decided scope of the project, the support expected from the information system is decided. Usually a model of the information system is created and then either an off-the-shelf solution is purchased if it is available, or a custom made system is developed. In either case, the organization does not change its business processes according to the software specifications.

An ERP system is a generic system that supposedly implements best business practices. These best practices, the vendors claim, are the results of extensive research and reflect the practices followed by the successful business across the globe.[10] An organization that implements ERP system is expected to adapt/change its business processes according to an ERP system.

Consider a multi-site organization that is spread geographically. If the organization does not have an ERP system, each site can follow its own naming convention for various components and products. If an ERP system is installed and all sites are integrated, everyone would have to follow the same convention. 'Nestle' USA was paying 29 different prices for vanilla to the same vendor because each factory used different name for it, and every factory was responsible for its own purchases. Then they implemented an ERP system, every factory had to use the same name for vanilla. The purchases were then consolidated impacting everybody in each factory including purchase, finance, materials management and production. Earlier each factory planned procurements according to their requirements. But now, the procurements happened according to the suggestions made by the ERP system. The people who had been running the factory saw many changes in business processes and roles. To quote:[11]

> When you move to SAP (an ERP system), you are changing the way people work. You are challenging their principles, their beliefs and the way they have done things for so many years.

1.9 SCOPE OF ERP SYSTEMS

ERP has been successfully implemented by automobile industry, consumer goods, chemical sector, pharmaceutical sector, banking, insurance, healthcare, telecommunication, and so on. All functional areas of an organization are supported by an ERP system. For a manufacturing organization, these include the following:

- Finance and accounting
  - Financial accounting
  - Treasury management
  - Enterprise control
  - Asset management
- Logistics
  - Production planning
  - Materials management
  - Plant maintenance
  - Quality management
  - Project systems
  - Sales and distribution
- Human resources
  - Personnel management
  - Training and development
  - Skills inventory
- Workflow
  - Integrate an employee in the value chain

For an academic institute, the ERP functionality would include the following:

- Academics
- Training and placement
- Hostel management
- Library management
- Admissions
- Human resource management
- Accounts
- Alumni relationships
- Research projects
- Seminar and events
- Purchases

There are ERP systems for various business verticals such as banks, oil industry and telephone service providers Figure 1.12 shows the functionality offered by ERP system for a bank and its operations.

1.10 GENERAL MODEL OF BUSINESS AND ROLE OF ERP

ERP systems are installed in big organizations to replace the legacy system. These legacy systems worked as standalone systems and were not integrated with other systems. One of the reasons is that these systems were added to the organization as and when required by each of the functional units of the organization. The organizations themselves evolve over years. An enterprise starts as a small business with small investment and few people. As the business grows, the organization also starts growing, more people are hired and the responsibilities that were earlier shared are divided among people. In other words, functional units get created. Each functional unit installs IT systems as per their requirements. The business processes also evolve along with the business and organization. The business processes that evolve over a period of time are not always efficient. Information systems are often used to automate or support the

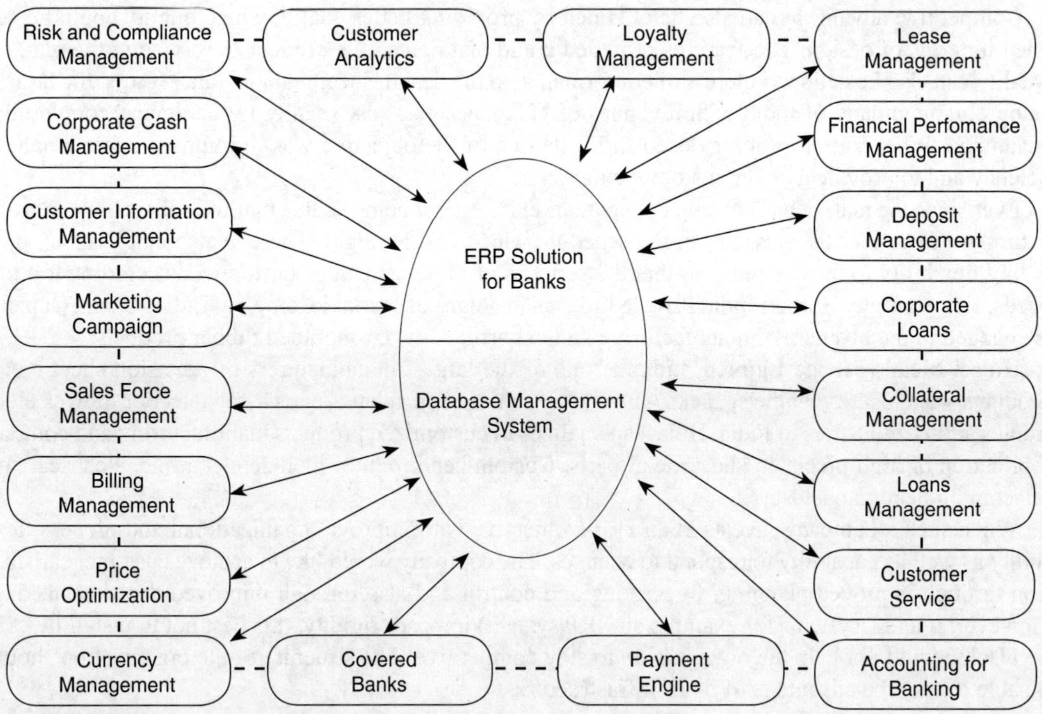

FIGURE 1.12 Functionality Offered by an ERP System for a Bank

existing processes. ERP vendors claim that they implement the best business practices in their ERP systems. When an organization implements an ERP system, its business processes also improve. ERP also affects the organization structure as it makes information to flow horizontally through the organization as opposed to vertically in traditional organization.[12] This calls for a relatively flat organization. An ERP is a software that affects all aspects of an organization. People have to be ready to accept ERP and the changes it brings about. A training program is required to prepare people technically and psychologically.

ERP system has to support competitive strategy of the organization. Competitive strategy of an organization refers to the basis on which it achieves competitive advantage. An organization's competitive strategy may be based on one or more of the following criteria:

- Price
- Quality
- Delivery (on time)
- Flexibility (deliver-customized product)

An organization may use price as a criteria and try to provide essential qualities in its services and products at a cost lower than its competitors.[13] For instance, Air Deccan, an Indian domestic airline clearly mentions on its Web site that it is a low-cost carrier. The company was formed in 1995 and since then it has successfully carved a niche for itself. Air Deccan has adopted a lean and mean approach to management and staffing stating, that it aims at maintaining a low aircraft-to-employee ratio. The airlines recently (December 2005) made a collaboration with Cafe Coffee Day (CCD) to serve its customers in the sky for which customers pay. CCD has the same criteria as Air Deccan for achieving competitive advantage.

Competitive advantage can also be obtained by providing better quality where quality could be defined in terms of design. The features provided could distinguish the product or service in the market. Quality can also be defined in terms of conformance to the design specification. Tata Motors, the largest automobile company of India with revenues of ₹20,483 crores, use quality for achieving competitive advantage. When Tata Motors invested in IT, its one of the objective was to improve operational efficiency and to provide a better customer experience.

Ever since the market has become buyers market instead of being sellers market, sellers have to work extra hard to deliver the services on the schedule which is often tight. There is also emphasis on providing flexibility to the customer so that the services or products can be customized according to their needs. For example, Horiaki India Private Ltd., a subsidiary of Horiaki Company Ltd of Osaka (Japan), is engaged in the business of manufacturing and exporting custom-moulded rubber products.

Hulasi Metals Private Limited, India, is one of the largest manufacturers of precision sheet metal products—enclosures/cabinets, racks, sub-racks, chassis and related parts—for telecom, power electronics and IT industries in India. Hulasi specializes in customized products manufacturing and contract fabrication of high-precision sheet metal parts. Customized products include electronic, electrical and telecommunication enclosures.

When such a company invests in an IT, its objective is to improve organizational and process flexibility as well its capability to respond to changes. The company would like to achieve customer satisfaction through improved planning, forecasting and control and also through improved decision making. However, if an IT system (for example an ERP system) imposes rigidity, it is best not to install it.

IT alone will not help the organization to stay competitive. The structure of the organization should be able to take the advantage of its IT infrastructure.

1.11 MAJOR ERP PLAYERS

SAP is by far the largest company, and has been in business since 1972. SAP has 26,150 customers, 88,700 installations across 120 countries with 12 million users. SAP has a market share of 56 per cent, Oracle/People Soft 23 per cent, Microsoft 12 per cent and Siebel 9 per cent. SAP has a total revenue of 7,514 million Euro, out of which 2,361 million Euro is the contribution of license fee. Their 50 per cent revenue comes from Germany and US, with equal contribution from each country and the remaining comes from the rest of the world. SAP has more than 32,000 employees. Some other ERP vendors are BaaN, Marshal, Protean, Prism, Advantis, J. D. Edwards, MFG\PRO, Rhythm, Avalon, BPCS, Mamis and RAMCO. The Sage Group is a leading provider of business management software for mid-sized companies worldwide, with annual sales of nearly $900 million and 3.6 million customers. Siebel Systems is a recent (about five-year old) company based in San Mateo, California, employs 1,200 people and with about $410 million in revenues.

There are companies that specialize in banking sector such as Nucleus Software, TCS and Infosys. There are companies that specialize in education sector such Dimensions Innovations.

1.12 IMPLEMENTATIONS IN INDIA

In India, many major corporate houses as well as small and medium enterprises have implemented ERP system and many more are in the process of implementing or considering an ERP implementation. A small list of ERP implementations in India are listed in Appendix A. The source is mainly the Web sites of the companies and ERP implementations partners/vendors. Once a company installs an ERP system, it will serve the company for atleast three years but it may serve for as many as 10 years. Only about four

TABLE 1.1 ERP System Life Span and the Percentage of Organizations That Could Use ERP System for the Specified Duration

ERP System Life (Years)	Per cent of Companies
<3	3.4
3–5	21.5
5–7	27.5
7–10	22.8
>10	24.8

per cent of the companies would retire an ERP system in less than three years. Most of the companies continue to use their ERP systems for longer than three years (refer to Table 1.1).

CONCLUSION

ERP systems are semi-finished software products that integrate all departments and functional units of an organization. An ERP systems uses a centralized database to store the data and provide graphical user interface for performing business transactions. Information technology systems have evolved from Transaction Processing Systems (TPS) to Management Information Systems (MIS) to Decision Support Systems and Executive Support Systems (DSS and ESS).

ERP systems fall in the category of TPS and MIS.The data that ERP system stores can be consolidated and analysed using various DSS and ESS. It is critical that the data is accurate since it is seen throughout the organization and an error/omission by one functional unit. For instance, if inventory is not updated in timely manner, the production and sales may suffer.

ERP systems are available for all types of organizations—manufacturing such as auto, oil and gas exploration companies, refineries; service such as banking, telecommunication, legal agencies, distribution; and academic etc. There are more than 200 ERP products that are available in the market. One needs to carefully choose an appropriate ERP system.

CASE STUDY

There is retail company in Delhi, India registered with the name RetailS. The company was formed in 1995. The company primarily deals in metallic packaging material. It also deals in some food products. The turnover of company is about 10 million USD and the company has less than 30 employees. RetailS has three managing directors, a sales department, a purchase department and an accounting department.

The organization structure (shown in Figure 1.13) use organizational model convention used by SAP. The conventions used in the organizational chart are quite self-explanatory. The data that is shared between these functional units is shown in Figure 1.14.

The data that is shared between a customer who is outside organization unit and sales is the following:

- Customer data
- Items details
- Order data
- Accounting data

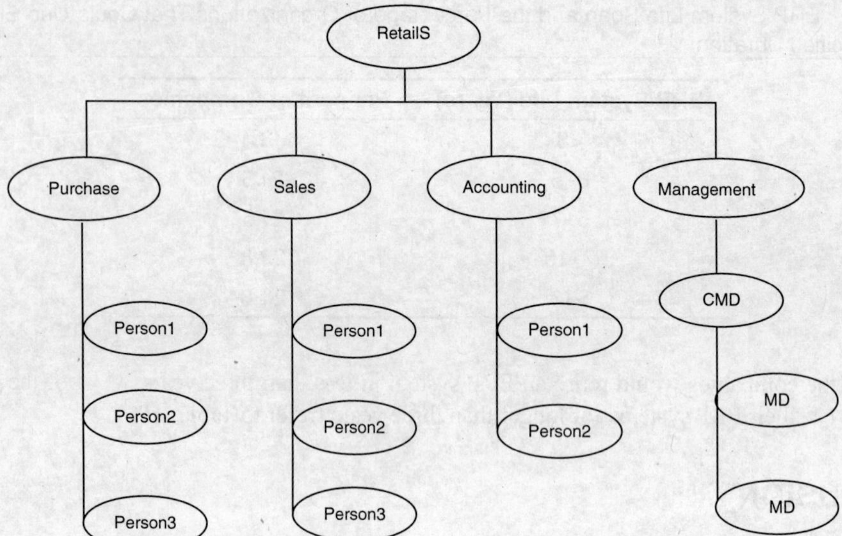

FIGURE 1.13 Organizational Structure of Retails

The data that is shared between sales and accounts is the following:

- Customer data
- Order data
- Accounting data

The data that is shared between sales and management is the following:

- Order data

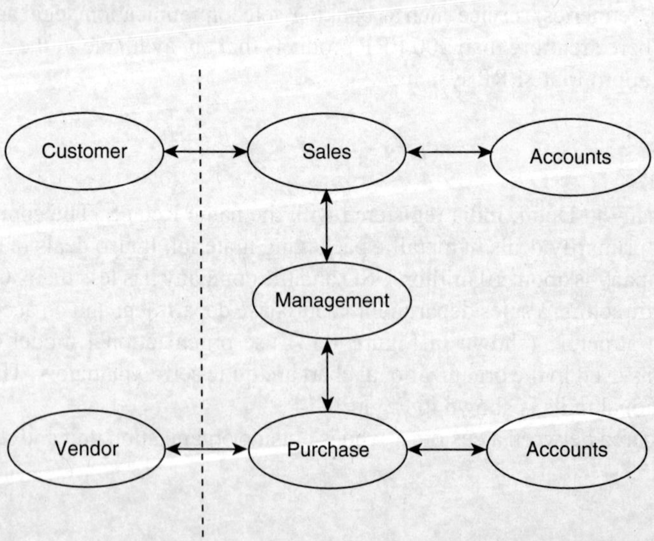

FIGURE 1.14 Interaction Between Various Organizational Units of RetailS and Outside Units—Customers and Vendors

You can enumerate the data that is shared between a vendor and the purchase, between the purchase and the accounts, and between the purchase and the management.

EXERCISES

Test Your Understanding

1. What is the value chain framework? How does each unit in this framework interact with others?
2. What are the problems that an organization faces if each functional unit maintains its own data?
3. Define and explain an ERP system. List major ERP players.
4. Explain evolution of ERP system using stages theory.
5. Explain three-tier architecture of an ERP system.
6. What makes an ERP system different from custom-made software products?
7. Compare and contrast MIS and an ERP system.
8. Describe your own IT usage pattern. Does it support stages theory?
9. What is the scope of an ERP system for a manufacturing system? Describe it with the help of Michael Porter's value chain network as well as functional view of the organization.
10. The scope of ERP system is industry specific. Justify this statement with the help of an example.
11. Who are the major ERP vendors?
12. What is the life span of ERP systems in organizations?
13. What are the different models of businesses? Do ERP support all business models?

Apply Your Understanding

1. Most likely, you are part of an organization. Identify some of the problems that you or your colleagues faced due to information being not available. Suggest some solutions.
2. Identify an organization that you can visit and study. For example, a retailing organization or a chain, a manufacturing organization, a bank, an academic institute or a law firm. You should be able to visit and talk to the managers and employees in the organization that you identify. It is not necessary for the organization to have information systems or an ERP system. Choose the organization carefully as you will work with the same organization throughout the book.
    a. Your task is to study information flow in the chosen organization. If the organization is big, restrict yourself to one functional unit but include its interface with other functional units. The objective is to identify the role that information plays in the organization and accessibility of the information.
    b. If the organization has information systems, study if they the systems are fragmented and isolated or integrated. Also, learn when were the information systems installed and how long they have been in use? Write down your learnings in a document.
3. Identify the functional units of your organization and draw an organizational graph similar to the one shown in Figure 1.13.
4. Identify the interactions among functional units of your organization and draw an interaction graph similar to the one shown in Figure 1.14.

ENDNOTES

1. T. H. Davenport, 'Putting the Enterprise into the Enterprise System', in *Harvard Business Review, 1998*, 76(4), July–August, 121–31.
2. E. J. Umble et al., 'Enterprise Resource Planning: Implementation and Critical Success Factors', in *European Journal of Operations Research*, 2003 146, 241–57.
3. Cited in Michael Hammer, 'Reengineering Work: Don't Automate, Obliterate', *Harvard Business Review* (1990), July–August.
4. T. H. Davenport, 'Putting the Enterprise into the Enterprise System', in *Harvard Business Review*, 1998, 76(4), July–August, 121–31.
5. Bakry and Bakry, 'Enterprise Resource Planning: A Review and a STOPE View', *International Journal of Network Management* 2005, 5, 363–70.
6. Y. Yusuf, A. Gunasekaran, and M. S. 'Abthorpe, Enterprise Information Systems Project Implementation: A Case Study of ERP in Rolls-Royce', in *International Journal of Production Economics,* 2004, 87(3), 251–66.
7. Richard L. Nolan, 'Managing the Computer Resources: A Stage Hypothesis', in *Communications of the ACM* (1973), 16(7), July.
8. Richard L. Nolan, David C. Croson and Katherine N. Seger, 'The Stages Theory: A Framework for IT Adoption and Organizational Learning', in *Harvard Business School* (1993), 9, March, 193–141.
9. Christopher P. Holland et at., 'An International Analysis of the Maturity of Enterprise Resource Planning (ERP) Systems Use', in *Proceedings of the 6th Americas Conference on Information Systems* (2000), 992–97.
10. T. H. Davenport, 'Putting the Enterprise into the Enterprise System' in *Harvard Business Review,* 1998, 76(4), July–August, 121–31.
11. Case: *Nestle's Enterprise Resource Planning (ERP) Odyssey*, Web site: http://www.cio.com/article/31066/Nestl_eacute_s Enterprise_Resource_Planning_ERP _Odyssey.
12. K. C. Laudon and J. P. Laudon, *Management Information Systems*, 7e, Pearson Education Asia (2002).
13. R. H. Hayes and S. C. Wheelwright, *Restoring Competitive Edge: Competing Through Manufacturing* John Wiley and Sons, (1984).

chapter 2

Life Cycle of an ERP Implementation Project

LEARNING OBJECTIVES

After reading this chapter, you will be able to understand:

- Life cycle of an ERP project and its phases
- Teams for an ERP project, their constitution and roles
- Interaction among various teams
- Time taken for an ERP implementation
- Life span of an ERP system

2.1 INTRODUCTION

In the last chapter, we learnt what ERP systems are, their characteristics and scope. ERP systems are semi-finished products that need to be configured at the site of the host company. The host company has to find the right ERP system among the options available in the market, based on their requirements. Identifying requirements is also a planned and budgeted activity. In this chapter, we will learn about various phases of an ERP deployment project. The entire project may take anywhere from six months to three years. There are various teams that are formed to take care of different aspect of the project. We will also learn about teams that are formed and their constitutions. The vendor who supplies the ERP software also gets involved either directly or through an implementation partner. Sometimes, the host company may also engage a consultant to guide them through the project. All teams work together to complete the project. The interaction among various teams is also part of learning from this chapter. A sense of implementation time, return on investment and life span should also get developed after reading this chapter.

2.2 LIFE CYCLE OF AN ERP PROJECT

An ERP implementation project encompasses the following stages (shown in Figure 2.1) that constitute its life cycle:

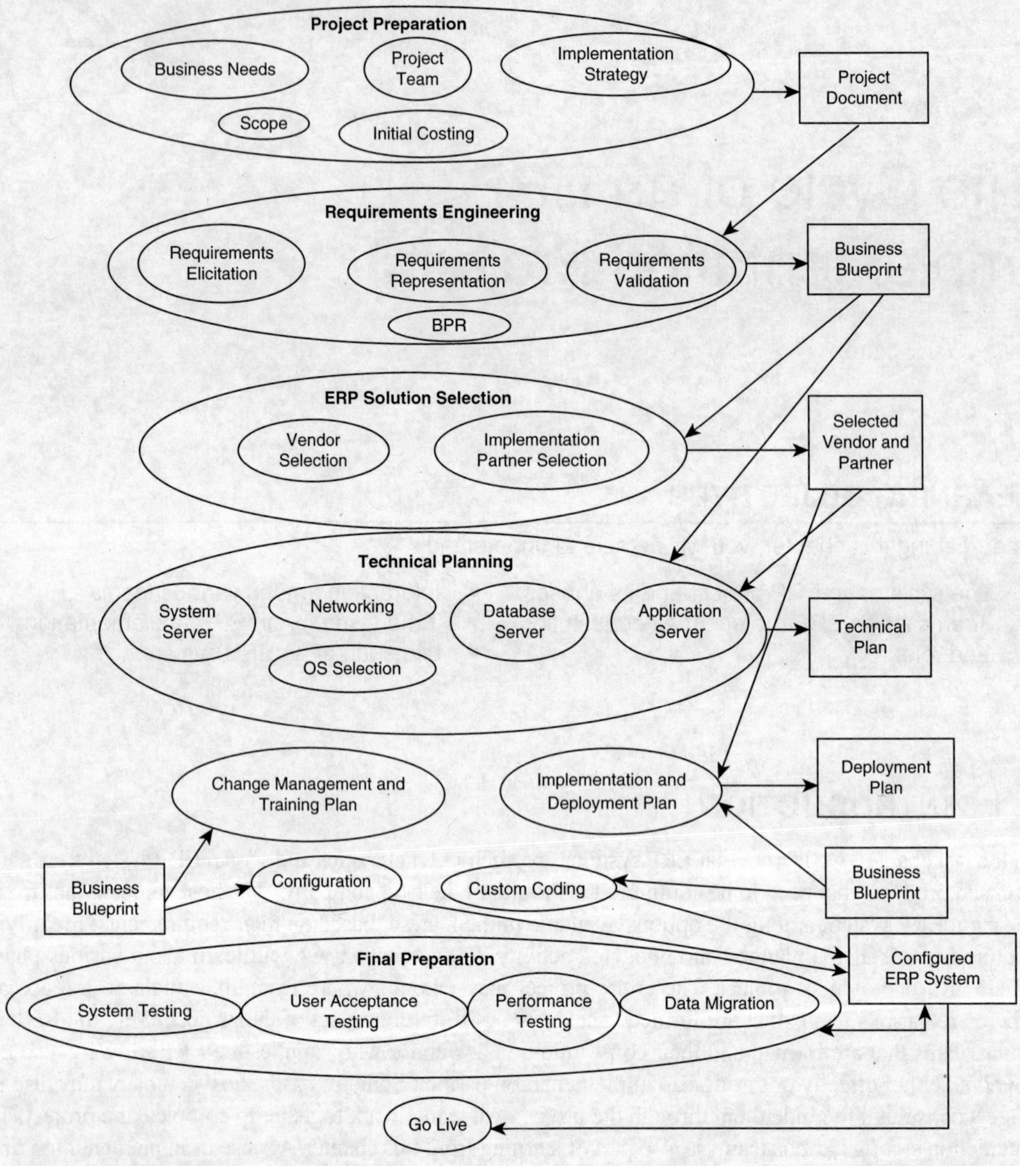

Outer ovals show high-level activities and inside ovals show sub-activities; rectangles show objects (data/document/software); an object is required by a process if there is an incoming arrow to the process; an object is produced by a process if there is an outgoing arrow from the process.

FIGURE 2.1 Stages in an ERP Implementation Project

1. **Project preparation:** This phase includes initial planning and preparation for an ERP project. It is also referred to as vision and planning phase. The tasks accomplished in this phase include the following:
   - Evaluate company's business needs by studying its business strategy and processes. Questions such as—do we need an ERP system? are we ready for ERP system? is installation of ERP system aligned with our business strategy? are asked and answered. These issues are discussed in detail in chapters 4 and 5.
   - Specify scope of the project in terms of the functional units that will be supported by an ERP system and business sites that will be covered.
   - Form steering committee and project team. The team composition and their activities are discussed in Section 2.3.
   - The two main approaches for deciding implementation strategy are big bang and phased approach. In phased approach, an ERP system is implemented in phases. Phases may be organized as follows:
     – *Functionality to be implemented in each phase*. For instance, an organization may decide to include sales and accounting in phase one, then include purchase in the second phase, and human resource module in the third phase. If the company is geographically distributed, all sites are likely to be covered in each phase to maintain uniformity.
     – *Sites/units to be covered in each phase*. The company may decide the functionality to implement, and implement all of it at one site in one go and then move on to the second one.

     In big bang approach, the complete ERP system is implemented in one go on all the sites/units of the organization. The complete ERP system refers to the functions that the organization has decided to implement and not to all functions that ERP system offers. Both approaches have their own benefits and risks.

     The distinction between the approaches is shown in Table 2.1. In big bang approach, it is either all or nothing situation. If the project fails then there is nothing at the end of the project. A company that is IT savvy, undertaking large projects that impact the processes, organizational culture and structure and brought them to a successful end, may go for a big bang approach. But otherwise, a phased approach may be preferred. In phased approach, communication among various units may become difficult and people may feel that ERP project has been going on forever. There may be a risk of adding more requirements in the next phase or widening the scope. At the same time, a phased approach gives an opportunity to learn and become better with each phase. Since each phase is relatively small, the risk involved is less than in a big bang approach. The management has to carefully choose the most appropriate approach for an ERP project.
   - **Initial costing.** An estimate of the cost is done right in the beginning to assess feasibility of the project. The initial assessment may be based on a similar project done elsewhere. A project

TABLE 2.1 Distinction Between Big Bang and Phased Approach

Big Bang Approach	ERP is implemented at all sites and all selected modules are implemented in one go
Phased Approach	• All selected modules are implemented, but at selected sites • Some of the selected modules are implemented at all sites • Some of the selected modules are implemented at some of the sites

may be termed similar if it was done in the same industry, with similar number of expected users, sites and functionality. The overall cost of an ERP project is between 1 to 3 per cent of the turnover of the host company which is a major expenditure. The management would need to know the expected cost to budget for the project.

During this phase, risk analysis may also be done. Risk mitigation and management are discussed in Chapter 9. At the end of this phase, a project document is created that serves as a reference document for future phases. The decision regarding the business needs, project scope, implementation strategy and expected cost are all documented. The high-level team that is formed during this phase is also mentioned in the document. These teams take the project further. The document created in this phase may be of 20 to 30 pages. This document serves as a reference document throughout the project. Once the project document is ready, the next phase of the project commences.

2. **Requirements engineering.** During requirements engineering (RE) phase, needs and objectives of various stakeholders are identified and documented. RE phase is divided into three sub-phases:[1, 2]
   - *Requirements elicitation*: Requirements are gathered from various stakeholders.
   - *Requirements representation*: Requirements are represented through a model.
   - *Requirements validation*: Correctness of gathered requirements are verified by end users and stakeholders.

   Outputs of this phase are documents containing requirements in the form of models (e.g., process, data, organization, etc.). These documents are also referred to as business blueprints. Various modelling techniques that are used for documenting ERP requirements are discussed in Chapter 6. Since all business processes are documented during this phase, it is an opportunity to improve or even radically change the existing business processes. This activity is known as Business Process Reengineering (BPR). BPR and related issues are discussed in Chapter 7.
3. **ERP solution selection:** Based on the requirements, an appropriate ERP system has to be selected. The selection process is discussed in Chapter 8. The selection process is followed by negotiation and contract with the software vendor and implementation partner. Most of the ERP vendors do not implement their ERP system themselves and outsource this activity to their certified implementation partners. Negotiations have to be done with ERP vendor as well as implementation partner.
4. **Technical planning:** System requirements including hardware and software are identified at this time. Hardware requirements such as technology including application servers, database server and networking should be gathered, based on the scope of ERP and performance requirements. Operating system has to be decided to run the ERP system where choices are Linux, Solaris and MS Windows. Most of the ERP systems would also require a database such as Oracle, DB2, MySQL and SQL server. Networking is a must, as most of the ERP systems are now based on client/server architecture that facilitates access across Intranet and Internet. Data security is another area that requires attention. System availability of 24 (hours) × 7 (days a week) is always required for which additional technical planning may be required in terms of backup systems. The data backup at regular intervals may also be required.

   One can also consider Software as a Service Option (SAAS) where instead of hosting the ERP system and database oneself, it is outsourced to an external agency. Cloud computing is another option now becoming available where the cloud computing service providers would provide the service but the servers may be distributed and shared. If the host company is not IT savvy and does not want to create the entire setup that would include acquiring hardware, database server and hiring manpower to maintain the system, SAAS may be an option. There are many companies who are now providing ERP as SAAS using cloud computing. The decision to opt for SAAS has to be taken considering privacy issues, cost effectiveness, credibility of the agency, speed of the network and so on.

Looking at the capability of the mobile phones that now have an operating system, many applications can be run on them successfully. Depending on the environment and working style of the host company, it may be desirable to have a mobile phone interface for the users of the ERP system. Touch screen interface is an another option that you may like to explore.

Disaster management planning should also be done upfront. Some companies would have a parallel server in a different seismic zone as a part of their disaster management plan. The technical team will have to work out these details.

The ERP project may be done using one setup where the implementation is done first, followed by testing and deployment. If an organization has more resources, two setups can facilitate parallel activities. Implementation and testing can be done on one setup which can then be deployed on another setup. It is a luxury to have three setups—one for implementation, one for testing and one for deployment. The decision to setup one, two or three systems would be taken by the management depending on the resources available and timeframe of the project. Business continuity is another factor that needs to considered. If ERP system crashes or malfunctions, the business should not come to a halt.

5. **Change management and training plan:** An important aspect in ERP system implementation is training of the end users. The employees who are end users of the ERP system may face difficulty in using the system and may offer some resistance. It is important to plan communication and training for the users to make the transition easy. A change management strategy should be worked out to mitigate the risk involved in implementing an ERP system that touches the culture of the organization impacting everyone. Change management is discussed in detail in Chapter 4.
6. **Implementation and deployment planning:** During the negotiation and contract signing, a clear ERP implementation plan should be worked out as well. A sample plan is shown in Figure 2.6. The plan should include the tasks that the team can comprehend and responsibilities should be clearly assigned. The start and end date is also part of the plan. Such a plan goes directly into the project management software. This is a high-level plan that does not include the deployment date of each module. Once the requirements have been finalized and the modules to be deployed have been identified, a detailed plan is worked out. An implementation may take anywhere from six months to four years. The largest percentage of companies takes between 13 to 18 months to complete the project (Table 2.2).
7. **Configuration:** ERP systems are generic, and functionality they provide serves a large variety of enterprises. Configuration is a process whereby individual components are assembled and adjusted to construct a working solution according to the requirements identified in the requirements engineering phase.[3] Output of RE phase is the input to configuration phase. Components of an ERP software are the following:
    - Relational database system that consists of large number of tables.
    - Functions that manipulate these tables.

TABLE 2.2 Implementation Time and Percentage of ERP Implementation That have Taken Specified Time

Implementation Time in Months	Percentage of Companies That Completed ERP in the Time Given in Left Column
<6	13.0
7–12	24.7
13–18	36.9
19–24	11.6
25–36	8.0
37–48	4.4
>48	1.4

Components are assembled by selecting tables and their attributes, and setting up relationships among them. We also configure relevant selected functions. An ERP project will always have a configuration phase. A relational database system associated with an ERP system may consist of thousands (30,000 in case of SAP) of tables (relations) and a large number of functions that operate on these tables. These components are assembled by selecting tables and their attributes and setting up relationships among them. These settings may impact the system at different levels.[4] The settings that impact the entire system are system level configuration settings. The object level settings affect entities or objects. Finally, the occurrence level settings affect a single instance of a process or an object.

An organization may make to order or may produce by lot size. The system level settings will permit one or both of these manufacturing styles and this setting will impact procurement. Such a setting is a system level setting. Some items may belong to make to order manufacturing process while another set of items may be produced by lot size. These settings impact every instance of the items produced and the processes related to the items. Such settings are object level settings. At the lowest level, setting such as bulk discount on an item is an occurrence level setting.

The organization may like to migrate legacy data to the ERP system for continuity. The legacy data may require cleansing, filtering and transformation before it can be loaded into the ERP system. The data migration and related activities should also be planned at this time.

8. **Custom coding:** Sometimes the chosen ERP system may not support a business process. There may be gaps between the business requirements and the functionality of the chosen ERP system. To close the gap, the client may do one of the following:
   - Alter its business processes so that the chosen ERP supports them. This strategy is well accepted and referred to as reengineering driven by ERP system. This is discussed in Chapter 7.
   - The organization strongly believes in efficiency and competitive advantages of its business process. In such a situation, the client may request the vendor to enhance the system's functionality. Such a request invariably would require the vendor to add or modify the code of the system. This activity is known as customization or custom coding.

It is a good idea to avoid customization as far as possible because the code that is written on the request of the client does not come with any warranty and support. Customization is expensive and risky because the vendor will work under time pressure and may not be able to do a thorough testing. The added code does not become part of the ERP system that vendor sells and supports. Consequently, the future releases will have to be customized too. Customization adds risk, time and cost to the implementation, upgrades and maintenance.

An ERP implementation that uses no custom coding is referred to as *vanilla* implementation. Vanilla implementation has the following characteristics:

- A company for whom the competitive advantage comes from the products that it sells, rather than from the information system it uses, may go for vanilla implementation. For a service industry, the differentiation may come from the information system of the organization and vanilla implementation may not suffice.
- The vendor generally takes care of the governing laws and the transactions are accepted by audit department. Customization may disturb the conformance to the governing laws.
- A client with no or little inhouse IT capability may choose to go for vanilla implementation to keep it less complex.
- When the vendor customizes their software for a client, it becomes a unique system for which the vendor is not able to provide same level of support as for the original product.
- Newer versions are released by the vendor. Upgradation of a customized system is more challenging.
- In any case if the system is customized, it should be used at all sites. Otherwise, the systems may not be able to communicate.

9. **Final preparation:** In this phase, the activities of consolidating nature are performed. The system has to be tested for accuracy, completeness and performance. Some adjustments may be required in the configuration of the ERP system if any discrepancy is discovered. Sometimes, when system is loaded, the performance (number of transactions performed per unit time) may not meet the requirements. Some changes in the hardware configuration may be required.
10. **Go-live:** ERP system is commissioned and is put in actual use. A helpdesk is also setup to ensure 24×7 availability. Some monitoring of key business processes may also be required till a reasonable level of confidence builds in the system.

The phases of ERP system are not sequential. Figure 2.2 shows activities and their sequencing in an ERP project. Many activities are done in parallel. For example, all activities related to technical planning—all server, relational database management system, operating system and networking related activities can progress in parallel. Figure 2.3 shows the sequencing as a spreadsheet. These details are used to create plans with the help of a project management tool by the project planning and monitoring teams. The project management will be discussed in detail in Chapter 9.

Maintenance: Support the system on an ongoing basis. This also involves upgrading to a new version every few years. ERP software is updated to incorporate new laws, to take care of changing business needs, to take advantage of new technology or to stay synchronized with the vendor.

As soon as the idea of implementing an ERP system surfaces in the organization, a team is formed for project preparation. Assuming that the organization decides to go ahead with the ERP project, many other teams would be formed. In the next section, we discuss various teams that are formed, their constitutions and roles.

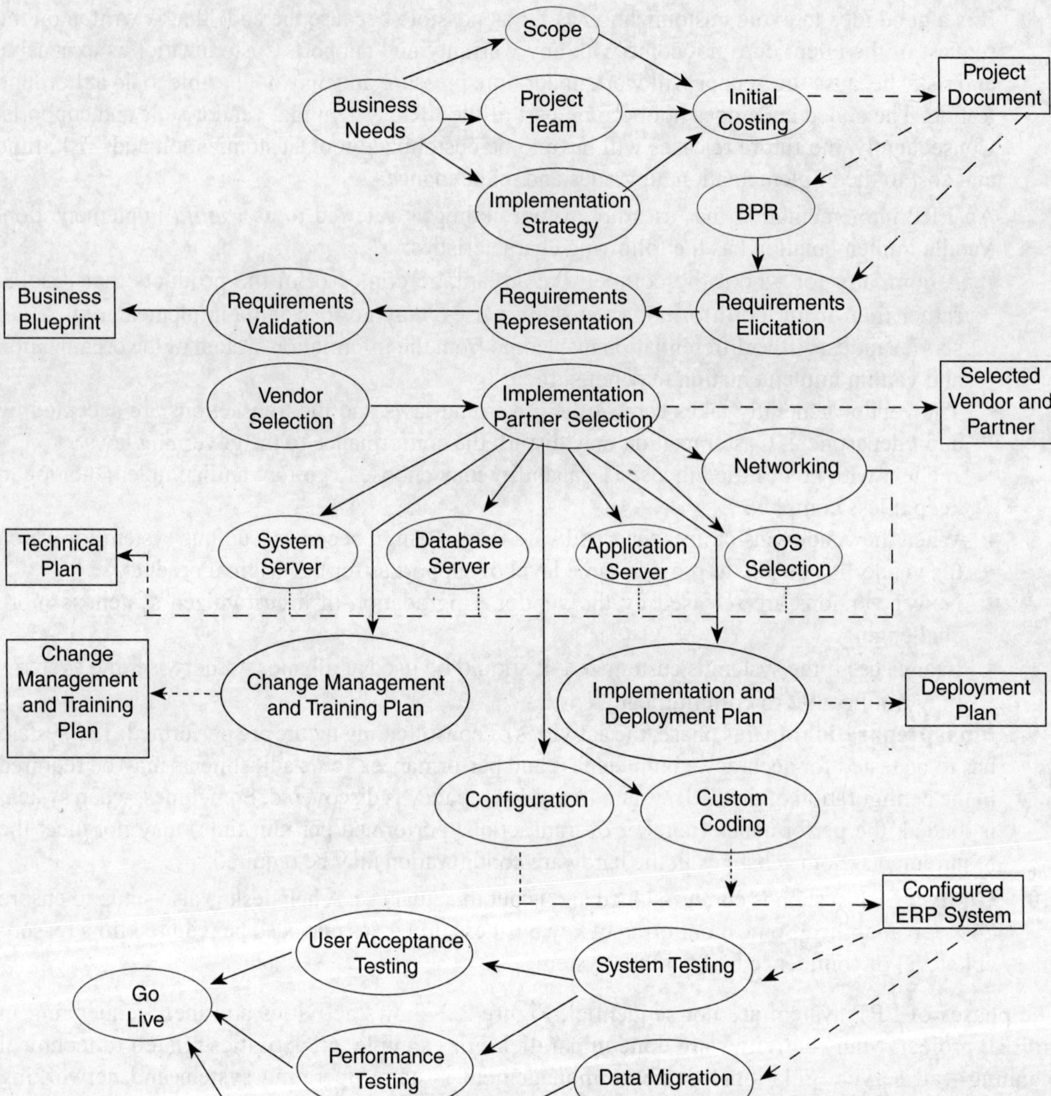

FIGURE 2.2 Sequencing of Activities Involved in an ERP Project

Phase	Activites	P1	P2	P3	P4	P5	P6	P7	P8	P9	P10	P11	P12
Project preparation													
	Business Needs	■											
	Project Team		■										
	Implementation Strategy		■										
	Scope		■										
	Initial Costing			■									
Engineering	BPR												
	Requirements Elicitation			■									
	Requirements Representation				■								
	Requirements Validation					■							
Slect Vendor and Implementation Partner							■						
	Vendor Slection							■					
	Implementation Partner Slection								■				
Technical Planning													
	Sever									■			
	Database Server									■			
	Application Server									■			
	OS Selection									■			
	Networking									■			
Change Management and Training Plan													
	Training Plan								■				
	Change Management				■								
Implementation and Deplyment Plan										■			
Configuration										■			
Custom Coding										■			
System Testing											■		
User Acceptance Testing												■	
Data Migration											■		
Performance Testing											■	■	
Go-Live													■

FIGURE 2.3 Phases of an ERP Project, Activities of Each Phase and Their Sequencing

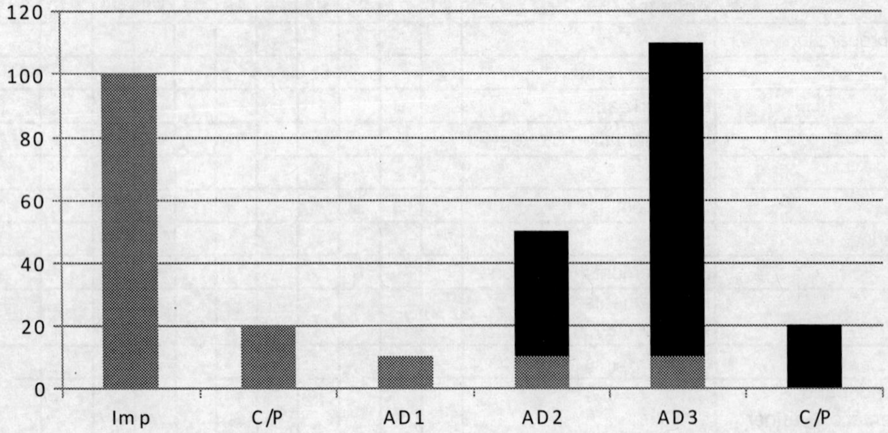

FIGURE 2.4 x Axis Shows the Effort and y axis shows the activity for 6 years; implementation (Imp) of an ERP system is done in year 1, corrective and perfective maintaince (C/P) is done in year 2 followed by adaptive maintenance (AD) in year 3 and 4. In year 3, new systems are explored and in year 5, new system is implemented. The cycle starts all over again.

The vendor often releases new versions, and the clients have no choice but update their ERP system. The vendor may release a new version for one of the following reasons:

1. Fix bugs or residual errors—corrective maintenance
2. Improve the system—perfective maintenance
3. Enhance the system—adaptive maintenance

Corrective and perfective maintenance may be incorporated using a patch requiring no major effort. But adaptive maintenance may result in a new version or release of the system. A maintenance step may be triggered due to data problems or error in the configuration. Figure 2.4 shows effort involved in maintaining the system for five years. Year 1 is when the system is implemented and the effort is used as a reference for the next seven years. Year 2 will require corrective and perfective maintenance and may be as high as 10–20 per cent of the implementation effort. Subsequent years will require little effort in maintaining the system. Assuming that the system has a life span of four years; at the end of third year an effort to explore new systems will start, and implementation of the new system will take place in the fourth year. Every time there is a change in the system, some training may be required for the end users.

2.3 TEAMS

ERP implementation team is carefully put together with the high-level management involvement. The management identifies team leaders who are committed towards the project. The team leaders then add operational managers to their teams considering their skill set. The following teams are formed for ERP implementation:

- Executive steering team
- Project manager

- Selection team
- Business process owners
- Implementation team
- Integration management team
- Change management team
- Rollout manager
- Functional team
- Extended team
- Project management office
- Technical team

Let us look at the constitution and responsibility of each of the team. Figure 2.5 shows interactions among various teams.

- **Executive steering team:** The team consists of CEO of the organization and two strategic level managers of which one will be designated as the primary sponsor of the project. The level of involvement of the executive steering team is the heaviest at the beginning of the project. The team needs to provide a clear direction about the project. Their job is also to make sure that the project has support of the shareholders and board members. It is already known that an ERP project costs anywhere from 1–3 per cent of the turnover and impacts organizational structure, culture as well as procedures. The committee may meet once in a month to check the progress of the project. The primary sponsor of the project continues to be involved on a weekly basis throughout the project. Their job is to be proactive and resolve issues quickly to avoid schedule slippage and cost overrun. They perform both substantive and symbolic roles to ensure that the implementation receives the necessary support and attention to succeed.
- **Project manager:** A full time project manager needs to be identified to lead the program from its onset till it goes live. There is another project manager from the implementation partner's side. Project managers (PM) must understand business and technology both. One can hire a technologist from outside the organization but not an expert for the business. PM may have to help business process owners to make decisions regarding changes in the business processes whenever there is a gap. The PM should have exposure in implementing large projects as ERP implementation is a large project involving staff from every department, vendor organization, external consultancy agency and implementation partner. There are (non-technical) public issues which are required to be addressed at PM level. Technical, non-technical, operational staff and managers at all levels get touched by the ERP implementation. Capacity to resolve issues and adapt according to the situation's demand with an accommodating attitude are essential attributes of a PM. A person liked by most of the people with appropriate skillset would make a better PM than an extremely skilled person who is difficult to get along.
- **Selection team:** Constitution of the selection team and their job is discussed in Chapter 8. Just to summarize, the team is responsible for working out the requirements of the organization, evaluate various ERP systems available in the market and determine the overall fit between the ERP system and the requirements. The team selects ERP system and implementation partner.
- **Business process owners (BPO):** The owner of business process(es) knows the business process(es) that they owns well and approves all changes to these processes. BPOs are generally the functional heads. They are involved in creating business blueprint during the requirement engineering phase. They work closely with the implementation partner and take the responsibility for mapping and

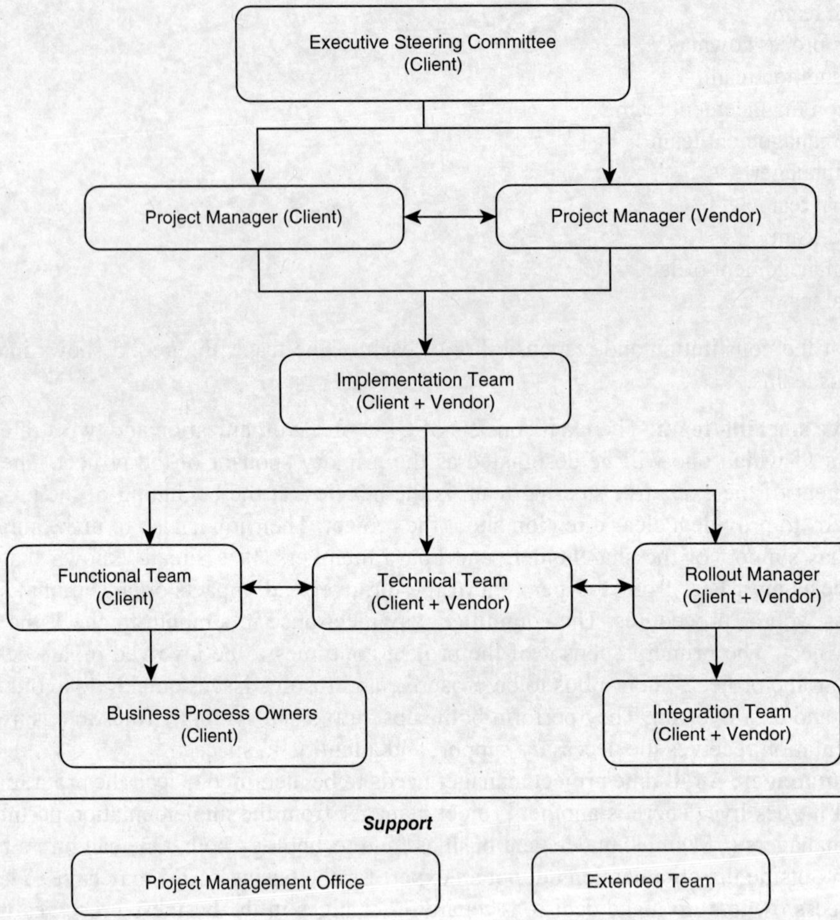

FIGURE 2.5 Teams for an ERP Implementation Project and Their Interactions

changing business processes to fit with the overall ERP system. Process owners need to be available as advisers and leaders in a timely fashion as key decision makers and direction provider during the implementation.

- **Implementation team:** The project manager works with an implementation team to do the detailed process design, system configuration and testing. The team constitutes people from IT department, business functional units, implementation partner and external consultants. The implementation team for a large organization could be as large as 100 people. Most of the ERP systems are modular and the implementation team is divided into groups to take care of individual modules. Each module team would have five to seven people and a module leader reporting to project manager. A group of users outside the implementation team would also test the system in parallel. These users are referred to super users.
- **Integration management team:** As mentioned earlier, ERP systems are mostly modular. Each module is configured and then integrated with each other. A team is constituted to perform integration of modules and test the integrated system. Their job is to test transactions from end to end. The system

is also ported to actual hardware and software platform and the performance is tested. The test could proceed with light load and then with heavy load to achieve the desired level of performance. This team largely consists of IT people from client and implementation partner.

- **Change management team:** A change management team consisting of middle level managers is formed at the beginning of the project. The responsibility of this team is to assess the organization's readiness to handle the changes that will be brought about by ERP system. Based on the findings, the team would draft a change management strategy. The strategy would include training and hand-holding of the end users, providing support during go-live and addressing individual issues. Communication, expectation setting and follow up are also part of the change management strategy. Large ERP projects would have a dedicated communication team whose job is to ensure sufficient and timely communication.
- **Rollout manager:** Rollout manager prepares a rollout strategy and time line for go-live. Their main job is to work with integration team and data migration team to release the system for use. Rollout manager is required after the implementation begins. Client as well as implementation partner work together with rollout management team.
- **Functional team:** This team consists of people who understand business processes well. This team works with BPOs during requirements engineering phase and later on move to configuration team. After the go-live, this team forms the user support group.
- **Extended team:** This team is a pool of people who can be assigned jobs that are short and bursty in nature. This team may also be assigned unanticipated and unplanned jobs. For instance, an individual may need extra training due to his skill set or job profile. Extended teams can handle these jobs.
- **Project management office (PMO):** The program management office team provides administrative support to the project team. Individuals providing support from the PMO typically are reassigned to another project as the project is closed out.
- **Technical team:** Dedicated and knowledgeable technical resources are required for the duration of the project. Depending on the size of the organization, number of sites and scope of the project, a strong technical team is required. Team members would come from client, vendor and possibly from an external agency.

CONCLUSION

Life cycle of an ERP system consists of the following phases:

- Project preparation
- Requirements engineering and ERP solution selection
- Technical planning
- Change management and training plan
- Deployment planning
- Configuration
- Custom coding
- Final preparation
- Go-live

There are multiple teams involved in an ERP system implementation. There are teams for each phase and there is also a steering committee that is a high-level team to manage the project apart from a project manager. The constitution of all teams and their roles are defined. These teams interact and work together. Broadly, teams include members who have functional and technical knowledge.

To walk through the life cycle of an ERP implementation, read the case on ERP implementation at BPCL.[5] The case examines in detail the ERP implementation at BPCL. It focuses on the IT infrastructure put in place and BPCL's IT initiatives before the ERP implementation. One can buy this case for a nominal charge.

CASE STUDY

We will continue with RetailS that we discussed in the last chapter. We will form teams and work out the time line as well.

The company has two sister organizations—one in Delhi and other in Dubai. This is their first major IT project and the company has no inhouse IT capability. Their only server is managed by an outside agency. RetailS wanted to move in a phased manner. They wanted to implement only sales and purchase modules of the ERP system. RetailS is happy with a proprietary software that they use for their financial accounting and did not want to include financial accounting in the ERP system. The modules to implement are just about 1.5 out of 14 using SAP as a reference.

- **Project document:** A project document is created in the beginning of the project that contains business requirements, scope, schedule and initial costing for the project. The document that was created for RetailS ran into couple of pages. The essential details are presented here as an example in Figure 2.6.
- **Time line:** We expected the entire project to take about six months, and the initial schedule shown in Figure 2.6.
- The project plan is shown in Figure 2.7. This plan is very elaborate and lists the activities on almost daily basis. Notice that some of the activities proceed in parallel. This document is signed by all the parties involved and used as a reference throughout the project. Progress of the project is measured against this plan.
- **Teams:** The ERP teams are shown in Table 2.3.

TABLE 2.3 Teams for ERP Projects of RetailS

People	Teams
CMD, RetailS	Champion and business process owner
Consultant	Interface between the implementation partner and RetailS
CMD, RetailS and Consultant	Selection team
Consultant	Project manager
Implementation partner and Consultant	Implementation team (no one from RetailS would be on the team)
External IT agency and consultant	Technical team

Since it is a small organization, there is no need to create other teams.

Project Document for ERP System for RetailS

Date: 09-04-2010

Author: Ms. V. Agarwal

Approved by: CMD, RetailS

Objective: The objective of the project is to deploy an ERP system covering sales and procurement process. ERP system will give an accurate and timely picture of all the sales and purchase orders. We will not include HR or financials in the ERP as of now.

Schedule of events: The following is the required schedule of events for this project. The schedule may change depending on the results of the responses and a final schedule will be established prior to contracting with the successful vendor.

S. No.	Events	Duration (Days)
1.	Informal requirements	10
2.	Meeting with potential vendors	10
3.	Award contract	1
4.	Requirements gathering and documentation	30
5.	Customization by the vendor of his product	60
6.	Testing, exploring and bug fixing (if any)	30
7.	Master data preparation entry	30
8.	Training	15
9.	Go-live preparation and go-live	6

Initial costing: The data collected from various sources indicates that an ERP implementation costs around one per cent of the turnover of the company. For RetailS, this figure turns out to be ₹50,000,00 because their turnover is ₹50 crore. RetailS plans to implement only sales and purchase modules. This is about one-tenth of the functionality an ERP system provides. We expect to spend around ₹5,000,00.

This price includes the furnishing of ERP solution, its implementation, data migration, maintenance, training, its source code, manuals, tools and the provision of all labor and services necessary or proper for the completion of the work.

RetailS involvement: RetailS has designated Ms. V. Agarwal as the PM. The team from RetailS consists of CMD and Ms. V. Agarwal. The PM will be the single-point contact for the project. RetailS will participate in requirements gathering, system testing, acceptance and user training.

Functional requirements: ERP must support all activities related to sales and procurement except the accounting part. These requirements are to elaborated in the requirements gathering phase.

Figure 2.6 A Sample Project Plan

Product: KN Retail
Project: RetailS, Delhi
Customer Project Coordinator: Ms V Agarwal
Contact number: +91 11 2509 2509
KN Project Coordinator: Mr Amit, Consultant to RetailS
Contact number: +91 11 0008 0088
Tentative Project Completion Date: 07 October 2010

S.No.	Activity	Days	Who	Scheduled Start Date	Expected Date of Completion
Project Kick Off Meeting		1	Joint	11 May 2010	11 May 2010
	40% Payment on commencement of Project		Retails		
Process Study and Product Demo					
1	Business Process Study	6	Joint	12 May 2010	18 May 2010
2	Sample Data Sheet Collection	6	Retails	13 May 2010	19 May 2010
3	Data Modelling as Per Study	9	KN	19 May 2010	28 May 2010
4	Product Demonstration to Retails	2	KN	31 May 2010	01 June 2010
5	Submission of SRS & Gap Document	1	KN	31 May 2010	31 May 2010
6	Business Process Study & Gap sign-off	11	Retails	02 June 2010	14 June 2010
Environment Set Up					
7	Customization of KN Product as per Gap Identified	29	KN	16 June 2010	19 July 2010
8	Product Installation at Retails	8	KN	20 July 2010	28 July 2010
9	Configuration	14	KN	29 July 2010	13 August 2010
10	Verification of Customized Solution by Retails	14	Joint	16 August 2010	31 August 2010
Master Data Preparation and Review					
10	Master Data Creation Workshop	7	KN	20 July 2010	27 July 2010
11	Master Data Collection	7	Joint	28 July 2010	04 August 2010
12	Verification of data before uploading to system.	4	Retails	05 August 2010	09 August 2010
13	Uploading / feeding of Masters in KN	7	KN	31 August 2010	07 September 2010
14	Verification of Masters after uploading in ERP	9	KN	08 September 2010	17 September 2010
15	Correction if any to be done	11	Joint	18 September 2010	30 September 2010
16	***Master Data Sign-off***	1	Retails	30 September 2010	30 September 2010
User Training					
17	User Training	16	Joint	01 September 2010	18 September 2010
18	***Training Sign-off***	1	Joint	09 September 2010	09 September 2010
Go Live Preparation					
19	Go Live Preparation	4	Joint	01 October 2010	06 October 2010
20	Go live sign-off	1	Joint	07 October 2010	07 October 2010
21	***Formal Implementation Completion Sign-off***	1	Retails	7 October 2010	07 October 2010

FIGURE 2.7 A Sample ERP Project Implementation Plan

EXERCISES

Test Your Understanding

1. Project planning in the life cycle of an ERP system is an important phase. Justify this statement.
2. Explain life cycle of an ERP system. What are the major activities and sub-activities performed in each phase?
3. Each phase has an entry and exit condition. Can you identify these conditions for all the phases?
4. What are the major teams that are formed for an ERP project? What is the constitution and role of these teams?
5. Why do we need business process owners to be part of the ERP implementation team? What is their role?
6. Why is it important to decide a priori interaction and reporting structure for the teams? What problems do you perceive if there are no such rules?

Apply Your Understanding

1. In the last chapter, you had chosen an organization to work with. Constitute teams for the ERP project. Do you perceive any problems in constituting teams? You may face multiple problems. Some of them are:
   a. The management may not be cooperative.
   b. There is a possibility that the organization does not have enough staff to free for ERP project.
   c. People you select may not be interested.
   d. People you left out of the ERP project teams may be unhappy.

   How would you handle these problems? Can you think of some other problems? List all of them and offer solution.
2. Assuming that your organization is implementing an ERP system, would a suggest big bang approach to your organization? Justify your answer. You can cross check your recommendation if your organization has already implemented an ERP system.
3. What will be the constitution of the technical team in your organization?

ENDNOTES

1. I. Sommerville, 'Software Construction by Configuration: Challenges for Software Engineering Research', in *Proceedings of the 21st IEEE International Conference on Software Maintenance (ICSM'05)* (2005).
2. P. Bollen, 'Enterprise Systems: Is There Still a Need for Requirements Determination' in *Proceedings of the 6th Annual ISOnEworld Conference*, (Las Vegas, NV, 2007), April 11–13.
3. A. B. Brown, A. Keller, and J. L. Hellerstein, 'A Model for Configuration Complexity and Its Application to a Change Management System,' in *9th IFIP/IEEE International Symposium on Integrated Network Management* (2005), 631–44.
4. Pnina Soffer, 'Aligning an Enterprise System with Enterprise Requirements: An Iterative Process', in *ICEIS* (2003), 147–55.

chapter 3

Benefits and Cost of an ERP System

LEARNING OBJECTIVES

After reading this chapter, you will be able to understand:

- Benefits of an ERP system
  - Strategic benefits
  - Operational benefits
  - Managerial benefits
  - Organizational benefits
- Intangible benefits
- Cost of an ERP system
- Cost-benefit analysis

3.1 INTRODUCTION

In the previous chapters, we learnt that an ERP system is a semi-finished product that has to be configured for the host company. We also learnt that an ERP project costs between 1 to 3 per cent of revenue of the host company if all modules of the ERP system are implemented. A company spends money on the ERP system because it expects to benefit from the system. An ERP system may deliver strategic benefits, operational benefits and managerial benefits. But a company would set an objective for implementing the ERP system and focus on the set objective. In this chapter, we will learn about these benefits in detail. A company can measure success of its ERP implementation by setting a quantitative objective and measuring the performance of the system against the objective. A quantitative benefit that the organization is looking for may be to reduce inventory by ten per cent, and a qualitative objective may be to increase customer satisfaction. Problems with qualitative objectives are those which cannot be verified. IT systems are known for bringing in many intangible benefits that may be difficult to measure directly. The objective of ERP should be aligned with the firm's competitive strategy. Benefits have to be weighed against the cost. An ERP project involves direct as well as indirect costs. Once we have a handle on the benefits and the costs, we can do a cost-benefit analysis to justify the project and get funding for the project.

3.2 BENEFITS

ERP may bring in many benefits that can be divided into four groups as shown in Figure 3.1. Let us look at the benefits that each of these groups offer.

3.2.1 Strategic Benefits

- ERP supports current and future business growth. The company can handle lot more transactions which are conducive to business growth. Since the data becomes easily available and the cycles become shorter, introducing new products and services are encouraged. The company can analyse data in timely manner at the desired grain level to identify niche geographical and functional areas.
- All business units get integrated. Moreover, if a company acquires another company, the newly acquired company may be integrated easily and faster through ERP system which facilitates business growth.
- Strategic planning needs timely and accurate picture of the organization. ERP system makes accurate picture available to the management in a timely manner that helps them come up with appropriate market strategy and identify new business process chains and areas.
- Streamlined and efficient processes help a company become cost leader in the market.
- ERP helps a company to provide customized products and services to its customers. World economy has moved from being a manufacturing economy to service economy. A manufacturing company now has to provide a solution to its client, not just a product. We see many such examples in India as well. A car distributor now worries about maintaining the car after its sale. The distribution centre or its collaborators follow up with customers to make sure that the car gets serviced on regular basis. The service is customized based on the customer data that ERP stores and provides. A manufacturer may shift their manufacturing strategy from make-to-store to make-to-order. Make-to-order will require linkages with suppliers, distributors and related business parties. ERP-II or extended ERP includes customer relation management and supply chain management to build external linkages. Suppliers, customers and your own marketing offices, manufacturing facilities could be spread globally. ERP is an international package and facilitates seamless (almost) integration of data across geographical limits. One can centralize world operations, manage global resources, deploy multiple tax rules and handle business transactions in multiple currencies and multiple time zones.
- ERP system may improve organizational and process flexibility.
- Customer/supplier satisfaction and relations can be enhanced by using ERP system.

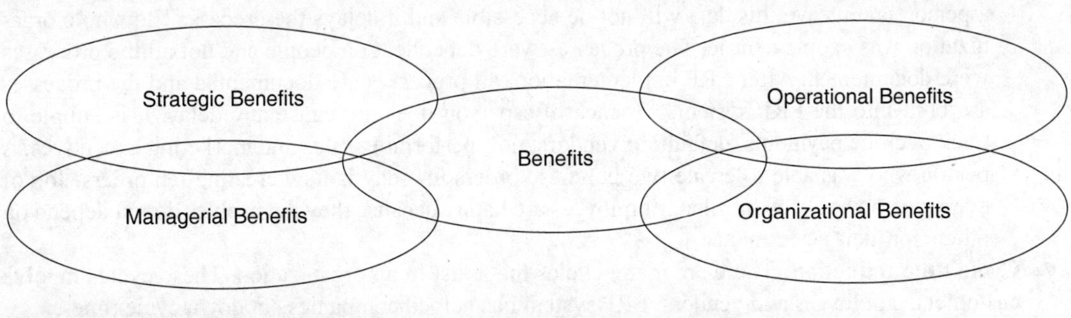

FIGURE 3.1 Benefits Offered by an ERP System to the Organization

- ERP system may help the organization to reduce marketing costs and improve market share.
- The organization may be able to establish itself as a leader in new technology.
- ERP system may help a company to gain competitive advantage and establish itself as market leader.

3.2.2 Operational Benefits

ERP help companies to improve data management, communication, decision making and reduce response time to queries. The companies that implemented ERP experienced operational benefits that can be largely classified into the following categories:

- **Cost reduction:** The following are the cost reductions:
  - ***Reduced labour cost:*** An ERP implementation will in the least automate and integrate business processes of an organization. Consequently, processes become efficient. Coupled with rationalization and reengineering, the process become even more efficient as the redundancy in processes and the redundant processes get eliminated. The required staff in customer services, production planning, order fulfillment, administrative processes, purchasing and financial management reduces.
  - ***Inventory cost reduction:*** The carrying cost reduces due to better material requirements planning, less efforts in inventory management and warehousing.
  - ***Administrative cost reduction:*** The paper work, printing effort, printing cost and moving papers around reduces. As an example, take the case of a company in Kanpur, Uttar Pradesh, India with a turnover of ₹60 crore that produces high-quality adhesives. According to the company's marketing manager after implementing ERP, their system has become very efficient even though they have not changed their processes. The integration and availability of data online has made a lot of difference—their sales have gone up by ₹1 crore in one month after they implemented Navision (ERP software). The reason being it was difficult to keep track of defaulters earlier. They buy 4,500 items from different vendors. In spite of their best efforts, they were not able to maintain three vendors for each item and bargain. At times, the purchase manager would create a crisis by saying that there is only one vendor in the market and there is shortage of the item that they supply. The management used to give them a go ahead for purchase at the vendor price because they did not want the production to suffer. A purchase order involved looking up many files for consolidating the information required including appropriate vendor, his address, request for quotation, vendor quotation, quality records of the vendor and his outstanding bills if any. The person responsible for placing an order had to contact many persons to get data. If a person is on leave, his data will not be accessible and it delays the process. The whole organization was people centric. The processes were dependent on people and not all the processes were documented. After ERP implementation, all processes are documented and the processes are built into the ERP system. Absence of a person does not cause any delay. It is simple to track overdue payments, defaulting vendors, non-performing sales and marketing executives. A person who was able to create two purchase orders in a day is now creating ten orders. Job of every person has been profiled. Employees are happy because they themselves do not depend on others for their performance.
- **Cycle time reduction:** There are many cycles that exist in an organization. These cycles involve customers, employees and vendors. ERP system has helped companies cut down cycle times.

- **Customer support activities:** These activities include order fulfillment time, billing, delivery and customer service activities become faster.
- **Employee support activities:** These activities include month-end closing, purchasing and reporting become fast.
- **Supplier support activities:** They have also become better. A company can combine multiple orders to get discounts from their vendors.

3.2.3 Managerial Benefits

In an organization, management is responsible for resource management, decision making and performance. The key ingredient to resource management and decision making is the data. The data helps management to manage their assets better. ERP helps in better production management due to the availability of the data required for production management. Management is better equipped for responding to changes that promotes proactive culture. The changes may be in the market, cost or business strategy. Planning and administrative procedures also improve. All these improvements lead to improvement in the service quality within the organization and to the customers. Manpower can be better utilized because job profiling for each employee can be easily done. The job allocation may also be changed according to the changing requirements. Monitoring is an important component of the management activity. One can sit in his own office and monitor the desired activities without having to worry about geographical proximity or distances. The activities that are closely monitored include financial performance, manufacturing performance, and overall efficiency and effectiveness of the management itself. In simple word, if one has access to timely and accurate data, management is sure to perform better in all its functions.

3.2.4 Organizational Benefits

The organization should experience the following benefits:

- ERP should facilitate business learning and broaden employee skills. The business processes get clearly defined that should help willing employees to enhance their business skills.
- Clearly defined and seamlessly integrated processes empower employees to be proactive problem solver. The overall responsibility and accountability improves. There is less of fire fighting, the role of management in routine activities decreases which results in better planning. An ERP system should help an organization in integrating clearly defined processes in a seamless manner. In some organizations, the number of management layers decrease and the organization becomes flatter.
- Another expected benefit is improved interpersonal communication, homogeneous business units that share common and consistent vision across the organization.
- ERP definitely cuts down on some mundane and repetitive activities.

The benefits have been summarized in Table 3.1.

3.2.5 Intangible Benefits

These are the benefits that cannot be easily quantified. Many of the benefits of ERP systems are intangible and there is no mechanism to measure these benefits in monetary terms. There is no way to account for intangible benefits into productivity measures. The information technology investments are no more a choice but necessary to survive in the market. The returns may not be direct and immediate. Here is a list of some intangible benefits of ERP systems.

TABLE 3.1 Benefits to an Organization from an ERP System

Strategic Benefits	Operational Benefits
• Business growth	• Reduced labour cost
• Business integration	• Reduced inventory cost
• Real time data availability	• Reduced administrative cost
• Best practices	• Cycle time reduction
• Better and personalized services to the customer	• Better customer support
• Lower marketing cost	• Better employee support
• Technology leader	• Better supplier support
• Competitive advantage	
Managerial Benefits	**Organizational Benefits**
• Improved resource utilization	• Employee empowerment
• Improved decision making	• Employees can enhance their skill set
• Better performance	• Less management layer
• Proactive management	• Efficient organization
• Improved planning	• Automation of routine jobs
• Better job-skill mapping	• Improved interpersonal communication
• Better monitoring	• Consistent vision across the organization

- Enhanced customer and vendor satisfaction
- Increased flexibility
- Improved resource utility
- Improved information accuracy
- Improved decision capability
- Better employee experience in the organization

The characteristics of intangible benefits are:

- Difficult to quantify
- Difficult to measure
- Difficult to put monetary value

3.2.6 What Benefits an Organization May Expect?

Benefits listed above are far too many to be realized by an individual company. Only some of these benefits are aimed at when an organization goes for an ERP implementation. The selection of groups of the benefits and sub-benefit should be done carefully. The objective of ERP should be aligned with the firm's competitive strategy. It is better to set quantitative objective; for example, the objective is to reduce inventory by five per cent in a year's time or to increase market share by two per cent, the data can be collected and analysed to show the performance. If, however, the objective is to increase customer satisfaction, then it is difficult to measure satisfaction level. The same objective may be stated as to reduce the number of customer complaints by 10 per cent from existing 50 complaints per 10,000 customers in one year then it becomes a quantitative objective.

Whatever the objective is, the management has to extend its full support. A project of the magnitude of an ERP implementation cannot succeed without the support of top management.[1] If the management is not convinced, the project will not get approved. However, if they lose interest after project has taken off, budget cuts or availability of proper manpower may become major threats to the success of the project. Project management itself is important. At organizational level, there are many concerns such as readiness of the organization and its people for ERP.

ERP systems are semi-finished products developed by others and require the host organization to change their processes according to ERP system.

3.3 COST OF AN ERP IMPLEMENTATION

One of the popular ways to assess cost of an ERP implementation is to benchmark the organization against a similar organization, if one is available. This method is referred to as analogy based cost estimation. The parameters that one can use to check similarity between two organizations are as follows:[2]

- Number of users
- Number of sites
- Number of interfaces required
- Number of modules implemented
- Number of companies of the organization
- Electronic data interface
- Number of modifications required in the software
- Number of distinct reports to be generated
- Number of plants that the organization has

Experiments have shown that number of modules, interfaces, users and sites are the parameters that decide effort required for ERP implementation.[3] The implication is that if these four parameters are similar, the effort and cost would be similar even if other parameters do not match.

Incidentally, there are no popular and well-established parametric algorithms for estimating cost of an ERP implementation.[4] A regression model has been built in 2001 using data[5] from 176 R/3 SAP implementations. The data were gathered from 1990 to 1998 in a multinational consultant organization.[6] The projects span many industries and countries in all regions of the world. The data have been reported by project managers who themselves use the database to plan and estimate future projects. The company has a standard ERP methodology. Therefore, the data presumably have been reported in a consistent manner.

The following is the regression model for estimating effort in workdays:

$$\ln(\text{Effort}) = 4.82 + 0.286 \times \ln(\text{No. of users}) + 0.093 \times \ln(\text{No. of sites}) + 0.314 \times \ln(\text{No. of interfaces}) + 0.746 \times \ln(\text{No. of modules})$$

The data that was used for building this model had missing data. Depending on the techniques used for handling missing data, the constant and coefficients varied as given in Table 3.2. We will plug in some

TABLE 3.2 Range of the Constant and Coefficients for Different Techniques of Handling Missing Data

Constant	4.82–5.26
Coefficient for number of users	0.110–0.286
Coefficient for number of sites	0.067–0.153
Coefficient for number of interfaces	0.153–0.393
Coefficient for number of modules	0.457–0.822

numbers to get an idea of the efforts required. Let us say, number of users are 1,297, number of sites are 45, number of interfaces are 39, and number of modules to be implemented are 5.2. When we plug-in these numbers in the above equation, we get effort as 14,827 work days that translate to 494 person months. Referring to Table 3.4, this effort accounts for consulting and project team. One can convert the effort into cost by accounting for cost of each resource. One of the popular equations to convert person month to calendar month is the following:[7]

$$\text{Time in calendar months} = 2.5 \times \text{PM}^{0.38}.$$

Using this equation, we get 26 calendar months. Divide 494 by 26 to get the team size of approximately 20. The project would take over 2 years and 20 full time staff to complete it. The equation to calculate effort will not work for very small projects. This effort covers primarily the consulting effort that includes configuration efforts from the vendor or implementation partner.

An organization may not be able to rely on this model alone for estimating the efforts. But the model can be safely used to get an idea of the effort that would be required. No model gives an accurate estimate of the effort. Some of the data from a survey[8] are given in tables 3.3 and 3.4. This survey was conducted in Sweden but the data obtained through this survey is universal. Implementing an ERP is very expensive and time consuming. The cost of implementation varies from 1–3 per cent of the turnover (Table 3.3). The cost of an ERP implementation is the same in India. Some data was collected and the cost of implementation was verified.

TABLE 3.3 Implementation Cost for ERP Project as a Percentage of Revenue

Revenue ($M)	Cost as Percentage of Revenue
<15	3.45
16–50	2.15
51–250	2.36
251–750	1.31
>750	0.38

TABLE 3.4 ERP Project Cost Components

Software	24.2%
Hardware	18.5%
Consulting	30.1%
Training	13.8%
Project Team	12.0%
Other	1.4%

Major cost components and their shares are shown in Table 3.4. Consulting is the largest cost component followed by the software. The cost associated with an ERP project may be divided into direct cost and indirect cost. Direct cost is what one can easily account for through an invoice or a bill whereas indirect costs are difficult to account for as there is no bill or invoice raised. Let us look at the direct and indirect cost heads.

3.3.1 Direct Costs

- **Hardware:** An ERP implementation would require a computer server to run the ERP server, as most of the ERP systems are based on client/server architecture.

- **Software:** ERP vendors usually charge for the software—client-side software and server-side software. In addition, they charge per user license fee which is essentially the number of logins you are allowed to create. Usually, number of concurrent users are much less, about one-third to half of the number of licenses. The cost of implementation and testing tools is covered by the license fee. But it is not a bad idea to verify with the vendor upfront.
- **Consulting:** An ERP implementation always requires an external consultant. Most of the non-IT organizations would not have core competence to handle ERP project. It is one of the major cost component.
- **Add-on hardware and software:** One may need additional hardware and software such as operating system, database, networking cables and router. ERP system stores every transaction in the database. At the end of the fiscal year, data is archived for which one may need a file server with plenty of disk space. One may also need an interface converter to facilitate communication between ERP database server and the back-up file system. Network setup may require a router and cables. Network security, data backup server and disaster management system are additional add-ons that must be allocated funds. One may include these costs under hardware and software heads.
- **Training costs:** The vendor and implementation partner would train handpicked people from the organization who in turn train all end users in the organization. This train-the-trainer program also costs and should be accounted for.
- **Project team cost:** The resources (people) put on ERP project team would account for this cost head. Most of the companies use time sheets to account for the resource cost.
- **Other:** One can put all miscellaneous expenditure under this head. These may include costs such parallel run cost. In the last chapter, we mentioned that business continuity is an absolute must. The legacy systems may have to run in parallel till the ERP system stabilizes and goes live. The parallel run cost may be included under this head.

3.3.2 Indirect Cost

- **Lost productivity cost:** The management and employees of the organization while working on ERP project are away from their otherwise assigned duties. There may be a loss of productivity and this may be a major source of indirect cost.
- **Dedication to explore the potential of the system:** In the beginning, users spend time exploring the system. The cost of this time is another indirect cost component which is very difficult if not impossible to account for. If learning happens through trial and error, the cost can escalate even further.
- **Employee motivation:** This is an interesting indirect cost factor. After ERP system has gone live, if motivation level of the employees is low and they do not use the system, there is a huge indirect cost that the organization incurs. Various methods of ensuring user buy-in are described in Chapter 4.
- **Changes in salaries:** There may be a change in salaries of employees as a result of improved employee flexibility and staff turnover. These changes are always in the upward direction. The employees expect an immediate gratification. There are numerous interesting examples available. In one SAP project, the project manager decided to quit his job in the middle of the project and start

his own consultancy firm. The company hired him at a much higher cost. In another instance, employees were given some incentive to learn and adapt the new IT systems that became a permanent perk. Some employees just move to another place instead of adapting new ways of working, costing a considerable amount to the company.

After the go-live stage, the following two budgets will be required:

- **Running cost:** The system would require system-support staff and infrastructure to run. One would include the running cost of the system under this head. A thumb rule is to make it 20 per cent of the total project cost.
- **Upgrades and maintenance:** For software products, maintenance involves three types of activities, namely—corrective, perfective and adaptive. Corrective maintenance refers to removing any bug that may get discovered by the users. ERP vendor releases new versions at regular intervals and may discontinue support for older versions. Some technology upgrades may also be required to possibly handle larger transaction volumes or to make system faster. These costs must be accounted for and included in the maintenance cost. A new upgrade is generally adaptive and perfective both. The host company would go for an upgrade to improve their existing information systems.

3.4 COST-BENEFIT ANALYSIS

Various studies[9] have been done to figure out the benefits that companies expect from ERP systems if they are in the process of implementing an ERP system and benefits they have been to realize if they have already deployed the system. The following tangible benefits have been highlighted:

- Inventory reduction
- Personnel reduction
- Productivity improvements
- Order management improvements
- Financial close cycle reduction
- IT cost reduction
- Procurement cost reduction
- Cash management improvement
- Revenue/Profit increases
- Transportation/Logistics cost reductions
- Maintenance reductions
- On-time delivery

A table similar to the Table 3.5 is created and expected benefits are documented.

The cost of the project is expected to be around ₹5,00,000,00 (1 per cent of the sales). Recall that the cost-benefit analysis is done prior to the commencement of the project when actual cost of the project is not known. In any software project, the initial estimates can be off by a factor of 4.[10] The annual running cost of the project will be close to 20 per cent of the project cost. Table 3.6 gives the cost-benefit analysis for this particular example.

The ROI is 12.6 per cent for this ERP project. Most of the companies would get a return of 5–25 per cent on their investment (Table 3.7).[11]

TABLE 3.5 Benefit Analysis

Business Area	Associated Figure	Associated Figure (in ₹)	Benefit (in ₹)
Sales		500,000,000	
Possible increase in sales	5% of sales	25,000,000	
Gross margin	50%		
Benefit			12,500,000
Inventory Carrying Cost			
Inventory holding cost	0.8% of inventory value		
Raw material inventory value	5% of sales	25,000,000	
Possible reduction in raw material inventory value	25%	6,250,000	
Benefit			50,000
Current work-in-progress and intermediate storage value	2.5% of sales	12,500,000	
Possible reduction in work-in-progress and intermediate storage value	50%	6,250,000	
Benefit			50,000
Current finished goods stock inventory value	12.5% of sales	62,500,000	
Possible reduction in finished goods stock inventory value	25%	15,625,000	
Benefit			125,000
Capital saving due to reduced inventory	25% inventory reduction	7,031,250	
Cost of capital	12%		
Benefit			843,750
Procurement Cost			
Cost of material purchased	30% of sales	150,000,000	
Procurement cost	2%	3,000,000	
Reduction is procurement cost	50%	1,500,000	
Benefit			1,500,000
Labour Cost			
Cost	10% of sales	50,000,000	
Possible reduction direct labour cost	2%	1,000,000	
Benefit			1,000,000
Shorter Debit/Credit Cycles			
Annual benefit	0.05% of sales	250,000	250,000
Total Benefits			**16,318,750**

TABLE 3.6 Cost-benefit Analysis for the Example

Head	Cost (₹)	Benefits (₹)
Total annual saving		1,63,18,750
On-going cost	1,00,00,000	
Net annual benefit		
One time cost	5,00,00,000	
One time cost saving		4,57,500
Net capital cost	5,00,00,000	

TABLE 3.7 Return on Investment (ROI) and Percentage of Organization That Achieved Specified ROI

Estimated Return	Per cent
<5	16.5
5–15	38.0
15–25	30.4
25–50	11.4
>50	3.7

CONCLUSION

There are different types of benefits that an ERP system may potentially deliver. These benefits can be categorized in strategic benefits, operational benefits, managerial benefits and organizational benefits. There are many benefits that are intangible and difficult to quantify. It is important to identify intangible benefits as well. An ERP system cannot deliver all the benefits. An organization should set objectives and benefits that it expects from the ERP system. It is important that the benefits are defined in quantitative terms so that it can be verified.

For estimating the cost of an ERP project, the general practice is to benchmark an organization with a similar organization who has already implemented an ERP system. The parameters used for checking similarity are number of users, sites, interfaces and ERP modules being implemented. There is no popular or standard algorithmic way of estimating the cost of an ERP project. Major direct cost heads include hardware, software, training cost and consultancy cost. An ERP project involves direct as well indirect costs. A sense of implementation time, return on investment and life span would help a project manager in managing an ERP project.

CASE STUDY

In this chapter, two topics—benefits and cost are discussed, and RetailS is used for discussing the benefits.

Benefits of Using ERP for RetailS

- **Strategic benefits: Prices and their validity**

  There is a sale price associated with each item RetailS deals in. Associated with each item that RetailS deals in, there is a sale price. The management fixes prices for the known items. These prices are generally valid for a month. In certain cases, the prices may fluctuate in positive or negative directions about which only the management knows. It is the responsibility of the management to update the price list. Since the management team consists of only three people and they are multi-tasking, it is not unusual for them to forget to update the price list. Sometimes, the monthly update of the price list is also not done. The sales staff may use the old list and cause loss to RetailS or overprice the customer that may result in loss of the customer, or his goodwill or both.

The sales price is dependent on the purchase price. The management negotiates the purchase price with the vendors before creating the sales price list.

The management wanted an IT system that will send a reminder to the management after a month to update the price list. The IT system should also prevent the sales staff to use a stale price.

- **Strategic benefits: Reduce errors**

  There are multiple parameters associated with a product that RetailS deals in. A mistake or omission of one of the parameters may result in delay, cancellation or rejection of the entire order. IT system can force the staff to check every parameter.

  Every order involve details that need to be carefully defined. For instance, the payment terms have to be defined and agreed upon by RetailS and the customer. Any omission or mistake may cause delay or confusion in the payments. IT system can help RetailS to create a master list of possible payment terms to avoid any errors.

- **Strategic benefits: Follow up**

  RetailS needs to frequently follow up with their customers, vendors and shipping agents. A customer is contacted multiple times during the process of a sale that also requires staff to contact the vendors multiple times as well. IT system can generate a reminder to the concerned staff for a follow up activity.

- **Managerial benefits: Trade secret**

  RetailS succeeds in their business by identifying customers, providing them the items of required quality at agreed upon prices in a timely manner. All this is possible if the vendors supply them quality items at a reasonable cost and on agreed time. RetailS has to protect price information from their existing competition and from the potential competition that may even shoot up from within RetailS. The information should be available in a very selective manner to the employees. IT system can help RetailS to make only the required information available to an employee.

- **Managerial benefits: Reports**

  IT systems can provide required reports to the management about the organization in real time in desired format.

Budget

Here is an attempt to budget the ERP project for RetailS. The data collected from various sources indicates that an ERP implementation costs around 1 per cent of the turnover of the company. For RetailS, this figure turns out to be ₹50,000,00 because their turnover is ₹50 crore. As mentioned earlier, RetailS is a very efficient company and this figure is way too high for an ERP project for a company that has less than 30 employees. Little calculation would show that if RetailS spends ₹50,000,00 on an ERP project, it would be spending ₹1,70,000 per employee on ERP project.

Accordingly, we expected to be able to find a solution for about ₹5,000,00. Since the cost of the project was estimated to be ₹5,000,00, RetailS did not feel the need to do any cost-benefit analysis. They had the infrastructure already and no new hardware was required. Their only indirect cost was the productivity loss when employees were getting trained. The strategy deployed by RetailS was to account the expenditure and not worry about doing the cost-benefit upfront.

EXERCISES

Test Your Understanding

1. Briefly describe various types of benefits that an ERP system may deliver.
2. What are the differences between tangible and intangible benefits? Give examples.
3. Why is it important to set quantitative objective for an ERP project? Give some examples of qualitative as well as quantitative objectives.
4. What are various cost factors involved in an ERP project? Explain each briefly.
5. How would you estimate cost of an ERP project?

Apply Your Understanding

1. Is there a relationship between the type of industry of the organization implementing ERP system and the types of benefits it expects from ERP system? You may take two different industries such as service and manufacturing industry and answer the question.
2. In the last chapter, you chose an organization to work with. Collect relevant information and estimate the cost for ERP project for your organization. If ERP system has already been implemented, the management may verify your estimates. Otherwise, check their willingness to invest the specified amount in ERP system. What are the lessons learnt?

ENDNOTES

1. P. Bingi, M. K. Sharma and J. K. Golda, 'Critical Issues Affecting an ERP Implementation', in *Information Systems Management* (1999), 7–14.
2. Ingunn Myrtveit, Erik Stensrud, and Ulf H. Olsson, 'Analyzing Data Sets with Missing Data: An Empirical Evaluation of Imputation Methods and Likelihood-based Methods', in *IEEE Transactions on Software Engineering* (2001), 27(11).
3. C. Francalanci, 'Predicting the Implementation Effort of ERP Projects: Empirical Evidence on SAP R/3', in *Journal of Information Technology* (2001), 16, 33–48.
4. E. Stensrud, 'Alternative Approaches to Effort Prediction of ERP Projects', in *Information and Software Technology* (2001), 43, 413–23.
5. Ingunn Myrtveit, Erik Stensrud, and Ulf H. Olsson, 'Analyzing Data Sets with Missing Data: An Empirical Evaluation of Imputation Methods and Likelihood-based Methods', in *IEEE Transactions on Software Engineering* (2001), 27(11).
6. C. Francalanci, 'Predicting the Implementation Effort of ERP Projects: Empirical Evidence on SAP R/3', in *Journal of Information Technology* (2001), 16, 33–48.
7. P. Jalote, *An Integrated Approach to Software Engineering*, Narosa, (2002).
8. Jan Olhager and E. Selldin, 'Enterprise Resource Planning Survey of Swedish Manufacturing Firms', in *European Journal of Operations Research* (2003), 146, 365–73.
9. *Deloitte Consulting, ERP's Second Wave*, New York, NY: Deloitte Consulting, 1998.
10. P. Jalote, *An Integrated Approach to Software Engineering*, Narosa (2002).
11. Jan Olhager and E. Selldin, 'Enterprise Resource Planning Survey of Swedish Manufacturing Firms', in *European Journal of Operations Research* (2003), 146, 365–73.

chapter 4

Change Management

LEARNING OBJECTIVES

After reading this chapter, you will be able to understand:

- Readiness of the organization for an ERP system
- Factors that influence attitude of employees
- Enhance attitude towards an ERP system
- Change management at organizational level
- Tools for change management

4.1 INTRODUCTION

An ERP project has associated with it—people, technical and organizational issues. Each organization has to work out a strategy based on their exposure, experience, precedence and suggestions from their consultants to handle the changes brought about by an ERP system. Broadly, the focus of the strategy[1] is one of the following three:[2–4]

- People issues
- Technical issues
- Organizational issues

Strategies to manage technical changes pay attention to ERP complexity, adequacy of inhouse technical expertise, and time and cost of the implementation.

We will discuss change management strategies to handle people and organizational issues. People issues are discussed in Sections 4.2, 4.3 and 4.4. Before the management decides to go for an ERP system, they should make an effort to check the attitude of the employees towards an ERP system. Attitude of employee can be checked with the help of a questionnaire. The chapter also discusses three different types of reactions from the employees in the form of resistance if they are not ready for ERP. Extended Technology Acceptance Model (ETAM) provides a framework to enhance the attitude of the employees. The earlier questionnaire can be used again to check the attitude.

Organizational issues are dealt with in sections 4.5, 4.6 and 4.7. An organization implementing an ERP system needs a change management strategy to manage the impact on the organization. We will discuss Lewin's model and improvisational model of change. We will also look at a general strategy for change management and three facilitating tools to execute the strategy. These tools are force field analysis and matrix of change.

4.2 PEOPLE ISSUES: ARE YOU READY FOR ERP?

An organization will need to change itself quite a bit to ensure success of ERP implementation in the organization. The change would involve and impact people in a big way. They will have to shed away their earlier ways of doing work. During the implementation phase, the anxiety may start due to the fear of unknown as well as the fear of known. People may also worry about the changes ERP system will bring about and their ability to adjust to the changes (fear of unknown). People may also fear getting laid off due to reduced manpower requirements (fear of known). Examining ERP implementation from a chronological process perspective aids in understanding when and how employee attitude play an important role.[5]

We are primarily concerned with the attitude of people during pre-adoption phase of an ERP implementation.[6] It is the phase where an organization begins to consider the need to change existing technologies and identify available ERP solutions.

The pre-implementation phase is time to identify and shape attitude of everyone in the organization. The attitude at the beginning is what finally shapes behaviour of the employees towards the technology. We need to figure out the following:

- What are the concerns people have when ERP system is considered for adoption by an organization?
- Possible relationships/interactions among these concerns.

These two will help the organization to address the concerns and put people at ease so that the chances of acceptance will increase manifold.

We can address people issues in two phases. In the first phase, we figure out the preparedness of people for ERP system. In the second phase, we prepare them for ERP system.

4.3 FACTORS THAT INFLUENCE PRE-IMPLEMENTATION ATTITUDE

There have been multiple studies to assess factors that influence pre-implementation attitude of employees towards an ERP system. Organizational demography is an important factor determining attitude towards ERP implementation. Demographics are characteristics of individual employees. An organization with a higher proportion of relatively new employees may find it easier to implement an ERP system. If the employees have not experienced previous IT initiatives, they may not have any reason to have negative attitude. Past failures in IT initiatives/projects may impact end-users in a negative way. Better IT project track record establishes IT as a trusted unit within the organization.[7] The managerial and professional employees are likely to have more positive attitude towards ERP system than the others. Managers and professionals are likely to have information about ERP system and their attitude would be based on this information. It has been shown that attitude towards ERP system is dependent on perceived usefulness and ease of use.[8] The relationship among these three is shown in Figure 4.1. Stages theory[9] which is discussed in Chapter 1 also supports these relationships.

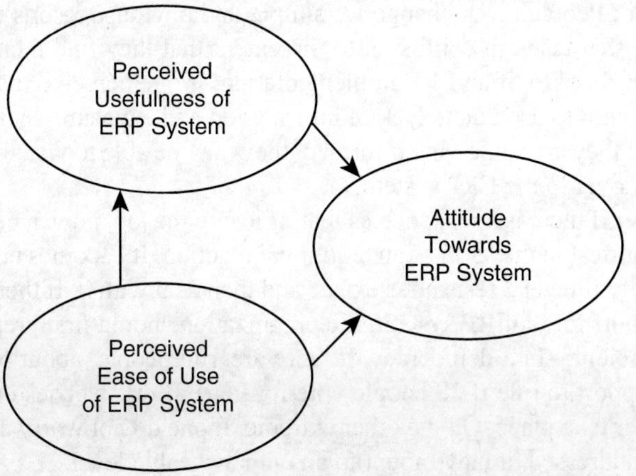

FIGURE 4.1 Factors That Influence Attitude Towards an ERP System

If an organization has used information systems (TPS, MIS, DSS) successfully, then the organization and its people would perceive ERP systems to be useful and easy to use. These perceptions would be based on past experience. On the other hand, if an organization has not used information systems or has not had much success, the attitude of people is likely to be negative. Organizations that have a history of trust and collaboration across hierarchical levels are likely to experience smoother implementation experience.

One can use a questionnaire[10] similar to the one shown in Figure 4.2 to assess the attitude of employees. It has been used to assess attitude of employees of a government organization in India. If employees have negative attitude, they will resist ERP implementation. Such resistance is due to perceived risk and habit.[11] The resistance may manifest in one or more of the following form:

Ease of Use

Q1. Learning to use the new system will be easy for me.

Q2. It will be easy to get the new system to do what I want it to do.

Perceived Usefulness

Q3. Using the ERP system will increase my productivity.

Q4. The new system will be useful in my job.

Attitude Towards an ERP System

Q5. The ERP system will provide access to more data.

Q6. The ERP system will make data analysis easier.

Q7. The ERP system will be better than the existing systems.

Q8. The ERP system will provide accurate information.

Q9. The ERP system will provide integrated, timely and reliable information

FIGURE 4.2 Questionnaire to Assess Attitude of Employees Towards an ERP System

- **Level 1 resistance:** People resist change for simple and obvious reasons such as lack of information and exposure that leads to confusion to the extent that they find themselves in disagreement with the idea itself. In case of an ERP implementation, if one perceive that the system will not be useful and will be hard to use due to lack of information and exposure, they are likely to resist ERP implementation. If they are somewhat informed, they may be able to visualize the amount of efforts required to switch over to the ERP system.
- **Level 2 resistance:** If there is a fear such as fear of losing the job, power, control or importance, the resistance will manifest in the form of an emotional reaction. It becomes necessary for the management to first identify if level 2 resistance exists, and then deal with it. If there is lot of resistance and not sufficient support for an ERP system, the organization should first prepare its people to accept ERP system (sufficient—In a democracy, if there are 100 people, about 55 of them vote and you have sufficient support to rule if 28 people vote for you). If one worries only about the resistance, no change will ever take place. On the other extreme, if one do not worry about the resistance at all and it remains unaddressed, it may mount to an unmanageable level.
- **Level 3 resistance:** Sometimes, people may dislike the person from whom they think that idea of ERP system has originated. They resist the person by resisting ERP system.

In Maurer and Associates,[12] it is cited that the primary reason for the failure of changes is resistance (according to a survey of Fortune 500 executives, reference not cited). We know from our school physics that resistance opposes movement. We also know that anytime there is a movement, resistance from somewhere or the other will be offered. In other words, resistance is inevitable. Then, is there a way out? It has been established that the management's (lack of) response to the resistance is the cause of the failure and not the resistance itself. Some authors[13] believe that resistance is good as it indicates that there is energy.

The objective is to reduce the resistance and increase the support level.

4.4 HOW TO ENHANCE ATTITUDE?

Assuming that people are rational, if a proposal is explained to them, individuals see that it is in their interest and subscribe to the change.[14] If the assumption that people are rational is correct, communication would resolve most of the issues. Level 3 resistance may be managed through communication. Level 2 resistance may also be managed to a great extent through communication and negotiations[15] such as trade short-term pains with long-term gains.

Some of the factors that help in preparing people and gaining their support identified in isolation are as follows:

- Top management support.
- A strong business justification for the project.
- A structured implementation team that performs well-defined jobs, both substantive and symbolic.
- Training of employees.
- Project communication.
- User involvement.

It does not help much to look at the factors in isolation and the above list may not be able to guide the change management team.

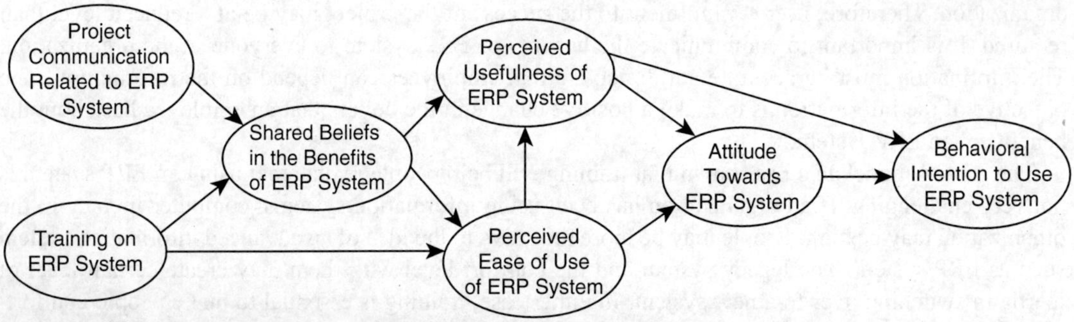

FIGURE 4.3 Extended Technology Acceptance Model

Extended Technology Acceptance Model (ETAM)[16] is a model that captures the issues and their relationships. ETAM is an extension of Technology Acceptance Model (TAM) model[17] that was developed for office automation systems. ETAM considers the issues involved in an ERP implementation.

4.4.1 Extended Technology Acceptance Model

There are two exogenous variables in ETAM:

- **Communications related to ERP project:** Informing the people about the project through multiple communication channels like newsletter of the company, Web site, demonstrations and presentations is important. Moreover, the change management team has to ensure that people are actually getting informed.
- **Training on ERP systems:** Training of adequate length at appropriate level of details to employees by knowledgeable trainers is important. The assumption is that the understanding of employees should improve after the training, that in turn should improve their perception about the usefulness and ease of use of the ERP system.

Various parameters and their relationships are shown in Figure 4.3. The actual usage of the system depends on the attitude towards the system. The direct communication from the company would lead people to start talking about ERP systems and issues involved. The positive beliefs about the ERP system get re-enforced if these dominate. The negative sentiments would soon start fading away due to mutual influence and shared beliefs with peers and supervisors. To achieve success, a sense of mutual trust and commitment must develop between the various participants to ensure a free exchange of beliefs and opinions.[18] Individual opinions and beliefs get influenced by others in the organization. These beliefs may be different for people at varied levels. If somehow the negative sentiments are stronger than positive sentiments, the organization may not be ready for the ERP system. Managers can proactively influence the beliefs and opinions through opinion leaders and liaison officers. Lack of communication has been identified as one of the reasons for project failures. People may form negative opinions about the system in absence of the information from reliable and competent authorities. It is essential to communicate with employees to help them form a coherent and accurate opinion about ERP system. Decision to implement ERP system in the organization mostly originates from senior management leaving the users, business units and the middle management out, even though its impact is felt across the organization. Therefore, user commitment to the success of the project may be at a reduced level than required. It is important to communicate the benefits of ERP system to everyone in the organization. The information must be accurate and timely so that employees can depend on the information. The objective of the information is to make a positive change in the beliefs that an employee has about the benefits of an ERP system.

The ETAM model also has shown that training will help people realize that using an ERP system is not very challenging. If an organization has been using information systems, computer literacy in the organization may be high. People may be more receptive to the idea of an advanced information system such as ERP system. The legacy system and the comfort level with them may create certain level of inertia in switching over to a new system. In either case, training is essential to make people comfortable with ERP system. Direct experience that people would get during the training sessions is essential irrespective of the level of computer literacy level in the organization. Training programs also provide a mechanism to disseminate useful and pertinent information about the ERP system. Training program would be different for different people depending on their roles and responsibilities. One tends to use an information system if they finds it easy to use. A system that requires no additional efforts on the part of the user after the training, is more likely to be used. While the implementation is in progress and in parallel training, sessions are organized for the employees, their perceptions about the usefulness of the system and ease of use would determine their attitude towards the ERP system. The user must be assured that the management is supportive of ERP system. The user themselves must consider the new system better than the legacy systems in providing accurate, integrated, timely and reliable information. Direct benefits to the user may include increased productivity and improved job profile. This model is also useful in addressing Level 1 resistance (reaction to fear of unknown—not knowing the impact of ERP system) and Level 2 resistance (fear of known—chances of being laid off, losing power in the organization). Communication about the project and training would reduce the fear of unknown and the anxiety would disappear.

Level 3 resistances can be handled by making the idea of ERP system look like an idea of a group of people rather than an individual.

The questionnaire given in Figures 4.2 and 4.4 can be used to assess the attitude of employees after training and communication. One can use Likert-type scale with choices such as strongly agree, agree, neutral, disagree and strongly disagree with numerical values 1 to 5 associated with the choices. The responses of the employees are evaluated to find out the readiness of the employees. For further details, the case is provided in later stages. The communication and training will bring about a positive change in the attitude of employees.

4.4.2 Summary

We have discussed a strategy for assessing and changing attitude of the employees that consists of the following three phases.[19]

- **Knowledge formulation phase:** Use questionnaire given in Figure 4.2 to evaluate the attitudes of individual users. An analysis of the data would reveal the attitude of groups or functional units provided the questionnaire request the individual to identify their functional unit. The data would also help in identifying their needs and concerns.
- **Strategy implementation phase:** Based on ETAM, the communication and training are two activities to focus on to address most of the people issues.

Communication

Q.1 I was well informed about the project through the company newsletters

Q.2 I was informed about the project through presentation, demonstrations, or road shows

Training

Q.3 The training provided to me was complete

Q.4 My level of understanding substantially improved

Q.5 After going through the training program

Q.6 The training gave me confidence in the new system

Q.7 The training was of adequate length and detail

Q.8 The trainers were knowledgeable and aided me in my understanding of the system

Beliefs in the Benefits of ERP System

Q.9 I believe in the benefits of the ERP system

Q.10 My peers believe in the benefits of ERP system

Q.11 My management team believes in the benefits of ERP

Behavioural Intention

Q.12 I expect to use ERP system

Q.13 I expect the information from ERP system to be used

FIGURE 4.4 Questionnaire to Assess Enhanced Attitude of Employees Towards ERP System Due to Training and Communication

- **Status evaluation:** Another survey should be done using questionnaire given in Figure 4.4 to evaluate effectiveness of the training and communication as well as their quality. If the attitude remains largely negative towards ERP system, it may be wiser to delay the adoption of the ERP system. The management should first focus on winning the support of the employees.

There are many other changes that the organization will experience. The management would have to work out a change management strategy to handle organizational issues which are discussed further.

4.5 CHANGE MANAGEMENT STRATEGIES TO HANDLE ORGANIZATIONAL ISSUES

An ERP system makes an impact on organizational structure and its culture. To quote,[20]

> An ERP system, by its very nature, imposes its own logic on a company's strategy, organization and culture. It pushes a company towards full integration even when a certain degree of business unit segregation may be in its best interest. And it pushes a company towards generic processes even when customized processes may be source of competitive advantage.

Change management is defined as the process of assisting the organization in the smooth transition from one defined state to another, by managing and coordinating changes to business processes and systems. Change management involves the effective communication with stakeholders regarding the scope and impact of the expected change; formal processes for assessing and monitoring the impact of the change on the stakeholders and their work processes, and identifying and developing effective and appropriate techniques to assist stakeholders to cope and adapt to the new technology.[21] There are different ways of looking at the changes.

4.5.1 Lewin's Model

An early model of change developed by Kurt Lewin describes change as the following three-stage process:

- Unfreezing
- Changing
- Freezing

The first stage[22] is *unfreezing*. It involves overcoming inertia and dismantling the existing mindset. Unfreezing and getting motivated for the change is all about weighing up the pros and cons and deciding if the pros outnumber the cons. This is the basis of what Kurt Lewin called the Force Field Analysis. There are lots of different factors (forces) for and against making change that we need to be aware of (analysis). If the factors for change outweigh the factors against change, we will make the change. If not, then there is low motivation to change. This unfreezing stage involves moving an entire business towards motivation for change.

In the second stage, referred to as *changing*, the change occurs. This is typically a period of confusion and transition. The old ways are being challenged but a clear picture of replacement has not yet emerged. The third and final stages are *freezing*. The new mindset crystallizes and one's comfort level starts returning. Lewin's concern is about reinforcing the change and ensuring that the desired changes are accepted and maintained in the future. Without this, the organizations tend to go back to its older state.

Lewin treats change as a planned event that occurs in a bounded period. This model works well for organizations that are stable and changes are always a planned activity rather than an activity that gets triggered by technological changes or market forces. Present organizations are flexible and turbulent. The change itself is flexible and ERP implementation itself is an open-ended project.

4.5.2 Improvisational Model

The model[23] suggests that the changes fall into the following three categories:

- **Anticipated changes:** Changes that are planned ahead of time and occur as intended. These changes may be identified before a technology project commences and the management prepares to deal with them.
- **Emergent changes:** Changes that arise spontaneously from local innovation which are not anticipated or intended.
- **Opportunity-based changes:** These changes are introduced purposefully and intentionally during the change process in response to an unexpected opportunity, event or breakdown.

The change management team makes a plan to deal with anticipated changes, but emergent and opportunity-based changes are the ones that the change management team will have to watch for and respond to. For instance, ERP may empower employees through integrated information more than the management anticipated, this is an emergent change. The management may respond by enhancing job profiles (positive approach) or by limiting access to data (negative approach). An opportunity, which has presented itself to many companies after ERP system implementation went live, is to start a business centre. The trained ERP manpower was utilized to start ERP consulting. Business intelligence and knowledge management at organization level and at industry level have emerged as an opportunity because of ERP systems. Bristlecone in India is one such company. In any case, we need to work out a change management strategy for handling the anticipated changes. The steps involved in creating a change management strategy are described in the next section.

4.6 CREATING A CHANGE MANAGEMENT STRATEGY TO HANDLE ORGANIZATIONAL ISSUES

It is now clear that an organization needs a change management strategy. Devising a change management strategy involves the following general steps (adapted from Hussey):[24]

- **Envision:** Determine the changes that the ERP project will bring about. This is the foundation step. The changes have to be identified and documented. It may not be possible to identify all the changes but the objective is to identify all major changes. There are certain tools available that can be used for the purpose such as force field analysis or matrix of change that we will discuss in Sections 4.7.1 and 4.7.2. Set the objectives of the change management strategy and the objective may be one or more of the following:[25]
  - Enhance acceptance of the ERP system.
  - Enhance sustainability of changes.
  - Create common orientation among all stakeholders.
  - Ensure motivation.
  - Make results felt.

  This list is not exhaustive. The management may set one or more objectives for the change management team depending on the anticipated changes. The next step is to communicate to the stakeholders so that they would support the change and would learn about the support system during the process of change.
- **Communication:** The changes identified in Step 1 need to be communicated to the stakeholders. The structure of the organization, decision-making process, control structure or reward system may change due to the ERP system. Since an ERP system impacts everyone in the organization, it is best to inform everyone about the changes. In literature, this approach is referred to as extensive participation. The stakeholders may have a say and may be allowed to provide feedback. For an ERP project, generally focused participation works better where business heads, process owners and influential people are communicated directly who in turn inform their subordinates. Some amount of persuasion may be required if the level of resistance is high. Persuading people may involve spelling out the need and benefits of the change. If the organization has a history of failed IT projects, a leader with strong commitment and integrity may be required to lead the ERP project.

  In any case, the communication has to include the change in a clear manner. The stakeholders should understand the changes and their impact on them.
- **Create change management team and assign tasks:** Depending on the outcome of Step 1, an appropriate change management team has to be created. The responsibility of the team is to make sure that changes occur as planned and retained. One way is to use a Balanced Score Card (BSC) Approach,[26] where every team member is provided a balanced score card that contains their objective, measures for performance, initiatives for achieving the objectives and targets. BSC is discussed in detail in Chapter 5.

4.7 TOOLS FOR ASSESSING THE ORGANIZATIONAL CHANGES

We will discuss two tools from literature for assessing the changes that are likely to be experienced by the organization implementing the ERP system.

4.7.1 Force Field Analysis

The objective of the force field analysis is to assess the current state of the organization to gather all the factors that would support the changes and the ones that would oppose the changes. The management can use this analysis in the change management strategy. The following steps are involved in force field analysis:

- **Define the desired change(s):** Write down the goals or visions of a future desired state.
- **Identify the driving forces:** Those that are favourable to change. Record these on a force field diagram as shown in Figure 4.5. We have shown forces that have been identified in the literature.
- **Identify the restraining forces:** Those that are unfavourable to or oppose change. Record these on the force field diagram (Figure 4.5).
- **Evaluate the driving and restraining forces:** One can do this by rating each force, from 1 (weak) to 5 (strong) and total each side.
- **Review the forces:** Decide which of the forces have some flexibility for change or which can be influenced.
- **Strategize:** Create a strategy to strengthen the driving forces or weaken the restraining forces or both.

Driving Forces	**Rating**
1. Organization is IT savvy[30]	
2. History of successful information systems implementation[31]	
3. Management commitment[32]	
4. Perceived risk is low[33]	
5. ERP implementation is aligned with business strategy[34]	
6. ERP system requires negligible change in existing business processes[35]	
7. Responsibility on individuals would decrease[36]	
8. Vendor support is good[37]	
9. Information quality would improve[38]	
Restraining Forces	**Rating**
10. Functional units have autonomy[39]	
11. Accountability is localized[40]	
12. Decision making is localized[41]	
13. Processes are person-centric[42]	
14. Management has local control[43]	
15. Most employees have more than 5 years of the tenure[44]	

FIGURE 4.5 Force Field Analysis for ERP System

Driving Forces		Rating
1.	Organization is IT savvy	1
2.	History of successful information systems implementation	1
3.	Management commitment	5
4.	Perceived risk is low	1
5.	ERP implementation is aligned with business strategy	4
6.	ERP system requires negligible change in existing business processes	3
7.	Responsibility on individuals would decrease	4
8.	Vendor support is good	4
9.	Information quality would improve	5
Restraining Forces		**Rating**
10.	Functional units have autonomy	5
11.	Accountability is localized	5
12.	Decision making is localized	5
13.	Processes are person-centric	5
14.	Management has local control	5
15.	Most employees have more than 5 years of the tenure	3

FIGURE 4.6 Force Field Analysis for ERP System

The relevant forces may be identified by the project leader. (*One can apply analytical hierarchical model (AHP)*[27] *to identify the forces that are important and the ones that are not so important to reduce the number of forces under consideration. A complete example of using AHP and expert*[28] *choice is presented in Chapter 8 for deciding important factors in selecting an ERP system.*)

We have considered all the force factors in our example. The managers and end users are requested to provide rating for each force. One can average all responses to get the final rating for each force. An example is shown in Figure 4.6. In this example, the driving forces sum up to 33 and restraining forces sum up to 28. There is enough insight that obtains from such analysis. The organization does not seem to be ready for an ERP implementation. This conclusion is consistent with stages theory discussed in Chapter 1 and with suggestion[29] that successful IT history is important. The management has to work out a change management strategy.

In this particular example, it seems that the organization does not have enough exposure and experience with information technology. One can use stages theory[45, 46] and McFarlan Matrix (Figure 7.1, Chapter 7) as a reference and decide to start with a transaction processing system instead of an ERP system. Once the organization is comfortable with TPS, more advanced and integrated information technology systems can be deployed. The organization would stay in low risk and low gain zone. The organization should give itself some more time before going for an ERP system.

If we look at the restraining forces, each unit has autonomy, and processes are people centric. An ERP system would take away the autonomy, and accountability will be more widespread across the organization. The management would also get more control as the data would become available to them in real time. The processes will become non-person centric and some employees may feel loss of power while others may feel empowered. ERP will change processes and structure of the organization. The organization would need to spend efforts in business process reengineering (BPR) (For more details, refer to Chapter 7). There is a strong possibility that standard business processes are not documented and not known across this organization. The processes may not be most efficient. The feedback mechanism and performance measurements may also be local. If any of these problems exist, the organization may not be ready to change its processes according to the ERP system. A careful look at the existing processes, business strategy and their alignment (refer to Chapter 5) would help the management in making the right decision.

In this particular case, if the management decides to go for an ERP system, they will have to make sure that old ways are totally abandoned and the new ways are adopted. To summarize, according to force field analysis model, an organization prepares to change, implements the change and then tries to stabilize as quickly as possible.

4.7.2 The Matrix of Change

It is a framework[47] that can help managers understand the complex interrelationships that exist in the organization. The matrix can be built to capture interactions among the existing practices in the organization. The interactions and interrelationships may be complimentary (+) or interfering (–). Some practices may not have any interaction with other practices.

Let us explore this framework through an example. We will consider a service organization that has the following prevailing practices.

- Narrow job functions
- Independent functional groups
- Multiple management layers
- Customer care department
- Multiple contact points for customer

In order to change the organization which is energized and empowered, the underlying practices would become as follows:

- Greater job responsibility
- Functional group boundaries eliminated using IT
- All employees contribute ideas
- Few management layers
- Single contact point for customer.

We start by building two matrices as one horizontal and one vertical. Horizontal matrix captures the current organizational practices and vertical matrix represents the target practices. Next step is to identify and label interactions among existing practices. We do the same with target practices. Finally, interactions among existing and target practices are looked at. Interactions that are re-enforcing or complimentary are labelled with a positive sign, and opposing interactions are labelled with a negative sign. A blank indicates weak or no interaction.

Sometimes, the interactions are obvious. Sometimes a model, survey, empirical data, theories of ownership, and operation management models may be required. A matrix for the above service organization is shown in Figure 4.7.

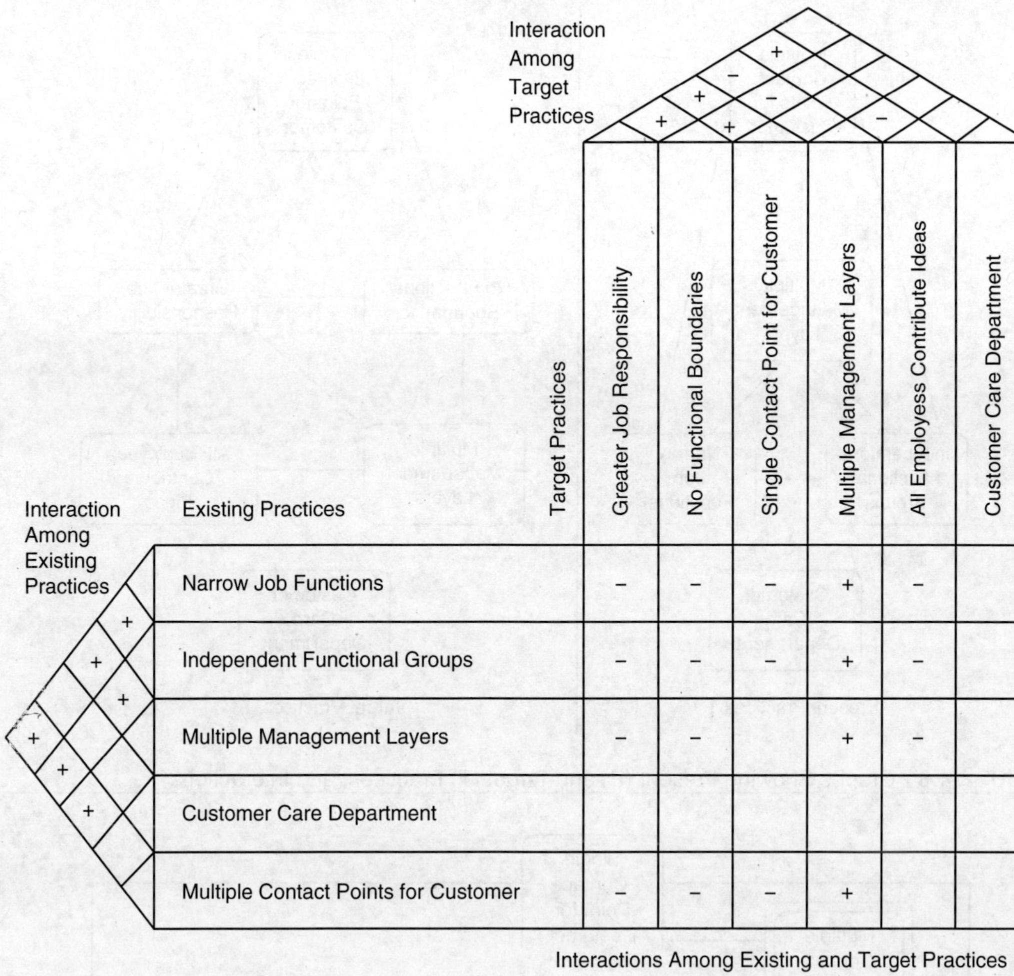

FIGURE 4.7 Matrix to Capture Existing and Target Practices, and Interactions

Analysis

The matrix of change is analysed to figure out the feasibility of the proposed changes and other issues involved.

Feasibility: The changes proposed have not been tried yet and the management may not feel confident about the changes. The matrix of change can show if the proposed system constitute a coherent and stable system. The same matrix can be used to figure out the stability of the present system as well. In Brynjolfsson,[48] matrix of change has been used to figure out the stability of the present and target system. In this book, we have taken the liberty to map these matrices to the graphs. Three graphs were made, one each for the present and target scenario which we will refer to as P and T graph (Figure 4.8) and one that includes both will be referred to as PT graph (Figure 4.9). A node in Graph P represents an element of the horizontal matrix for mapping the present scenario. There will be an arch between two nodes if the corresponding elements

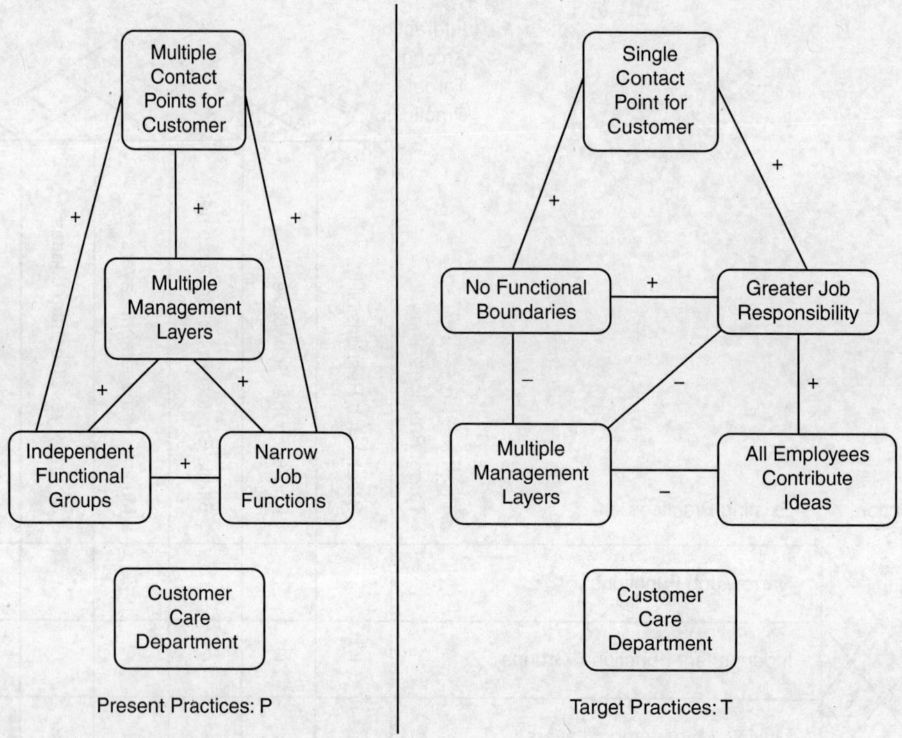

FIGURE 4.8 Graphs Showing Present (P) and Target (T) Practices, and Interactions

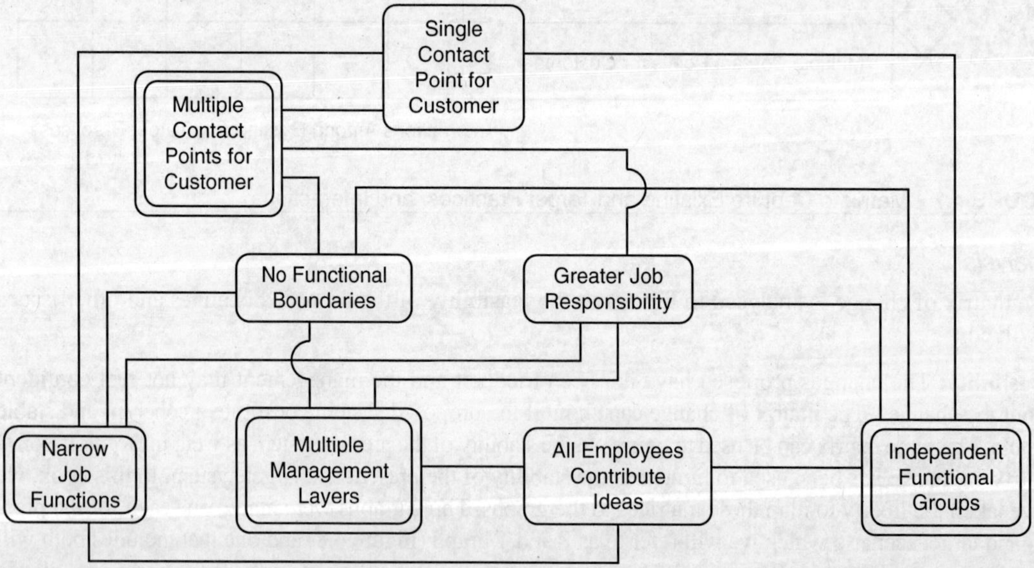

FIGURE 4.9 Graph (PT) Showing Negative Interactions Between Present (P) and Target (T) Practices; Nodes of P Graph are Drawn as Double-lined Rectangles and Nodes of T Graph as Single-lined Rectangles

interact in the matrix. The arch will be labelled with a positive/negative sign as the case may be. Similarly, in the T graph, the nodes will represent elements of the vertical matrix. In the PT graph, we have drawn nodes of P graph as double-lined rectangles and nodes of T graph as single-lined rectangles. Figure 4.9 includes only negative interactions. There are 14 negative interactions and only four positive interactions.

The transition will be difficult and unstable if there are many arcs with negative labels on them in PT graph. The existing practices and the target practices do not support each other which usually would be the case (recall the definition of re-engineering). The target practices once implemented will face the initial problems that any new system faces, possibly to the extent that the manager will start suspecting the new practices and may revert back to old practices even though they are in direct conflict. A short-term view will even be able to justify the resistance to change back to the practices that work. But the success of the entire exercise of reengineering becomes doubtful.

Sequence of Execution

Where should change begin? How does the sequence of change affect success? Are there reasonable stopping points? Let us consider a simple situation where there are only two nodes in P and two nodes in T.

- One possibility is that all nodes interact and their interactions are positive which implies that the existing practices reinforce each other and the target practices behave in the same way. Moreover, the target practices are not in conflict with the existing practices. It seems a happy situation and one would be tempted to make changes in a phased manner by first replacing one existing practice followed by another. But such a situation should be carefully reviewed to find out if we are re-engineering or simply rationalizing.
- Now consider another extreme situation where all nodes interact with each other and all interactions are negative. Such a situation will arise only if our present system in unstable and we are trying to make a transition to another unstable system. The present state of an organization is unlikely to be unstable as the processes over a period of time grow to a stable state. If indeed, the present and target states are both unstable, a relook at the policy, process and practice level is required before attempting any re-engineering exercise.
- In all other situations, there will be some positive and negative interactions. Now we can handle arbitrary number of nodes in P and T. There will be some coherent groups in P as well as in T. There will be some nodes in P which will support some nodes in T. This is the true picture of a re-engineering project. One simple heuristic is to replace one coherent block of activities from P by corresponding new practices in T in one phase without stopping in the middle. An old activity, policy or process that belongs to a group of coherent activities in P if allowed to remain in existence, may for its own convenience, cause other old practices to roll back into the system. Multiple management layer is one such practice in the graph shown in Figure 4.9.

  The nodes in T that interact positively with nodes in P can build the bridge for reengineering and help the management gain confidence in the re-engineering project. However, this approach runs the risk of making people feel that re-engineering is not going to change things much. In fact, the old practices may get reinforced further.

The practices that are somewhat independent can be handled later.

- **Location:** Are we better off instituting the new system in a Greenfield site or can we reorganize the existing location at a reasonable cost? The number of disruptive changes can be used to decide the location for re-engineering project. If the changes are too disruptive, it is better to shield the re-engineering project from the existing practices and start the project at a new or Greenfield site. Greenfield site will be characterized with the new processes, fresh attitude and mental models involving goals, values and causal structure. For radical changes, a company may need an outside change agent to help people see processes differently. A fresh team of management may also be required to rapidly change the old ways. Some more issues may surface that may need addressing, sooner than later. Dismissing these issues as trivial may be too expensive for the re-engineering project. We will have more to say on the role of the management little later.

- **Pace and nature of change:** Should the change be slow or fast? Incremental or radical? Which groups of practices, if any, must be changed at the same time? The pace and nature is largely determined by the nature of proposed changes. The proposed practices that do not build on the existing practices can be introduced by a radical change. Let us recall that radical change is introduced where the existing practices are completely discarded. On the other hand, if the proposed changes build on the existing practices, an incremental change may introduce new practices. As far as the pace is concerned, a coherent block will have to be introduced in one go. In other words, the pace can be determined by the task interdependence. Another important factor is the organizational culture. If the present state of the organization is too stable and the organization has been in the present state for a reasonable duration, the employees as well as management may not be ready for any change unless there is an immediate market pressure. The willingness of the stakeholders to accept change is an important factor. A change in the atmosphere and attitude may be brought about by running some training programs.[49]
- **Stakeholder evaluations:** Have we considered the insights from all stakeholders? Have we overlooked any important practices or interactions? Do a survey to find out the importance stakeholders attach to existing practices and target practices? Compute the net value by subtracting cumulative value for present practices from target practices, and if the net value is positive, there is support for the change. If the net value is negative, the stakeholders are not in favour of the changes.

CONCLUSION

An ERP system touches the culture of the organization. Before the management decides to go for an ERP system, they should make an effort to check the attitude of employees towards ERP system. A questionnaire can be used to check the attitude of employees. If employees are not ready for an ERP system, they may react negatively and offer resistance. ETAM can be used as a framework to check and then enhance the attitude of employees.

In this chapter, we have pointed out that an ERP system impacts culture and standard operating procedures (SOPs) of an organization. ERP may require changes in the culture and SOPs of the organization. The organization needs a change management strategy to manage the impact on its people. We discussed Lewin's model that consists of three stages, namely—unfreezing, changing and freezing. This model assumes that the change happens and then the system returns to a stable state. The improvisational model is based on the assumption that change is a continuous process and the management cannot anticipate all the changes beforehand. There are three types of changes: anticipated, emergent and opportunity-based changes. The management can use Lewin's model to prepare for anticipated changes but will have to watch for other changes and respond accordingly.

CASE STUDY

RetailS that we have been using as our company for the case study is a very new company with a young population of employees. The CMD was very sure of buy-in by the employees and no effort was made to assess the readiness of the employees.

We did a study in a larger organization that we will refer to as ABC in Hyderabad using the questionnaire given in Figures 4.2 and 4.4. We will present our findings here.

ABC is an arm of Defence Research and Development Organization (DRDO), Ministry of Defence and is dedicated to the R&D activity of defence equipments. The organizations have various departments termed as directorates and several programs that run concurrently. Being a R&D organization, ABC has taken the right initiative to implement SAP ERP system which is a great enabler for collaborative R&D. This ERP system will integrate all the functional directorates and work centres and will provide the data/status/analysis online at a single window on your desktop and thus it will IT enable the entire organization. We did this study when ABC was starting the project.

The data given in Table 4.1 gave us an idea about pre-project attitude of the employees. ABC can use these results to decide their change management strategy.

The major implications of the study are as follows:

ERP project communication: As mentioned in discussion of ETAM, project communication plays very important role in developing shared belief in benefits of ERP systems, which in turn improves perceived usefulness and perceived ease of use. Collected data revealed that this is somewhat ignored aspect in ERP implementation in ABC. Most of the people who participated in the survey indicated that they were not adequately informed about ERP project. Virtually no one had seen any presentation and there has been no direct communication.

The implication is that ABC should pay attention to communication about ERP project to their employees.

Shared belief in the benefits of ERP system: As suggested by ETAM, acceptability of an ERP system depends on personal and shared belief in the benefits of the ERP system. As per the data collected, 72 per cent of the respondents believe in the benefits of the ERP project at an individual level. But people are hesitant to share their beliefs or have just not shared their beliefs as only 40 per cent people perceived others to share their belief. Most probably, this is due to lack of communication among them regarding ERP project. ABC need to encourage their employees to share their beliefs.

Perceived usefulness of ERP system: The respondents were asked questions about their perception on data accessibility, data analysis capabilities and information availability due to ERP system. About 70 per cent people had a positive perception of the usefulness of the ERP system in terms of improved data accessibility and data analysis, availability of accurate integrated, timely and reliable information. About 70 per cent respondent believed that ERP would be better than the old system.
The employees have a very positive perception about the usefulness of the ERP system.

Perceived ease of use: Perceived usefulness along with perceived ease of use leads to behavioural intentions of using the system. Only 40 per cent considered that learning to use ERP system will be easy or very easy while 50 per cent considered it from moderately difficult to very difficult.
ABC should plan very focused training programs.

Attitude towards ERP systems: About 70 per cent respondents believed that ERP will increase their productivity and will be useful in their job.
ABC has a strong support for their ERP project.

Behavioural intention to use: As suggested by ETAM, perceived usefulness and attitude towards the system lead to behavioural inattention to use ERP systems. About 60 per cent of respondents had all the intention to use the system as well as information available due to ERP system.
Employees of the ABC have very positive attitude towards using the ERP system.

TABLE 4.1 Data Collected from ABC

All Figures are in Percentage of Responses						
	Communication	**Strongly Disagree**	**Disagree**	**Neutral**	**Agree**	**Strongly Agree**
Q1.	I was well informed about ERP implementation in ABC through ABCNet.	13	20	18	18	18
Q2.	I was well informed about ERP implementation in ABC through ongoing discussions.	28	34	18	15	5
Q3.	I was well informed about ERP implementation in RCI through presentations/demonstrations	49	23	10	8	8
	Shared belief in the benefits of ERP system					
Q4.	I believe in the benefits of ERP system	0	0	28	26	46
Q5.	My colleagues believe in the benefits of ERP system	0	3	36	33	13
Q6.	My departmental team believes in the benefits of ERP system	0	10	41	26	13
	Perceived usefulness of ERP system					
Q7.	It will provide access to more data	3	3	8	20	51
Q8.	It will make data analysis easier	2	3	20	26	46
Q9.	It will be better than the OLD systems	0	0	15	26	49
Q10.	It will provide accurate information	0	3	28	31	28
Q11.	It will provide integrated, timely and reliable information	0	2	26	36	28
	Perceived ease of use					
Q14.	Learning to operate it will be easy for me	2	15	31	36	8
Q15.	It will be easy to get it to do what I want to do	0	13	44	33	5
	Attitude towards ERP system					
Q12.	It will increase my productivity	0	5	26	43	26
Q13.	It will be useful for my job	0	5	26	44	23
	Intention to use ERP system					
Q16.	I expect to use it	0	0	26	33	31
Q17.	I expect information from ERP system to be used	0	0	33	31	36

Important factors for change management at ABC: As per the data collected, lack of communication in ABC about the ERP project is a major concern. All three modes of communication must be used:

1. ABC Net
2. Meetings and discussions
3. Presentations about ERP

Another major concern is perceived ease of use. A training plan should be developed. This plan should identify:

- Which groups or individuals require training?
- What are the training requirements?
- How, where and when it will be delivered?
- Who will deliver the training?

This should result in a well-defined training plan that will ensure that the ABC community acquires skills to play their role in the ERP project and as end users.

There a slight concern about the openness and sharing the beliefs. Group meeting and forums can be created to encourage people to share their beliefs.

There are no other major concerns.

EXERCISES

Test your Understanding

1. What are some of the indicators that management can use to judge readiness of the employees?
2. What are three different levels of resistance? Explain the reasons for all the three levels of resistances and their solutions.
3. Explain Extended Technology Acceptance Model (ETAM) in the context of ERP system. Why is ETAM used?
4. What is Lewin's Model and where is it used?
5. Is Lewin's Model applicable to an ERP implementation in an automotive industry? Is it also applicable to a service industry?
6. Explain force field analysis and its application to decision making with an example.
7. Explain matrix of change framework with an example. How will you determine sequence of change from matrix of change? What are other decisions that you can make with respect to an ERP project using this framework?

Apply Your Understanding

1. Identify the latest IT system that is installed in the organization that you are part of. Talk to people at different levels and find out if there was any resistance from the employees. What steps were taken by the management prior to introducing the IT system to reduce the resistance?
2. You identified an organization to work with in Chapter 1. If the organization has already implemented ERP system, find the resistance offered by its employees, if any. In case, the management faced no resistance, find out the steps that management took by talking to stakeholders. In case, there was resistance, find out how it was handled by the management.

3. Identify the latest IT system that was installed in the organization that you are part of. Talk to the department head or functional unit head where the IT system was installed. If the IT system is being used by the entire organization, talk to the management and find out the changes brought about by IT system. Categorize changes into anticipated, emergent and opportunity-based changes.
4. Identify the latest IT system that was installed in the organization that you are part of. Do a force field analysis to figure out if the IT system should be implemented or not. Do a reality check against your analysis.
5. Talk to the management of your organization to find out the changes they would like to introduce in the organization. Contrast the changes with the existing practices in the organization. Create matrix of change to capture interaction among existing practices, target practices and between them. Analyse the matrix of change to suggest to the management the following:
   - Feasibility of introducing the changes.
   - Sequence for introducing the changes.
   - What are different styles of leadership? What is the most appropriate style of leadership for a BPR project?
6. You identified an organization to work with in chapter one. If the organization has already implemented ERP system, find out their change management strategy. Was the strategy successful?

ENDNOTES

1. Adel M. Aladwani, 'Change Management Strategies for Successful ERP Implementation', in *Business Process Management Journal* (2001), 7(3), 266–275.
2. M. Al-Mashari and M. Zairi, *Electronic Journal of Information System in Developing Countries* (2000), 2(4), 1–15.
3. G. Gable and G. Stewart, *SAP R/3* 'Implementation Issues for Small to Medium Enterprises', in *30th DSI Proceedings* (1999), November, 779–81.
4. S. Sarker and S. Sarker, 'Implementation Failure of an Integrated Software Package: A Case Study from Far East', in *Annals of Cases in IT Applications and Management* (2000), 2, 169–86.
5. Sue Abdinnour-Helm, et al., 'Pre-implementation Attitudes and Organizational Readiness for Implementing an Enterprise Resource Planning System', in *European Journal of Operational Research* (2003), 146, 258–73.
6. D. M. Herold, S. M. Farmer, and M. I. 'Mobley, 'Pre-implementation Attitudes Toward the Introduction of Robots in a Unionized Environment', in *Journal of Engineering and Technology, Management* (1995), 12, 1551–73.
7. Yolande E. Chan, Rajiv Sabherwal, and Jason Bennett Thatcher, 'Antecedents and Outcomes of Strategic IS Alignment: An Empirical Investigation', in *IEEE Transactions on Engineering Management* (2006), 53(1), February, 27–47.
8. Kwasi Amoako-Gyampah and A. F. Salam, 'An Extentsion of the Technology Acceptance Model in an ERP Implementation Environment', in *Information and Management* (2004), 41, 731–745.
9. Richard L. Nolan, David C. Croson and Katherine N. Seger, 'The Stages Theory: A Framework for IT Adoption and Organizational Learning', in *Harvard Business School* (1993), 9, March, 193–41.
10. Kwasi Amoako-Gyampah and A. F. Salam, 'An Extension of the Technology Acceptance Model in an ERP Implementation Environment', in *Information and Management* (2004), 41, 731–45.
11. J. Sheth, 'Psychology of Innovation Resistance', in *Research in Marketing* (1981), 4, 273–82.
12. Maurer and Associates, web site: http://www.rickmaurer.com
13. W. Warner Burke, *Organization Change: Theory and Practice, 3e*, Sage Publications Inc., (2011).

14. R. Chin, and K. Benne. '*General Strategies for Effecting Changes in Human Systems*', *In the Planning of Change*, third edition, Bennis, Warren G. (ed.) (New York: Holt, Rinehart, and Winston, 1976).
15. W. Warner Burke, *Organization Change: Theory and Practice, 3e,* (Foundations for Organizational Science), (Sage Publications Inc., 2011), January.
16. Kwasi Amoako-Gyampah and A. F. Salam, 'An Extentsion of the Technology Acceptance Model in an ERP Implementation Environment', in *Information and Management* (2004), 41, 731–45.
17. F. D. Davis, 'Perceived Usefulness, Perceived Ease of Use, and User Acceptance of Information Technology', in *MIS Quarterly* (1989), 13(3), 319–39.
18. Kwasi Amoako-Gyampah and A. F. Salam, 'An Extentsion of the Technology Acceptance Model in an ERP implementation Environment', in *Information and Management* (2004), 41, 731–745.
19. Adel M. Aladwani, 'Change Management Strategies for Successful ERP Implementation', in *Business Process Management Journal* (2001), 7(3), 266–75.
20. T. H. Davenport, 'Putting the Enterprise into the Enterprise System', in *Harvard Business Review* (1998), 76(4), 121–31, July–August, 121–31.
21. S. Foster, P. Hawking, and C. Zhu, 'The Human Side of ERP Implementations: Can Change Management Really Make a Difference?, in *IFIP International Federation for Information Processing*, Volume 254, Research and Practical Issues of Enterprise Information Systems II, Volume 1, eds. L. Xu, Tjoa A., and Chaudhry S. (eds.) (Boston: Springer, 2007), 239–49.
22. K. Lewin, *Field Research in Social Sciences*, New York: Harper & Row, 1951.
23. W. J. Orlikowski and J. D. Hofman, 'An Improvisational Model of Change Management: The Case of Groupware Technologies', in *Sloan Management Review, Winter* (1997).
24. D. E. Hussey, *How to Manage Organizational Change*, Kogan Page, (2000).
25. S. Foster, P. Hawking, and C. Zhu, 'The Human Side of ERP Implementations: Can Change Management Really Make a Difference?' in *IFIP International Federation for Information Processing, Volume 254, Research and Practical Issues of Enterprise Information Systems II, Volume 1,* L. Xu, Tjoa A., and Chaudhry S. (eds.) (Boston: Springer, 2007), 239–49.
26 W. V. Grembergen and Ronald Saull, 'Aligning Business and Information Technology Through Balanced Scorecard at a Major Canadian Financial Group: Its Status Measured with an IT BSC Maturity Model', in *Proceedings of the 34th Hawaii International Conference on System Sciences*, 2001.
27. T. L. Saaty, *The Analytic Hierarchy Process, NY: McGraw Hill (1980).*
28. *Expert Choice*, www.expertchoice.com.
29. Q. Hu and C. D. Huang, 'Aligning IT with Firm Business Strategies Using the Balance Scorecard System', *Proceedings of the 38th Hawaii International Conference on System Sciences*, 2005.
30. Richard L. Nolan, David C. Croson and Katherine N. Seger, 'The Stages Theory: A Framework for IT Adoption and Organizational Learning', in *Harvard Business School* (1993), March, 9 193-141.
31. B. H. Reich and I. Bensabat, 'Factors that Influence the Social Dimensions of Alignment Between Business and Information Technology Objectives', in *MIS Quarterly* (2000), 24(1), 84–113, 2000.
32. Albert Y. T. Sun, et al., 'Achievements for Enterprise Resource Planning (ERP) System Implementation Based on Critical Success Factors (CSFs)', in *International Journal of Production Economics* (2005), 98, 189–203.
33. G. Stewart, et al., 'Organizational Readiness for ERP Implementation', in *Americas Conference on Information Systems* (2000), 966.
34. J. C. Henderson, N. Venkatraman and S. Oldach, *Aligning Business and IT Strategies*, J. N. Liftman (ed.), Competing in the Information Age: Strategic Alignment in Practice, (New York: Oxford University Press), 21–42.
35. Kyung-Kwon Hong and Young-Gul Kim, 'The Critical Success Factors for ERP Implementation: An Organizational Fit Perspective', in *Information and Management* (2002), 40, 25–40.
36. G. Stewart, et al., 'Organizational Readiness for ERP Implementation', in *Americas Conference on Information Systems* (2000), 966-9–71.

37. Princely Ifinedo and Nazmum Nahar, *Prioritization of Enterprise Resource Planning System Success Measures: Viewpoints of Two Organizational Stakeholder Groups* (2006), SAC'06, 123–27.
38. ibid.
39. T. H. Davenport, Putting the Enterprise into the Enterprise System, in *Harvard Business Review* (1998), 76(4), July–August, 121–31.
40. ibid.
41. ibid.
42. ibid.
43. ibid.
44. Sue Abdinnour-Helm, et al., 'Pre-implementation Attitudes and Organizational Readiness for Implementing an Enterprise Resource Planning System', in *European Journal of Operational Research* (2003), 146, 258–73.
45. Richard L. Nolan, 'Managing the Computer Resources: A Stage Hypothesis', in *Communications of the ACM* (1973), 16(7), July.
46. Richard L. Nolan, David C. Croson and Katherine N. Seger, 'The Stages Theory: A Framework for IT Adoption and Organizational Learning', in *Harvard Business School* (1993), 9-193–141.
47. E Brynjolfsson et al., 'The Matrix of Change', in *Sloan Management Review, Winter* (1997), 38(2) 37–54.
48. ibid.
49. Y. V. Everdingen et al., 'ERP adoption by European Midsize Companies', in *Communications of the ACM* (2000), 43(4), April 27–31.

chapter 5

Business and IT Alignment

LEARNING OBJECTIVES

After reading this chapter, you will be able to understand:

- The alignment between information technology and business in an organization
- The factors involved in alignment and their interconnection
- Different ways of approaching alignment
- Balanced score card (BSC), a tool that can be used for alignment

5.1 INTRODUCTION

The Information and Communication Technology (ICT) literature[1–4] has demonstrated that the alignment between business and IT has a positive effect on business performance and effectiveness. In fact, this alignment may be the basis of a sustainable competitive advantage for organizations. The concept of alignment between IT and business strategy surfaced around 1980s. Till then, IT was primarily used as transaction processing systems for generating standard report (MIS) and to automate standard operating processes (SOP) of the organization. But as the IT evolved to become integral part of the processes, its impact on business increased. Due to globalization, most businesses have to compete in a borderless environment. Success in global market demands more flexible and agile business structures. In global economy, business and IT alliance has become more important than ever before.

If business strategy and IT strategy are not aligned, the following mishaps would result:

- No mechanism for investing in IT may be devised.
- IT would be looked at as a cost centre and not gain credibility.
- Difficulty in measuring contribution of IT to the business.
- Inability in communicating business strategy to IT employees.

Organizations that have successfully aligned IT and business strategies on an average pay 17 per cent less on IT per user than those who fail to align.[5] To begin with, alignment requires a set of steps and procedures followed by a continuing process to stay aligned in spite of contingencies and inevitable changes in the organization, environment and technology. The two questions need to be answered:

- How to obtain a state of alignment?
- How to maintain a state of alignment over time?

It would be nice to have one uniform process/procedure that all organization can follow and achieve alignment. But as it turns out that there is no such process or at least it has not emerged. The challenge is to identify procedures that work for an organization from various options that exist in literature. Alignment is required irrespective of country, industry, size and turnover of the organization, and business strategy.[6]

The components which play role in the alignment are discussed Section 5.2. A framework for strategic alignment is presented in Section 5.3. The alignment process in the organization may be looked at as a project whose success depends on various factors. Balanced scorecard (BSC)[7] is discussed in Section 5.5. BSC is a tool that can be used to measure the performance of the alignment project.[8, 9] This chapter is largely based on the work presented in Luftman, Brier, Henderson and Venkatraman.[10–13]

5.2 COMPONENTS OF ALIGNMENT

Our target is to align business and IT. Therefore, it is necessary to identify the components that constitute business and the ones that constitute IT. In literature, the following components have been identified for the purpose of alignment of business and IT:[14, 15]

- Business strategy
- Organizational infrastructure and processes
- IT strategy
- IT infrastructure and processes

5.2.1 Business Strategy

Business strategy has following three components:

- **Business scope:** It include decisions that determine where the enterprise would compete. These choices define the types of products, niches, customers and geography that determine the reach or range of the enterprise. Business scope includes the competitive forces described by Porter which are buyers, suppliers, substitutes, potential entrants and existing competition.[16]
- **Distinctive competencies:** It includes focus on areas that determine how the enterprise will compete in delivering its products and services. These decisions determine those attributes of the strategy that create the capability of the enterprise to differentiate its products and services from competition. The strategy may be based on pricing, quality or superior marketing channel.
- **Business governance:** These choices include entering a market as a single entity through alliance, partnerships or outsourcing.

5.2.2 Organizational Infrastructure and Processes

- **Administrative structure:** It includes roles, responsibilities and authority structure of the enterprise. An organization may have functional units or product offering units. The decision-making process may be distributed or centralized. The management structure may consist of different number of layers. These choices establish the administrative structure within which the management and work processes operate.

- **Processes:** The manner in which key functions operate or flow is determined by the processes that are followed in the organization. The capacity of IT to integrate with processes, and restructure processes for improving their effectiveness and efficiency depends on the characteristics of processes and work flows. The characteristics of processes are discussed in Chapter 4.
- **Skills:** Skill set consists of experience, competences, values and norms of the employees. The skill set must be appropriate for carrying out the business strategy of the organization.

5.2.3 IT Strategy

The IT strategy has to be defined in the same way in which business strategies are defined. The scope of IT and governance structure are important constituents of IT strategy. The scope defines critical and necessary information technology for the organization.

Analogous to skill set in the business strategy is the systemic competencies in IT strategy. Systemic competencies are defined in terms of characteristics of information technology such as information accessibility, reliability, response etc. There are various models such as full ownership, partnership, outsourcing etc. for IT governance. These choices are part of IT strategy.

5.2.4 IT Infrastructure and Processes

Similar to business processes, there are IT processes. These processes are followed for developing, acquiring and managing IT applications and architectures. The policies and priorities that are used to make choices of the hardware, software, applications and to put them together lead to IT infrastructure in the organization. To be able to create and maintain the IT infrastructure, skilled manpower is required. Experiences, competencies, commitments, values and norms of individuals working to deliver and maintain IT products and services constitute the skillset of IT employees.

All these components and their interactions are shown in Figure 5.1. The objective is to achieve a harmony between business strategy and information strategy through coherence between IT infrastructure and processes, and organization infrastructure and processes. The IT strategy must be aligned with business strategy to make best use of IT. Information technology can help in creating competitive and strategic advantage. These two roles of IT can be distinguished. In a scenario, where a business strategy is at start, then explores and exploits IT potential to shape/adapt business processes and organization structure, IT is used for strategic advantage. If the IT potential can be used to decide business strategy (new products, services and marketing opportunity), then IT is used for competitive advantage. The competitive advantage and strategic advantage that IT may provide soon become necessary. Few of examples are given in Table 5.1 from customer's perspective.

If an organization does not pioneer in identifying these opportunities, it will have to quickly deploy them to survive. The usage of IT then becomes defensive and the IT strategy is reactive rather than proactive. IT strategy—whether reactive or proactive—is always iterative and consequently alignment is also an iterative process.

5.3 STRATEGIC ALIGNMENT FRAMEWORK AND ITS APPLICATION TO STRATEGIC ALIGNMENT

The four components that participate in IT and business strategies alignment are shown in Figure 5.1. To initiate, it is assumed that either the business strategy is defined or the IT strategy is defined and stable.

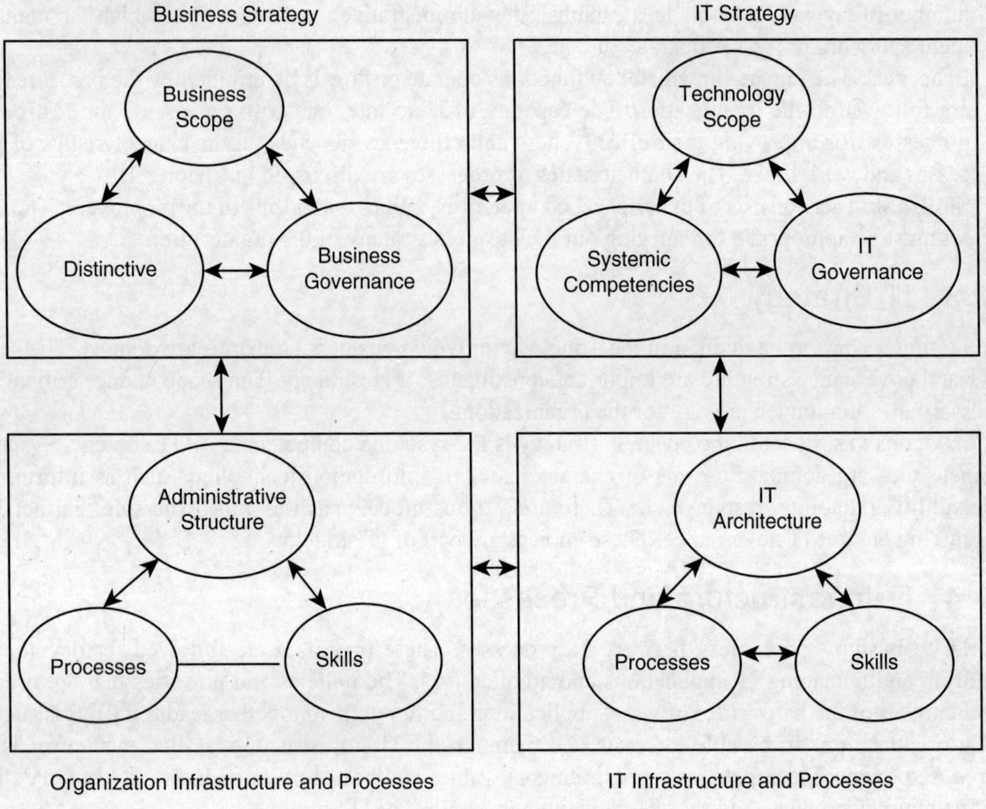

FIGURE 5.1 Strategic Alignment Framework[17, 18]

TABLE 5.1 Competitive and Strategic Advantages That have Become Necessity

Field	IT Advantage That Became a Necessity
Education	Online application form, online fee payment.
Bank	ATM, online banking, core banking.
Travel	Online reservations, real time status of trains, planes.
Manufacturing	Online customer interaction shift from make-to-stock to make-to-order shift from product to solution provider.
Market	Seller's to buyer's.

What is picked as stable will depend on the alignment perspective and various possible perspectives will be described in this section itself. What is picked as stable is referred to as anchor. Then a domain pivot is picked from the remaining three components. Domain pivot is the area that can be improved based on the anchor. Finally, an impact domain is picked that is modified, adapted or re-engineered to align it with the pivot domain. The fourth component is left unmodified to provide stability to the alignment process. To summarize, there are three steps:

1. Select a anchor domain that acts as a catalyst or an enabler for the alignment.
2. Select a pivot domain that has problems or opportunities. Improve it.
3. Select an impacted domain that will be affected by the changes to the pivot domain. Reengineer it.

The selection of these three components would depend on the specific business and information technology issues faced by the organization. Let us say, an organization feels that it is not making best use of the potential of information technology. It identifies IT strategy as the anchor, then decides to adapt its business strategy to exploit the opportunities presented by its IT strategy. The modified business strategy may require changes in the business processes and organizational infrastructure. The alignment team then needs to plan and carry out these changes.

As mentioned earlier, alignment is a continuous process. After one alignment cycle is complete, changes in the component that was left untouched may be required that will start another alignment cycle. Depending on what the anchor, pivot and impact domains are, one is looking at alignment from the following different perspectives.[19]

- **Strategy execution:** The organization has a business strategy that has been articulated and serves as the anchor domain. Organizational infrastructure and processes are the pivot domains. The pivot domain may require changes to support execution of business strategy. Changes in the pivot domain may require support from IT infrastructure and processes. The impacted domain is IT infrastructure and processes. This is a very traditional top-down approach and fairly well understood. IT is more of a facilitator than driver for business strategy. Driver continues to be business strategy and the role of top management is to formulate business strategy. IT management facilitates implementation of business strategy by devising a supporting IT infrastructure and processes. IT infrastructure is treated as a cost centre. The methods used for evaluating IT are usually return on investment (ROI) which is not a very effective instrument for measuring performance of IT.[20] Strategy execution perspective fails to use full potential of IT.
- **Technology potential perspective:** Start with an articulated business strategy (anchor) and then explore and devise an IT strategy (pivot) that would best support the business strategy. Change IT infrastructure according to new/modified IT strategy. Implement the business strategy through appropriate IT strategy that may require transformation in IT infrastructure and processes. The driver or anchor is business strategy and the top management works closely with IT managers as technology visionaries and technology architects. Executives and business strategists would be able to exploit IT better if they are aware of its potential. It is not really a sequential process. If business and IT strategists work together, potential of IT can be better utilized and the organization can pioneer technology usage.
- **Competitive potential perspective:** One can base a business strategy on IT strategy. Start with an IT strategy based on emerging IT capabilities, and figure out the ways with which the IT strategy can influence or enable new business strategies including new products/services for competitive advantage. These business strategies may need changes in organizational structure and processes (refer to Figure 5.2). The management tries to figure out opportunities to use IT creatively and for competitive advantage. The driver is IT strategy for framing business strategy.
- **Service level perspective:** This perspective focuses on building a world class IT service organization. Start with IT strategy and develop IT infrastructure to realize IT strategy. Redesign organizational infrastructure to make best use of the IT strategy and infrastructure. The role of top management is to set up the priorities, and the role of IT management is to provide leadership. The performance criterion is customer satisfaction. The IT department within the organization is looked

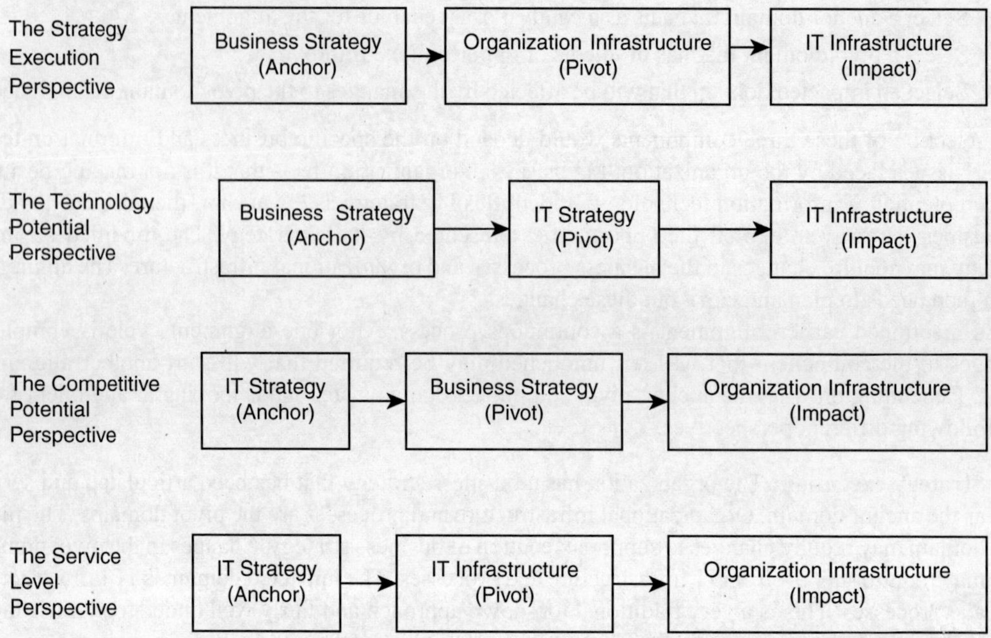

FIGURE 5.2 Four Different Perspectives for Business and IT Strategies Alignment

upon as a service provider to the organization. The objective of the IT department is to provide world class services to its customers. For instance, BPCL[21] came up with a competitive strategy based on IT strategy. They decided to deploy an ERP system and the organization was restructured accordingly. The business strategy and processes were all based on the availability of the ERP system 24 × 7. The IT department has to provide world class services to the organization. The processes were re-engineered according to the ERP system.

- There will be short-term goals such as respond to customer needs/requests through new applications/interface, and the long-term objectives to stay at the forefront of technology. The management has to set priorities to balance short-term and long-term priorities.

It is required to identify an anchor, a pivot and an impact domain. The anchor and one other component remains stable during the alignment process, and provide stability. Anchor is always either business strategy or IT strategy. The strategic level management needs to define and freeze at least one of the two. From the alignment framework, it is clear that the pivot domain is being aligned. Two external factors may cause a pivot domain to get misaligned—changes in the market place and changes in the information technology. The pivot domain should contain issues external to the organization, where opportunities typically exist. For example, an organization uses strategy execution perspective and makes significant changes to its IT infrastructure and processes. It is not hard to see that these changes may call for a new IT strategy that in turn may impact/influence business strategy. A new cycle begins after the very first cycle completes or sometimes even before the first one completes. That brings us to the point made right in the beginning of this chapter that alignment is a continuous activity. The first cycle is the most difficult because an anchor has to be identified for which lot of information (implicit and explicit) will have to be extracted and collated, and various techniques will have to be deployed to introduce changes.

Some organization will find that they have been implicitly performing alignment. It is important to treat alignment as a planned and budgeted activity for which manpower and budget is allocated. Judging the alignment between IT and business is also a challenge.

5.4 ARE BUSINESS AND IT ALIGNED?[22]

Some degree of alignment may exist in each functional unit and the organization may perceive it as organization level alignment. IT and business both need to check if they are aligned with each other. The parameters that business strategist can use to check their alignment followed by the parameters that IT can use are listed below. Business strategist can use the following parameters to check if they are aligned with IT strategists:

- **Liaison with IT:** The level of communication between IT and business managers is an indicator of the alignment between the two. A formal channel that facilitates communication at regular frequency, say once a month is required to achieve the alignment. In addition, informal communication between IT head and other business heads must take place.
- **Perception of IT by business:** The IT could be treated as cost centre in the organization indicating poor alignment between the business and IT. Next higher level of treatment to the IT is when it is utilized for efficiency. If IT enhances efficiency of whatever business is doing, IT will be aligned better than when it is treated as a cost centre. The best possibility is that IT is treated as a partner in business and IT is perceived as a partner for creating value. Business processes may be designed keeping IT capabilities in the focus. If IT is treated as a partner, the corporate strategy document clearly lays out the objectives of IT department. The perception of IT has been going through a change since last 50 years as IT evolved. A successful IT track record tends to improve perception of business managers.[23]
- **Inclusion of IT in formal business planning:** If IT is not invited to business strategy meeting or is invited as an observer, there is poor alignment between the two. If IT is included in all meetings as partner, better alignment exists.
- **IT metrics aligned with business metrics:** Every organization uses a set of metrics to judge its performance. If IT uses the same metrics, chances are that IT and business are better aligned than if both use different metrics.

IT strategist can check if their strategy is aligned with business strategy using the following parameters:

- **Liaison with business:** IT will have its strategy planning meetings and other regular meetings. For an alignment to exist between IT and business, business head should participate in key IT meetings. Some informal communication channels must exist between IT and business.
- **Perception of business by IT:** IT people should understand business domain and language, share their vision and understand the business strategy. IT must understand their role in the business. If IT understands its role in the overall business, chances are IT and business will be better aligned.
- **Formal IT planning:** IT head and IT department must work with CEO and business strategists to gain their confidence and attain the level of business partners. IT planning should not be done in isolation. The business heads must be involved.
- **Standards and benchmarking:** One of the common complaints of business and IT is the lack of understanding of each others domain. Since it is the IT that is a new thing and evolving, it is logical for IT to work towards defining standards and use them to facilitate interaction within and with business team. Capability maturity models (CMM levels that has level 5 as highest that) and unified

modelling language (UML) strives to follow same standards and procedures across organization. It has become easy for companies across the globe who follow these standards to coordinate and work together with business.

- **Innovation partners of the IT systems:** If IT works with internal customers and partners towards providing innovative solution then IT and business are better aligned. If IT avoids innovation or works towards achieving only efficiency, the alignment is limited.
- **Business metrics is aligned with IT metrics:** If IT management utilizes the same evaluation metrics as the business, then the two are well aligned. This is similar to discussion of business strategist's perspective section.

The objective of IT in the 1960s was to provide operational efficiency but now IT plays a strategic role in the organization. The IT, and business executives and strategists must work together to use IT as a strategic weapon. The balanced scorecard that has been used as a tool for implementing and sustaining alignment between IT and business is discussed in the next section.

5.5 BALANCED SCORECARD: AN ALIGNMENT TOOL

Balanced scorecard[24] (BSC) has been used as a tool or framework for implementing and sustaining the alignment between IT and business strategies. The BSC evaluates the alignment from four different perspectives.

A BSC has four perspectives to translate business strategy of an organization into objectives. Figure 5.3 shows these four perspectives and their interactions. These four perspectives are:

- **Financial perspective:** It is one of the oldest and widely used perspectives. This perspective captures financial objectives and performance of the organization.
- **Customer's perspective:** Customer's perspective reflects customer's perception of the services and products of the organization. The management must know if their organization is satisfying the customer's requirements.
- **Operational perspective:** Operational perspective or internal business process perspective is for evaluating/assessing business processes of the organization.
- **Learning and innovation perspective:** The fourth perspective, learning and innovation, is for assessing the readiness for future. Does the organization innovate itself enough to be able to remain in synchronization with the external changes and meet external challenges?

The management can use this tool to translate the strategy into objectives and initiatives to achieve the objective for all four perspectives. The management would need quantitative measures (and possibly some qualitative ones) and corresponding targets. The BSC would be different for individuals. A manager's BSC would be different from that of an employee in operations. The objectives, measures, targets and initiatives will all be different.

The relationship[26] between IT and business can be explicitly expressed through a cascade of balanced scorecards (Figure 5.4). If business strategy is the driver for IT strategy (strategy execution perspective), the flow will be as shown in Figure 5.4(a) and if IT strategy is the driver for business strategy (competitive advantage perspective), the flow will be as shown in Figure 5.4(b). Cascading works as an alignment instrument between business strategy and IT strategy. A BSC similar to the one shown in Figure 5.3 may be created for translating business strategy to objectives and initiatives. CIO, CEO and their teams can work together to figure out the contribution of IT to the initiatives. The

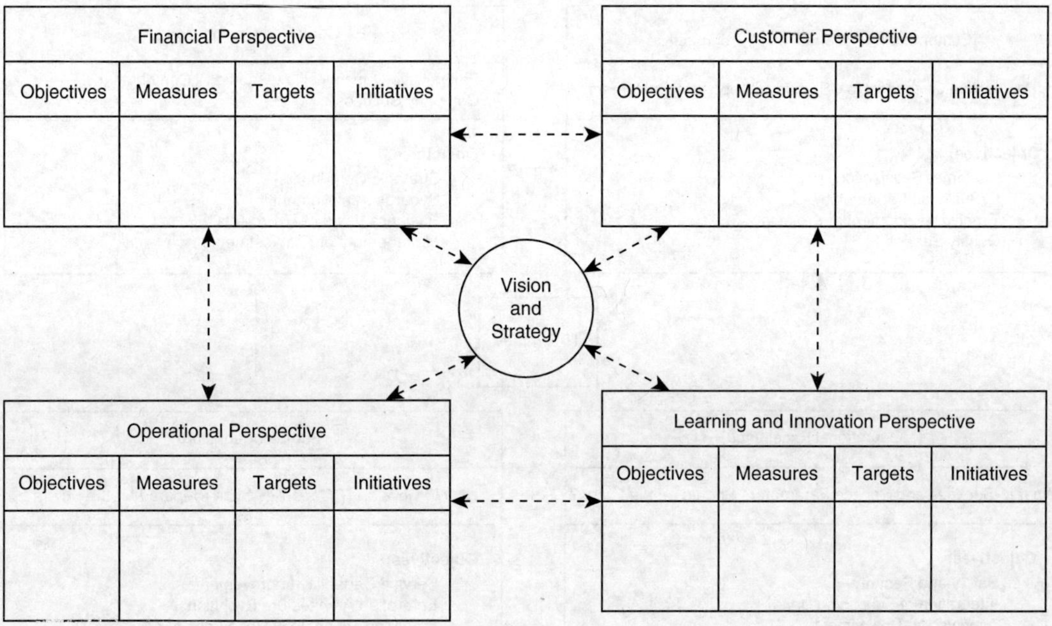

FIGURE 5.3 Balanced Scorecard Consisting of Four Perspectives for Translating and Strategy into Objectives[25]

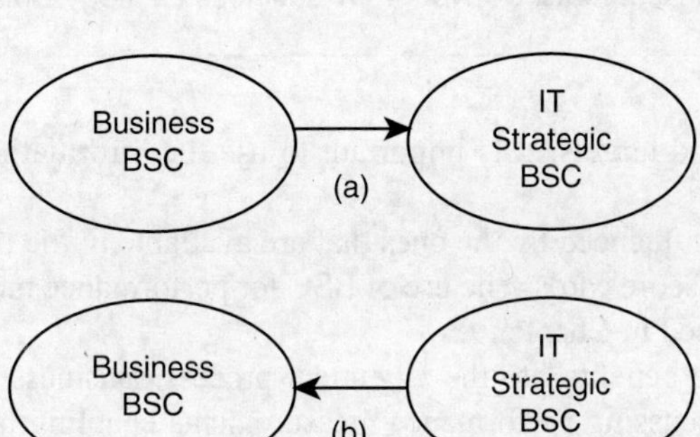

FIGURE 5.4 IT Balanced Scorecard Derived from Business Strategy Balanced Scorecard and Vice Versa

initiatives may be consolidated from all four perspectives which are financial, customer, operational perspective, and learning and innovation. The consolidated view would give direction to IT strategy that is converted to objectives and initiatives using a BSC similar to one shown in Figure 5.5. The financial perspective is mapped to corporate contribution. Customers of IT are functional units of the organization. CIO could create two more BSC—one for managing development/new projects and another one for the operational ones incorporating direct financial perspective, processes used for IT development projects, etc. These score cards should contain quantitative objectives, initiatives, measures and targets. Some organizations use BSC for individuals as well with their objectives based

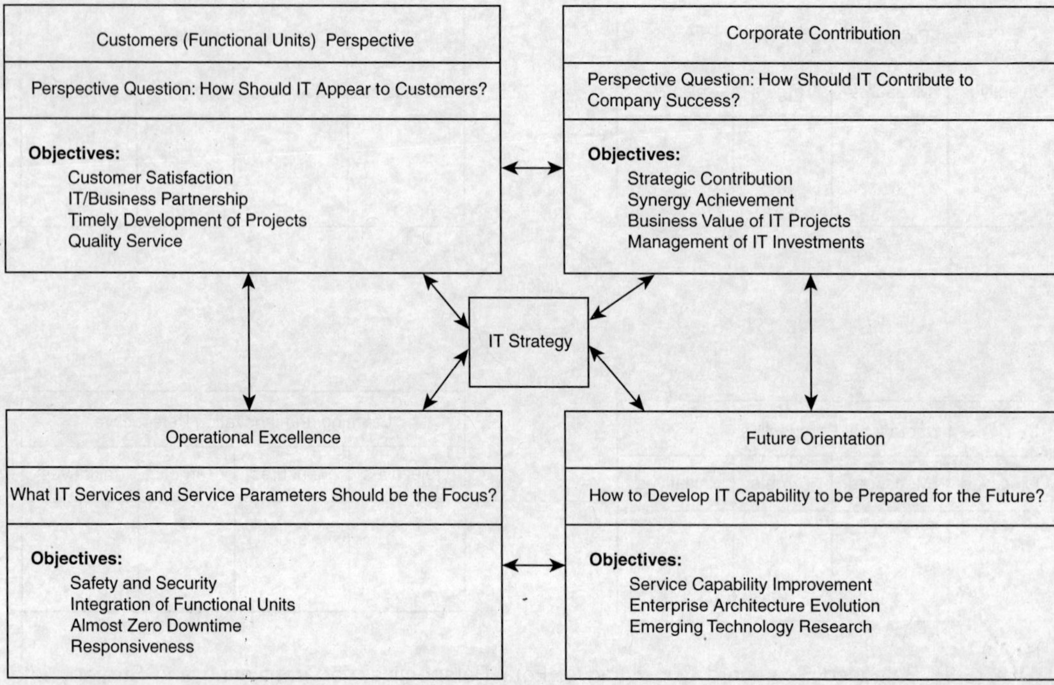

FIGURE 5.5 IT Balanced Scorecard Derived from Business Strategy Balance Scorecard Consisting of Four IT Perspectives

on their role, measures and targets. It is important to use the information from BSC for further improvement.

These score cards are influenced by the ones that are available in the literature.[27, 28] An organization would have to create their score cards. The use of BSC for performance measurement of an ERP project and ERP system is discussed in Chapter 9.

BSC offers two unique benefits[29] to the alignment process. Business and IT management can use the same language for discussing performance measurements enabling both parties to understand the capability and limitations of IT. Information technology can be managed using an integrated planning and evaluation cycle as other business processes. BSC helps the departments to look beyond their own departments and in communicating the company's goals and strategies. The corporate BSC is set up for basic corporate planning and then every business division plan including the IT plan becomes part the BSC. IT develops its own score card, using the measures based on the corporate scorecard. Automatically, reflection and linkage gets created between IT, and corporate vision and strategy. IT can align its cost structure, service levels and capital investments according to business scenario.

The leadership and culture of the organization play an important role in achieving organizational level alignment.

The following are some of the parameters that work as enablers[30] for achieving alignment:

- Senior executive support for IT
- IT involvement in strategy development

- Mutual understanding between business and IT
- Business and IT partnership
- IT demonstrates leadership

CONCLUSION

IT and business must be aligned. The factors that play role in alignment are IT strategy, business strategy, IT infrastructure and processes, and organizational infrastructure and business strategy. These four components interact with each other. There are four different ways of approaching alignment depending on the maturity level of the organization, namely—strategy execution, technology potential perspective, competitive potential perspective and service level perspective. Success of the alignment effort depends on multiple factors such as support of the top management and understanding between CIO (and his department) and CEO. Balanced score card (BSC) is a tool that can be used for alignment. The first alignment cycle is the most difficult one because the team is new and the team challenges the established strategy, processes and structure. The cycles one after the other must be carried out to make sure that business and IT stay aligned. The frequency and efforts required may be guided by the expected changes and returns.

EXERCISES

Check Your Understanding

1. Define business and IT alignment. What are various components of the alignment?
2. Alignment is not a state, but a journey. Do you agree with this statement? Justify your answer.
3. Describe strategic alignment framework and its components.
4. Describe balanced score card and how it can be applied to achieve business and IT alignment.

Apply Your Understanding

1. You picked an organization to work with in Chapter 1. Analyse your organization for the level of alignment. What parameters did you use to check the alignment?
2. If your organization is not aligned to your satisfaction, suggest the perspective they should use and start an alignment effort. Clearly identify anchor, pivot and impact domain. Justify your choice.
3. Create a balanced score card for a manager in business and for an IT manager of your organization.

ENDNOTES

1. David Wainwright and T. Waring, 'Three Domains for Implementing Integrated Information Systems: Redressing the Balance Between Technology, Strategic and Organizational Analysis', in *International Journal of Information Management* (2004), 24, 329–46.
2. J. C. Henderson and N. Venkatraman, 'Strategic Alignment: Leveraging Information Technology for Transforming Organizations', in *IBM Systems Journal* (1993), 32(1), 4–16.
3. J. C. Henderson, N. Venkatraman and S. Oldach, 'Aligning Business and IT Strategies', in J. N. Liftman (ed.) *Competing in the Information Age: Strategic Alignment in Practice*, New York: Oxford University Press, 21–42.

4. J. N. Luftman et al., 'Transforming the Enterprise: The Alignment of Business and Information Technology Strategies', in *IBM Systems Journal* (1993), 32(1), 198–221.
5. R. Szgenda, 'Information's Competitive Edge', in *Information Week* (1999), 720.
6. B. Cumps et al., 'An Empirical Study on Business/ICT Alignment in European Organizations', in *Proceedings of the 39th Hawaii International Conference on System Sciences* (2006).
7. R. Kaplan and D. Norton, *The Balanced Scorecard: Translating Vision into Action,* Boston: Harvard Business School Press (1996).
8. Q. Hu and C. D. Huang, 'Aligning IT with Firm Business Strategies Using the Balance Scorecard System', in *Proceedings of the 38th Hawaii International Conference on System Sciences* (2005).
9. W. V. Grembergen and Ronald Saull, 'Aligning Business and Information Technology Through Balanced Scorecard at a Major Canadian Financial Group: Its Status Measured with an IT BSC Maturity Model', in *Proceedings of the 34th Hawaii International Conference on System Sciences* (2001).
10. J. N. Luftman et al., 'Transforming the Enterprise: The Alignment of Business and Information Technology Strategies', in *IBM Systems Journal* (1993), 32(1), 198–221.
11. J. N. Luftman and T. Brier, 'Achieving and Sustaining Business-IT Alignment', in *California Management Review* (1999), 42(1), 109–22.
12. J. C. Henderson and N. Venkatraman, 'Strategic Alignment: Leveraging Information Technology for Transforming Organizations', in *IBM Systems Journal* (1993), 32(1), 4–16.
13. J. C. Henderson, N. Venkatraman and S. Oldach, 'Aligning Business and IT Strategies', in J. N. Liftman (ed.) *Competing in the Information Age: Strategic Alignment in Practice*, New York: Oxford University Press), 21–42.
14. J. N. Luftman et al., 'Transforming the Enterprise: The Alignment of Business and Information Technology Strategies', in *IBM Systems Journal* (1993), 32(1), 198–221.
15. J. N. Luftman and T. Brier, 'Achieving and Sustaining Business-IT Alignment', in *California Management Review* (1999), 42(1), 109–22.
16. Michael E. Porter, 'The Five Competitive Forces that Shape Strategy', in *Harvard Business Review* (2008), January, 86–104.
17. J. N. Luftman et al., 'Transforming the Enterprise: The Alignment of Business and Information Technology Strategies, in *IBM Systems Journal* (1993), 32(1), 198–221.
18. J. C. Henderson and N. Venkatraman, 'Strategic Alignment: Leveraging Information Technology for Transforming Organizations', in *IBM Systems Journal* (1993), 32(1), 4–16.
19. J. N. Luftman et al., 'Transforming the Enterprise: The Alignment of Business and Information Technology Strategies, in *IBM Systems Journal* (1993), 32(1), 198–221.
20. E. Brynjolfsson, 'The Productivity Paradox of Information Technology', in *Communications of the ACM* (1993), 36(12), December, 67–77.
21. A. Teltumbde, A. Tripathy and A. K. Sahu, http://www.icmrindia.org, Case number ITSY005 (2002).
22. J. W. Weiss and D. Anderson, 'Aligning Technology and Business Strategy: Issues and Frameworks, A Field Study of 15 Companies', in *Proceedings of the 37th Hawaii International Conference on System Sciences* (2004).
23. Q. Hu and C. D. Huang, 'Aligning IT with Firm Business Strategies Using the Balance Scorecard System', in *Proceedings of the 38th Hawaii International Conference on System Sciences* (2005).
24. R. Kaplan and D. Norton, *The Balanced Scorecard: Translating Vision into Action,* Boston: Harvard Business School Press, 1996.
25. ibid.
26. W. V. Grembergen and Ronald Saull, 'Aligning Business and Information Technology Through Balanced Scorecard at a Major Canadian Financial Group: Its Status Measured with an IT BSC Maturity Model', in *Proceedings of the 34th Hawaii International Conference on System Sciences* (2001).

27. ibid.
28. J. T. M. Van Der Zee and B. De Jong, 'Alignment Is Not Enough: Integrating Business and Information Technology Management with the Balanced Business Scorecard', in *Journal of Management Information Systems* (1999), 16(2), 137–56.
29. Q. Hu and C. D. Huang, 'Aligning IT with Firm Business Strategies Using the Balance Scorecard System', in *Proceedings of the 38th Hawaii International Conference on System Sciences* (2005).
30. J. N. Luftman and T. Brier, 'Achieving and Sustaining Business-IT Alignment', in *California Management Review* (1999), 42(1), 109–22.

chapter 6

Requirements Engineering

LEARNING OBJECTIVES

After reading this chapter, you will be able to understand:

- What is requirements engineering?
- Document requirements using the following
  - Structured English
  - Event process chains by SAP
  - Object-oriented modelling
  - Object Process Model
  - Data Activity Model for Configuration (DAMC)

6.1 INTRODUCTION

As mentioned in Chapter 2, an ERP implementation has multiple phases (refer to Figure 2.1). This chapter concerns the second phase of ERP implementation namely requirements engineering (RE). This phase is also referred to as creation of business blueprint. In the RE phase, needs of different stakeholders are identified and documented using some standard modelling technique for subsequent communication and realization purpose.[1] This phase consist of requirements elicitation, requirements representation and requirements validation.[2, 3] Requirements are gathered from customers, system users and others who have a stake in the system during requirements elicitation phase. Requirements are represented through various models.

An ERP system automates and integrates business processes across the organization. Therefore, requirements are expressed in terms of business processes that are being considered for inclusion in ERP system. Defining and documenting the requirements involve the following:

- Establishing a high-level project scope by working with senior executives to determine the processes to be included in the ERP implementation.
- Establish ownership for the business processes included in the ERP implementation.
- Designate team leaders for documenting business processes.
- Produce business process documents.

As described in Chapter 1, an organization and its business processes evolve over a period of time. Business processes may not be documented or the documents may not be up-to-date. It is a challenging task to gather requirements for ERP system. But once business blueprints are created, they can be used for multiple purposes.

- Use these documents to invite quotations or bids from the perspective ERP vendors.
- These documents serve as baseline documents for establishing the gap between the solution offered by the vendor and the requirements. One would like to select an ERP solution with minimum gap. The gap is a factor in the ERP implementation risk, time and cost.
- These documents are used as reference for ERP configuration.
- These documents also serve as reference in education and training.
- In future, if a change is required in a business process, these documents serve as reference documents, a new version of the document is created and a log is maintained.

A big question is whether *an organization should model its business processes from the scratch or not*. Modelling business processes of an organization is expensive and time consuming. If the organization has never documented its processes, its staff may not have modelling expertise. Simple mistakes such as focusing on functions rather than processes can render the whole effort worthless. For example, if modelling focuses on individual's activities rather than the processes of the organization, the model will unnecessarily proliferate and the larger picture may be lost. Sometimes, an amateur may misrepresent processes specially in the absence of any documentation.

An alternative is to do a preliminary shortlisting of potential ERP vendors and then choose business models of one of the vendors as reference. Business process modelling involves identifying the common components, adding the missing components and deleting extra/irrelevant components. The advantages of this approach are easy gap analysis and communication with the vendor because of the common reference.

Some researchers oppose the idea of using an ERP specific modelling technique; rightly so, since the issue addressed by the enterprise requirements are independent of the specific ERP package.

All companies manging from small and medium enterprises (SMEs) to large, seem to gather basic information about ERP vendors and then shortlist them based on some very high level factors such as their past clients, implementation time and cost, etc. Then the requirements are documented using either structured English or questions (discussed in Section 6.2). The shortlisted vendors are asked to make a presentation. Equipped with a reasonable knowledge of the systems, they make a selection by analysing the prototype, examination by consultants and/or taking the studies done by companies like Gartner etc. The vendor is then involved in modelling the business processes using its own modelling techniques.

Another approach is to pick an ERP solution that has minimum gap and then adapt its business processes discarding the existing business processes of the organization. This approach is referred to as IT-driven re-engineering. Business process re-engineering is discussed in Chapter 7.

Irrespective of the approach taken for modelling the business processes, it is a good idea to start with critical business processes. Business processes that give competitive advantage to an organization are referred to as critical business processes. These processes are added to the requirements first, and in the next iteration more generic requirements are added. The generic processes will be supported by almost all ERP solutions.

The business blueprints will have to be managed and maintained to counter the following problems:

- **Simultaneous update:** Multiple persons may have to work separately on the same document or different parts of the document. If everybody works on the same copy, the last one to make changes may easily destroy the work of others.

- **Shared document:** If multiple copies of the document are created, a change in one copy may not reflect in all other copies.
- **Common document:** A document that has been finalized becomes a reference document and multiple people may refer to it. If for some reason, a change is made to the reference document, every user must be informed. That means someone has to know who all are affected by the change in the reference document.
- **Versions:** A change in the document may fix one issue but may introduce another one. Sometimes, one may have to go back to what was discussed and rejected earlier.

The primary requirement is management of documents including sharing, version and change management. A librarian will manage the documents. Once a document is finalized and becomes part of the library, it cannot be changed casually. The change has to be justified, costed and approved by the concerned authority. The change approval strategy has to be worked out a priori. The librarian has to maintain record of all references (people and documents) to the documents in the library. In case, a document from the library is changed, all concerned people are informed (a policy is required to know how changes are communicated) and all documents are cross checked for any conflicts or discrepancy. The documents such as requirement documents, re-engineering documents, test plan and technology documents are all maintained by the librarian. Thumb rule is that all the documents that go through multiple revisions, developed by multiple people and refereed to by multiple people and documents should be maintained and managed.

ERP vendors offer help for modelling business processes using their own reference models. For instance, SAP suggests that you model your business processes using their reference EPC models (discussed in Section 6.3). Some techniques used for capturing requirements are discussed next.

6.2 STRUCTURED ENGLISH AND STRUCTURED INTERVIEWS

SMEs do not adopt any formal method for modelling their processes. Often times, the inhouse team may not have skillset to undertake the business process modelling task. They rely on the implementation partner to a greater extent. Recall that an ERP implementation involves a vendor (who supplies the ERP software), an implementation partner (who configures the ERP software according to the business needs of the client) and a consultant (who advises the client and protects the client's interests). In the beginning, the client team prepares an informal description of their processes by talking to business process owners. In SMEs, processes are mostly people centric. On a visit to two SMEs in Kanpur, and after having discussion with their project leader and implementation leaders, it was found that they did not use any specific modelling technique. Incidentally, processes were not documented anywhere and it was a challenge to get a description of the business processes. Employees were the business process owners who showed some resistance (refer to Chapter 4) in sharing their business processes with the implementation partner and the consultant.

One popular method for capturing requirements informally is through structured interviews. The client will need to detail company profile and processes. Some of this information may seem trivial but it is important for the vendors and consultants to understand the organization. A set of high-level questions for capturing the organization structure that are seen across client organizations, software vendors and consultants is shown in Figure 6.1.

1. Type of industry
2. The products and services provided (has a bearing on implementation complexity and cost)
3. Number of employees (license cost)
4. Vision statement (for aligning ERP with vision of the company)
5. Mission statement (ERP methodology must match with mission)
6. List and prioritize business area (all three parties need to understand business priorities)
7. Prioritize business area for improvement (required for re-engineering)
8. Organization structure (ERP maps organizational structure)
9. Relationship among businesses (ERP needs this information)
10. Geographical locations (ERP, hardware and networking needs this information)
11. Accounting profile (ERP setup this information)
12. Accounting calendars (ERP setup this information)
13. Currencies and conversion policy (ERP setup needs this information, client and vendor will also need this information for gap analysis)
14. Naming/Numbering standards (ERP setup needs this information, client and vendor will also need this Information for gap analysis)
15. Business functions that are performed centrally
16. Naming/Numbering standards (ERP setup needs this information, client and vendor will also need this information to check gap)
17. Business functions that are performed by each business unit (ERP setup needs this information, client and vendor will also need this Information to check gap)

FIGURE 6.1 Questions for Capturing the Organization Structure Using Structured English

To summarize, a written document about organization's vision, mission and structure provides a common baseline to the clients, the vendors and the consultants. During the process, the client gains a better understanding of its organization. The next step is to detail each process that will be included in the ERP implementation using structured interviews and recording the responses using structured English. A sample set of questions for material requirement planning process of a manufacturing organization is shown in Figure 6.2.

These questions partially capture MRP process of an organization. This list of questions is not exhaustive. An organization will come up with questions to represent their own concerns and process specific details. One can add another 30 questions easily. The questions and their answers are organization specific but vendor independent. Structured interviews may compliment any of the formal techniques for capturing requirements.

6.3 EVENT-DRIVEN PROCESS CHAINS

We already know that SAP is the largest ERP company. SAP has its own proprietary modelling technique called event-driven process chain (EPC).

SAP uses EPC as basic modelling technique. An EPC captures tasks or functions (what should be done), events (when should something be done), organization (who should perform the task) and communication (what information is required to perform the task). In EPC diagrams, events are passive elements. They describe the circumstances that trigger a function. Examples of events are sales order

- How is a purchase order created?
- How planned purchase orders are executed? Possibilities are
  - Automatically go to a specific vendor.
  - Automatically become part of a master order.
- Is purchasing decentralized?
- Does material requirement planning tales sales orders into account?
- What is the nature of your requirements—seasonal, highly variable etc.?
- Does raw material change from season to season?
- Do you stock material to respond to seasonal requirements?
- How long is the typical forecast cycle?
- Is forecast algorithm automated or human intervention is allowed?
- Does capacity play a role in MRP?
- Does MRP take input from demand forecast, on hand stock, order policy, safety stock policy etc?
- Can planner change planned orders?
- Do you have multiple distribution centre?
- How do you store material? Is it a networked warehouse?
- Do you run any MRP simulations?
- Do you keep track of individual inventory at different locations?
- Do you have flexibility in estimating material requirements?
- Do you setup vendor schedule?
- How is vendor selection done?
- How does a purchase requisition get converted into a purchase order?

FIGURE 6.2 Questions for Finding About the Purchase Process of an Organization

entered, stock not available, quality test failed, etc. In the EPC diagrams, an event is represented as a hexagon. Functions are active elements in EPC. They model the tasks or activities within the company. Examples of functions are create sales order and check stock. A function is represented as a rounded rectangle. A function in EPC diagram may end with more than one mutually exclusive events. There are objects such as information, material or resource objects that portray objects from the real world. A function may use these objects as input or may produce them as its output. Examples are material data, purchase order data, etc. An object is represented as a rectangle. The organizational unit that performs the activity is represented as an oval. Example organization units are sales department, purchase department, quality department, etc.

A control flow connects events with functions creating chronological sequence and logical interdependencies between them. A control flow is represented as a dashed arrow.

Information flow shows connection of a function with input and output objects. Input objects are read, and the output objects are changed or created. Information flow is represented as a solid arrow. The legends are shown in Figure 6.3. The sales and order processes using EPC are shown in Figure 6.4. EPC shown in Figure 6.4 is not a standard reference model of SAP. It is a generic process. For reference model of SAP, the book on SAP business blueprint can be referred.[4]

This process creates a sales order for a particular customer after verifying their credit limit. Then the availability of items is checked. If items are available, the material is packed and dispatched updating the inventory. Customer invoice is created and the financial records are updated. If ordered items are not available, they have to be procured from the vendor by first creating a purchase requisition

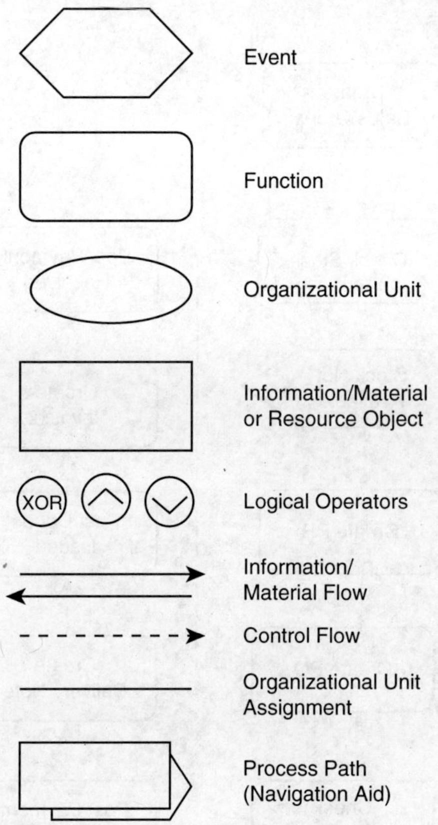

FIGURE 6.3 EPC Legends

and then converting it to a purchase order. The purchase order will be given to a selected vendor who will supply goods. The received goods/items go through a quality check and finally goods receipt is created. Inventory is also updated. When invoice is received from the vendor, payment is made and necessary postings to the financial accounts are also made. The pending sales orders can now be processed.

Each function in EPC accesses global data and communicates with other functions through global data. EPC reference models can be viewed in the following four different ways.

1. **Component model:** Component model captures all the functions performed by an organization. If we retain only the functions that are performed and do away with all other details contained in an EPC, then a component view is seen. A component view looks like a tree that may have multiple levels as follows.
   - Level 0 describes an application as a whole.
   - Level 1 contains the functional areas covered by the application.

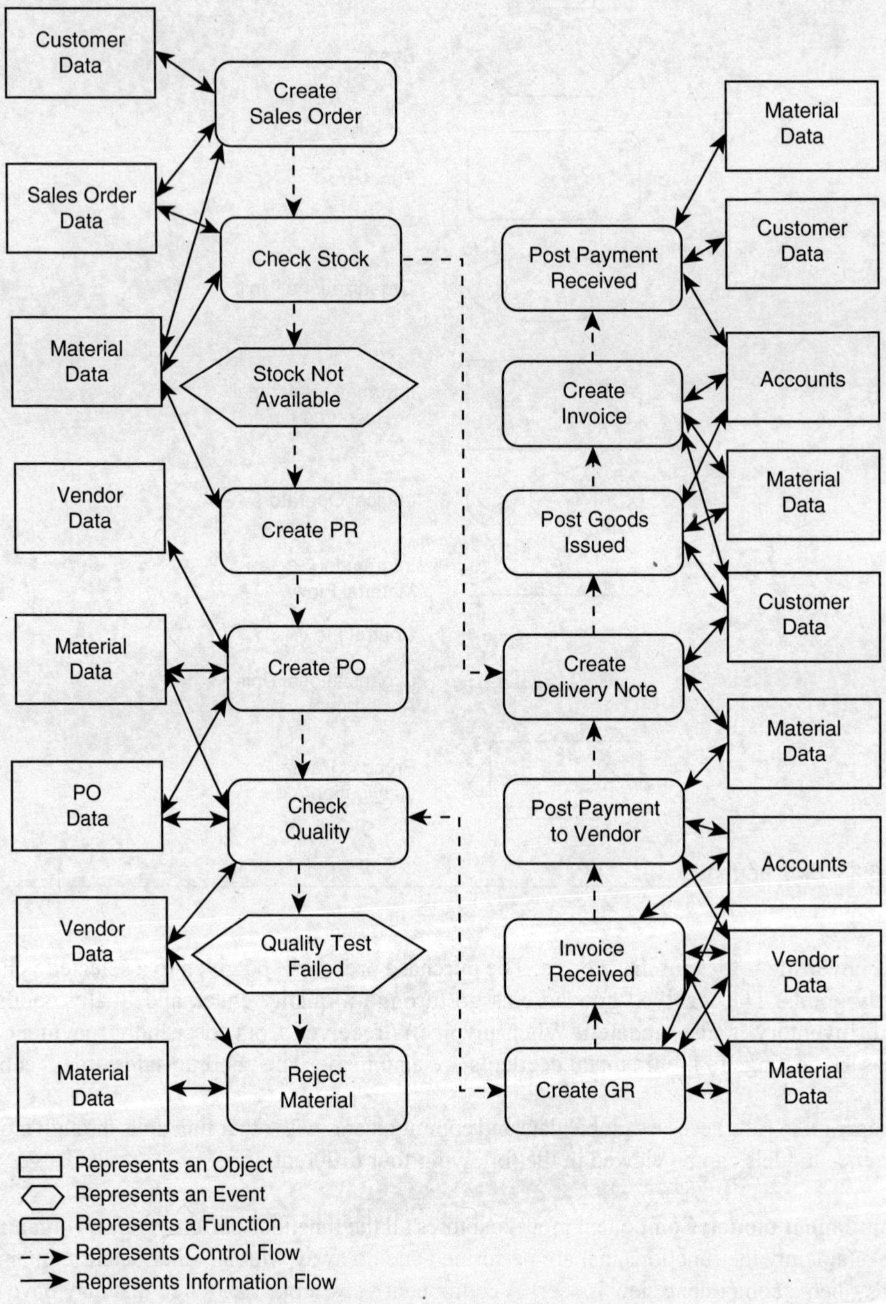

FIGURE 6.4 Event Process Chain for Sales and Order Process

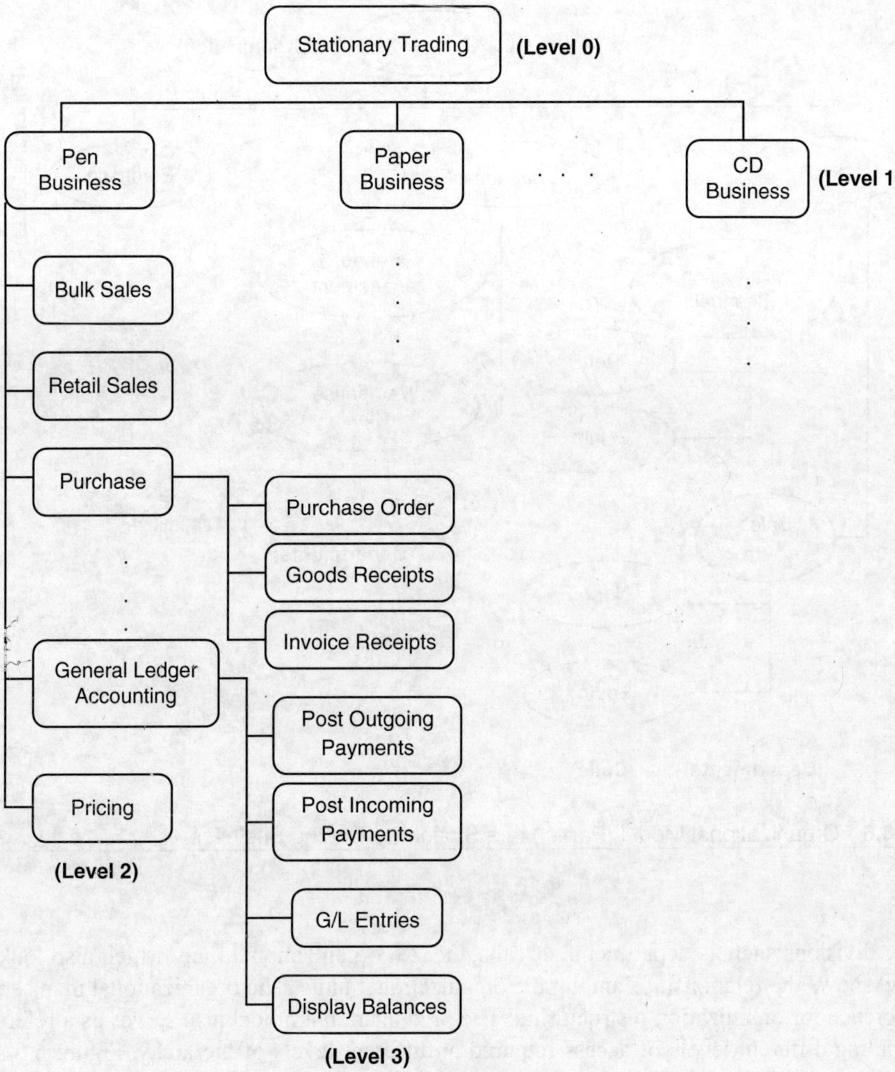

FIGURE 6.5 Component Model (Partial) of a Stationary Trading Business

- Level 2 contains the main tasks of a given functional area.
- Level 3 contains the individual tasks performed within the scope of a main function from the reference models.

Figure 6.5 shows a partial component model of a company that trades stationary.

2. **Organization model:** The organizational model captures the structure of the organization. An organization is divided into functional units and business units. A functional unit may have fur-

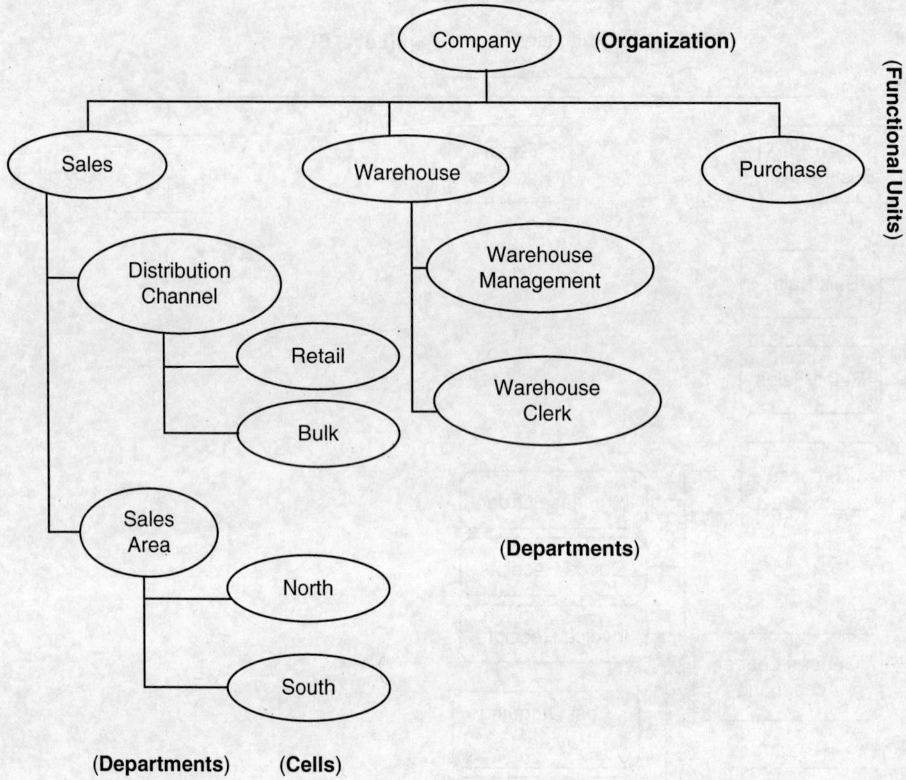

FIGURE 6.6 Organizational Model (Partial) of a Stationary Trading Business

ther divisions such as departments or cells, etc. An organizational map, which also looks like a tree, shows the relationships among the organizational units. The organizational map serves as a reference for organization restructuring. The organizational model also serves as a reference for deciding different levels of access required at different levels of hierarchy. Figure 6.6 shows a partial organizational model of a company that trades stationary. This company has units to manage sales, purchase and warehouse. There would be other units that have not shown. Each unit may have further subunits. Such a figure captures the organizational structure and the division of responsibilities.

3. **Data model:** The data required by functions is captured by the data model. The model that SAP uses is different from the standard techniques such as entity relationship diagrams (ER) or extended ER diagrams. The data/information and resources are represented as rectangles. Arrows are used to show specialization/generalization and a two-headed arrow with a stroke is used to show a relationship between data entities. In Figure 6.7, a customer could be an orderer, a receiver of the goods or a debitor. A customer is associated with an account that could be a general ledger account (payable/receivable).

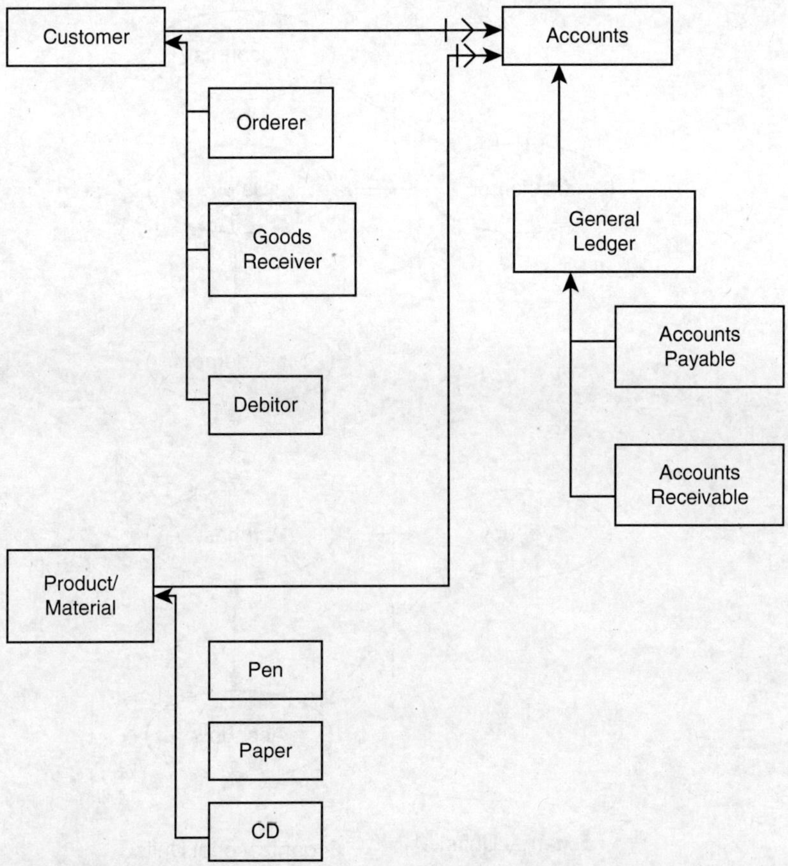

FIGURE 6.7 Data Model (Partial) of a Stationary Trading Business

4. **Interaction model:** Firstly, it is required to club together the functions that an organizational unit performs, then an interaction map to show interaction between organizational units is created. No details are included in the interaction map. For example, a customer interacts with sales units of the organization and sales unit interacts with accounting. An interaction map shown in Figure 6.8 captures these interactions.

Variation of EPC called configurable EPC also exists in which a function can be marked as optional. SAP has 3,000 reference business processes represented as EPC models. SAP claims that these reference models capture best business practices followed across the globe. An organization should be able to find almost all of their business processes among these reference models. These models include business processes from all business units of an organization such as financial accounting, inventory management, organizational management, plant maintenance, procurement, production planning, project management, quality management, sales and distribution, etc. There are multiple versions of the same process to cover variations in the processes. SAP also claims that their reference models cover all options for a pro-

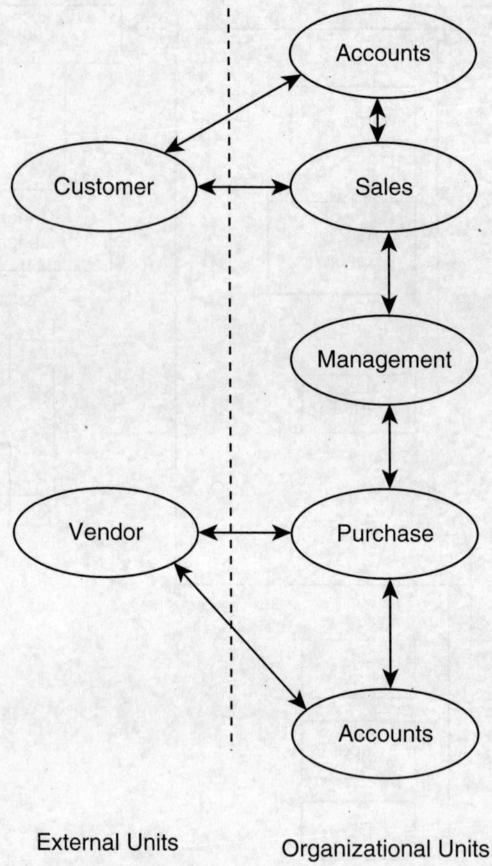

FIGURE 6.8 Interaction Model (Partial) of a Stationary Trading Business

cess and these represent best practices. If a client is doing a process in any other way, they should consider changing their business process. The question whether an organization should change its process or not falls under the general discipline of business process re-engineering. Business process re-engineering is discussed in Chapter 7.

6.4 OBJECT-ORIENTED MODEL

It is observed that 70 per cent or more of flow within an organization (manufacturing or service) is information. This result confirms the claim by Toffler,[5] that we are living in an information society and organizations have become *information organizations*.[6] For a business process, data is important and a business process should be analysed in terms of data and information that it modifies. Data is an important constituent of business processes and one needs to look at how data is defined, created, modified and used. In fact, enterprise resource planning software models an organization in terms of data and their relationships, and a set of functions that operate on the data.

Object-oriented (OO) model supports this view point and focuses on the data entities. The building block of OO model is named class that consists of data and methods (functions) that operate on the data. A class has relationship with other classes and interacts with other classes. A class may request another class to perform some action and/or provide data. The modelling may proceed in two different ways:

- **View integration approach:** Translate informal individual requirements into formal representation and merge.
- **Centralized schema design approach:** Merge informal individual requirements and then create formal representation.

Since OO modelling technique is not directly supported by any of the major ERP players, no reference models would be available. Starting point for capturing requirements would be legacy systems if they exist. The existing documents explaining the existing business processes may also provide inputs to the requirement gathering phase. The team who is creating OO model may also interview the business process owners (BPOs) for details. It is important to make the BPOs feel comfortable during the interviews. BPOs would open up and tell the details, strong points, trouble spots and bottlenecks only if they do not feel intimidated, undermined or threatened. The team consolidates information gathered from all sources. It remains a challenge to filter out what is information and what is not; what is to be retained and what is to be discarded.

The legends used in an OO model are shown in figures 6.9 and 6.10. There are classes or objects (shown in Figure 6.9(a)) that have attributes (or data part) and methods. A class can be specialized form of a general class (Figure 6.9(b)). The objects are related other through associations (Figure 6.9(c1) and (c2)) that have multiplicity (Figure 6.9(d) that defines the number of instances that can relate. A relationship or association may itself have attributes (refer to Figure 6.9(c3)). A class may request another class to perform functions (refer to Figure 6.9 (e1) and (e2)).

There are some guidelines that one can follow during modelling. One should start with the set of nouns that have been mentioned during interviews and found in the legacy systems. Out of the nouns with similar meanings, retain the one which is most general and descriptive. For example, out of client, buyer, receiver and payer, retain client as other words explain the role played by the client. The nouns which are out of the scope and irrelevant, are also deleted. The nouns that do not convey specific meaning and are vaguely defined should also be deleted. Nouns that describe individual objects and whose independent existence is not required are attributes that belong to an entity and not entities. For example, weight, price and colour are all attributes of an entity item. The verbs or actions are the methods or relationships. A verb that describes a relation between two classes is an association. Any dependency between two or more classes is also an association. A reference from one class to another is an association as well. Associations correspond to stative verbs, and verb phrases such as next to, part of, contained in, drives, talks to, has, supplies, works for and manages. An association should describe a structural property of the application domain, not a transient event.

Associations between entities provide path for data sharing and collaborations. Ask questions that should be answered by the model to make sure that there are enough entities, attributes and associations to answer your questions. If multiple paths exist between classes, eliminate the redundant ones. For a detailed description of OO modelling, refer to Rumbaugh et al.[7] Figures 6.10 and 6.11 shows OO model and collaboration model for the processes shown in Figure 6.4. There are six data items namely

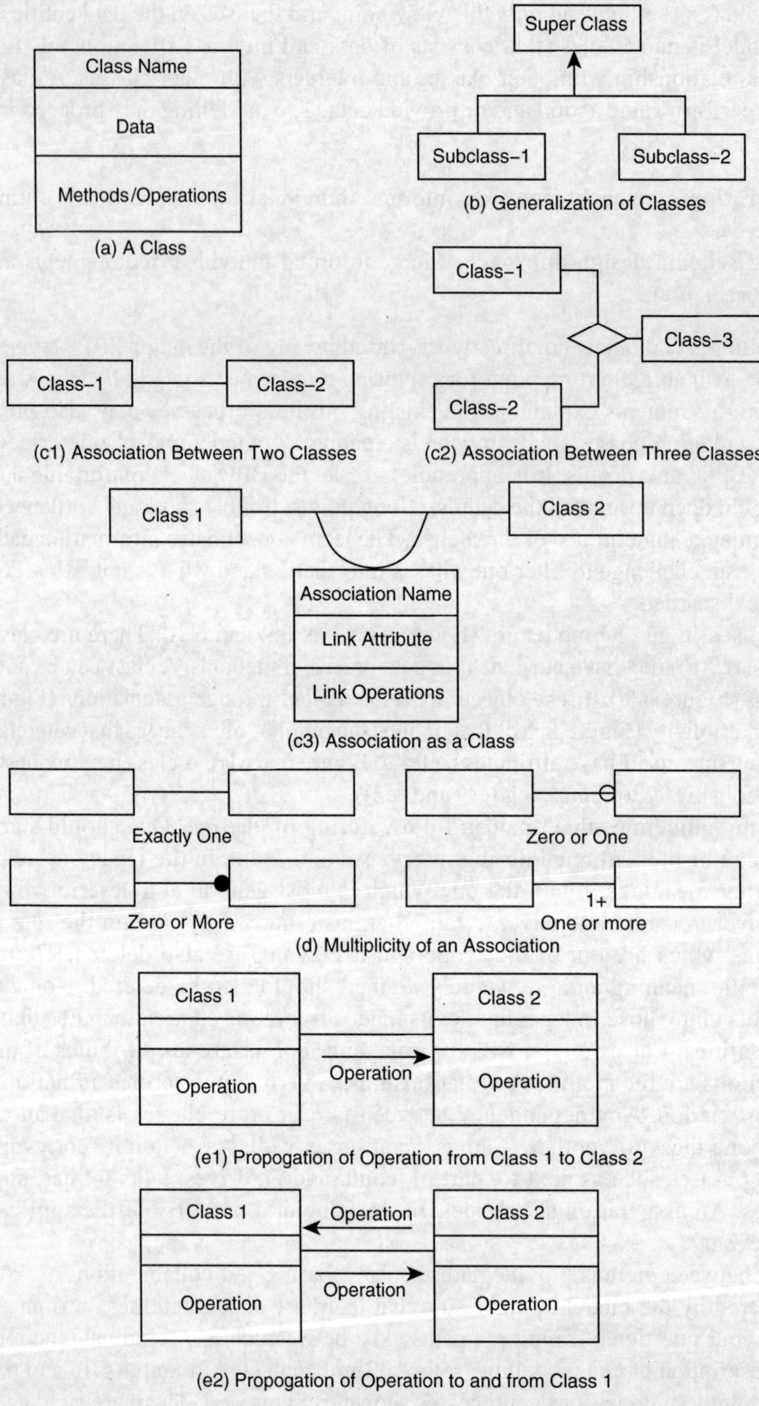

FIGURE 6.9 OO Legends

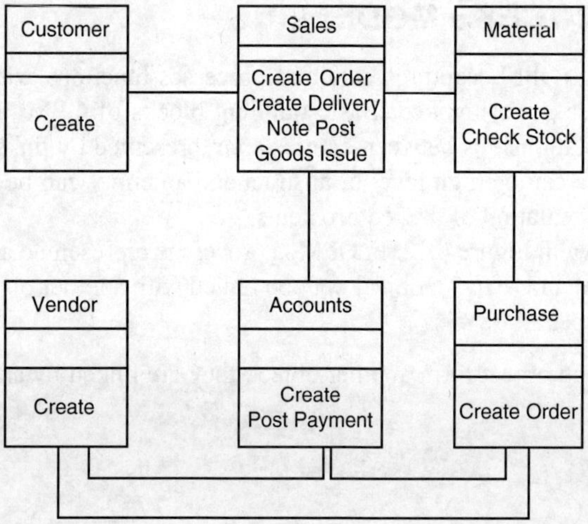

FIGURE 6.10 Example of Data Model

customer data, sales order data, purchase order data, vendor data, material data and accounts in Figure 6.4. The corresponding OO model has the same classes. With each class, we have methods/functions associated that cover all functions shown in the Figure 6.4. OO model provides a different view than EPC model. These two complement each other nicely. We can also create a collaboration model as shown in Figure 6.11 to capture the interaction among classes.

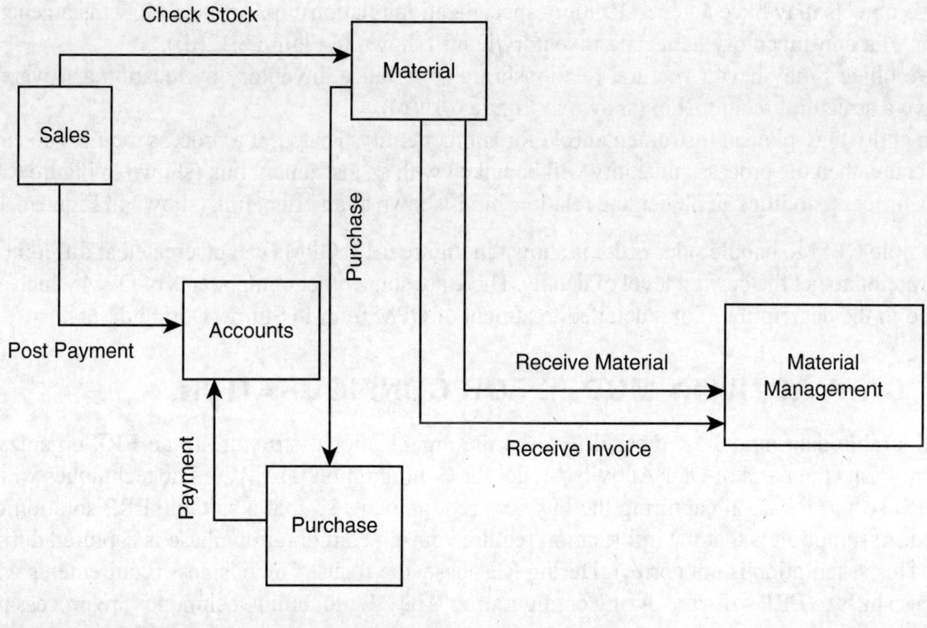

FIGURE 6.11 Example of Collaboration Model

6.5 OBJECT PROCESS MODELLING

Object process modelling (OPM) captures data and processes/functions without worrying about the sequence in which processes are invoked. Basic building blocks of OPM[8] are entities that represent processes and objects. Relationships between entities are represented by links that are either structural or procedural. The entities can be high level or abstract and an entity can be detailed in another OPM creating a top-down representation of the requirements.

OPM legends are shown in Figure 6.12. In OPM, a process is represented as an oval and an object as a rectangle (Figure 6.12(a) and (b)). An object may be linked with another object or process with a link of one of the following types:

- If many instances of an object form another object, they are linked by an aggregation link (shown in Figure 6.12(c)).

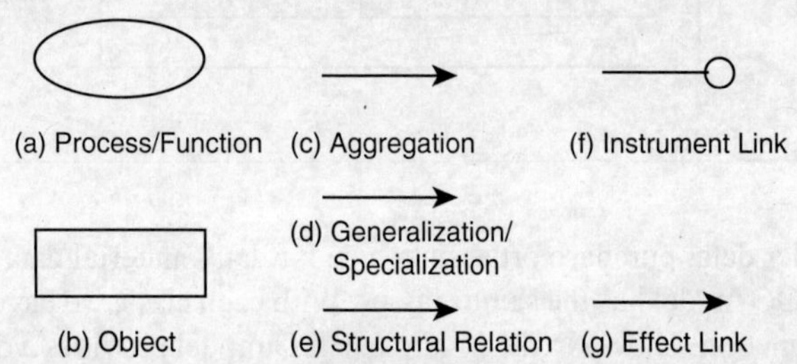

FIGURE 6.12 OPM Legends

- Two objects may have a generalization–specialization relationship. An item object is a generalization of a non-inventory items and inventory items (shown in Figure 6.12(d)).
- Two objects may have structural relationship. For instance, inventory by location and warehouse have a structural relationship (shown in Figure 6.12(e)).
- An entity may play an instrumental role for another entity. That is, if a process requires an entity to execute, then the process and entity will be linked with an instrument link (shown in Figure 6.12(f)).
- If a process modifies an object, the relationship is shown as an effect link (shown in Figure 6.12(e)).

An example OPM to handle sales order is shown in Figure 6.13. OPMs can be created at different levels of abstraction to get the desired level of details. There are some other components of OPM which are not included in the description. For a detailed treatment of OPM refer to Sturm, Dori and Shehory.[9]

6.6 DATA ACTIVITY MODEL FOR CONFIGURATION

A configurable data model[10, 11] created to align the organizational structure to an ERP organizational structure forms the basis of Data Activity Model for Configuration (DAMC). The techniques which are described so far, focus on capturing the business requirements so that a suitable ERP solution can be selected. Assumption is that the information required during configuration phase is captured during RE phase. This assumption is not correct. During RE phase, the focus is on business requirements whereas the focus shifts to ERP software during configuration. The RE modelling techniques are process model-

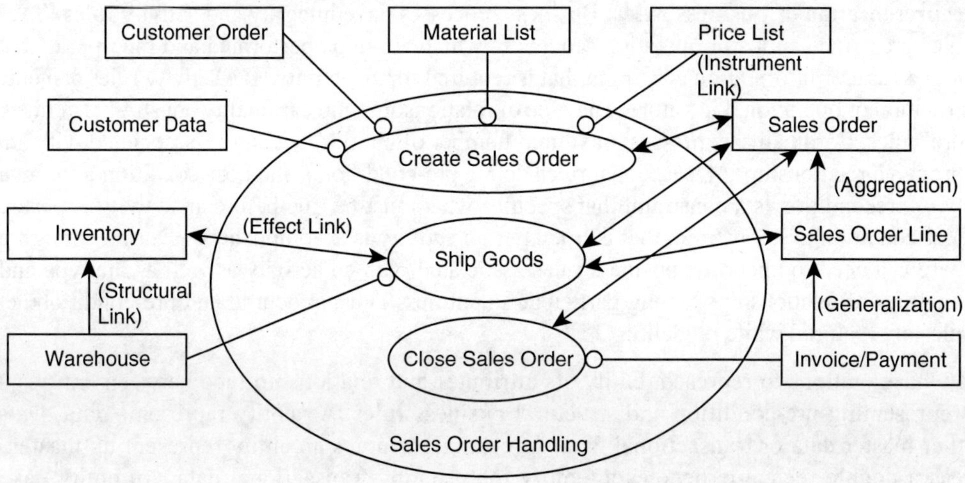

FIGURE 6.13 OPM to Handle Sales Order

ling techniques which emphasize on functions, processes, their interactions and required data. Configuration involves defining a business process in terms of data, their interrelationships and interactions to accomplish a task. The process modelling techniques used in RE phase may capture data elements but they fail to show their interactions and interrelationships. DAMC is suitable for capturing configuration specific requirements for ERP system.

The following information about data and processes is significant for configuration:[12, 13]

- Information regarding processes, functions, control flow and data is required for configuration. Process should be defined in terms of its functionality and control flow.
- While configuring an ERP system, many decisions about alternative functions, tables and parameters have to be made. Configuration reference models should be able to capture these decisions. The decisions can either be mandatory or optional in nature. Some configuration decisions are critical while others are non-critical. Critical decisions have significant impact on the business processes. The decisions should be differentiated between critical and non-critical decisions.
- There should be a logical sequence to take decisions for configuration. A decision may include processes and data objects. The logical sequence is through interrelationships within one process model, between one or more process models or between process and data models.
- ERP-specific configuration details may also be required. For instance, SAP configuration is done through its IMG. Such information may provide valuable information to the configuration team.
- Reference data models are important for configuration. ER diagram or its variants are used for data models. We need to distinguish between optional entities and required entities. An entity is connected to another entity through a relationship. A relationship may be optional. Distinction between mandatory and optional relationship is required.

In addition, following information is also important:

- Distinction between persistent (master) and transactional data is important. Transactional data is created when a transaction is executed after a successful configuration. It is master data that is used for configuration.

- **Representation of business rules:** Business processes have integrity and activity rules.[14] Activity rules prescribe actions or operation sequences which are to be performed and incorporated in any process and/or information constraint that is required for an activity.[15, 16] Activity rules can either be structural or operational in nature. The type of relationships and cardinality constraints define structural rules. Cardinality expresses maximum number of entities that can be associated with another through a relationship.[17] Operational rules define pre-condition/s and post-condition/s for an activity. A precondition is a constraint that specifies what must be true before an activity is performed. Post-condition is a constraint that is true after an activity is accomplished.[18] During configuration, there is a need to know the business rules associated with an activity as well as the type and cardinalities of relationships among participating entities. Thus, structural and pre-condition activity rules are required while modelling.

DAMC has notations to represent entity, its attributes and relationship type between entities along with representing pre-condition and structural business rules. An entity represents data. Data can be either master data or transactional data. A rectangle denotes an entity representing master data, whereas a double rectangle denotes an entity representing transactional data. An entity has attributes. An ellipse represents an attribute. A relationship connects entities and can either be mandatory or optional in nature. It represents an activity and has a unique name. A solid line represents a mandatory relationship whereas a dotted line denotes an optional relationship. The entities participating in an optional relationship may themselves be optional. In other words, one may not depict entities participating in an optional relationship. A required (mandatory) entity is represented with an *r* and an optional entity is depicted with an *o* written in the corner of an entity representing master data. One-to-one, one-to-many and many-to-many cardinality constraints depict structural rules. Precondition rules check availability of external or transactional data and output of an activity/relationship. Conditions/constraints associated with a relationship represent precondition business rule within curly brackets just below the name of a relationship. Figure 6.14 summarizes the notations of DAMC.

Figure 6.15 shows a simple DAMC containing *A* and *B* entities that participate in the relationship *T*1 and has precondition: *C*1 to be true. These entities represent master data. Activity *T*1 creates transactional data that is stored in an entity *M*. *T*2 is an optional relationship between entities *B* and *C* that represent master data. T2 has precondition *C*2 associated with it. For the optional activity *T*2, entity *B* is required entity whereas entity *C* is optional. Activity *T*3 reads entity *A* if precondition *C*3 is true. *A*1 and *A*2 are the attributes of entity *A*.

DAMC for creating a sales order activity is shown in Figure 6.16. A sales order consists of the customer details, and the material details that are fetched from persistent entities customer and material. The sales orders are stored in a transactional entity sales order. A sales order is created if either a quotation or a purchase order is available.

Credit of a *customer* may be verified under any of the following conditions. For one time sales order, *credit* of a customer is verified (*using verify credit status*) whereas for *recurrent sales orders*, this is an optional activity. Similarly, if a customer is a one time customer then his credit limit may be verified but for regular customers it may be an optional activity. *Discount* may be associated with a *customer* and *material* depending upon the discount strategy and/or customer type and discount strategy and/or material type, respectively. For this optional relationship, entity *customer* is required whereas the entity *discount* is optional. Tax may be associated with material depending upon its type and/or taxation

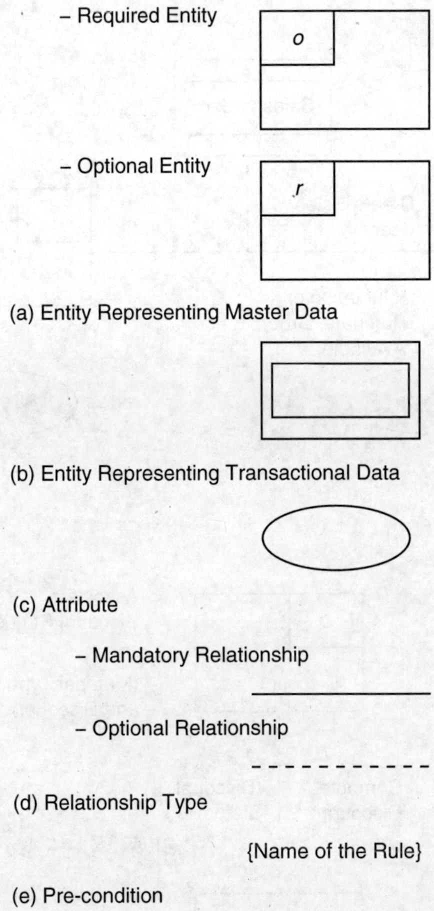

FIGURE 6.14 DAMC Legends

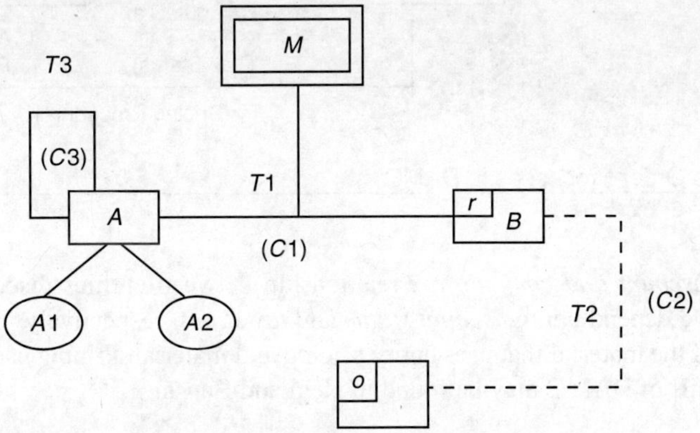

FIGURE 6.15 Small Example of DAMC

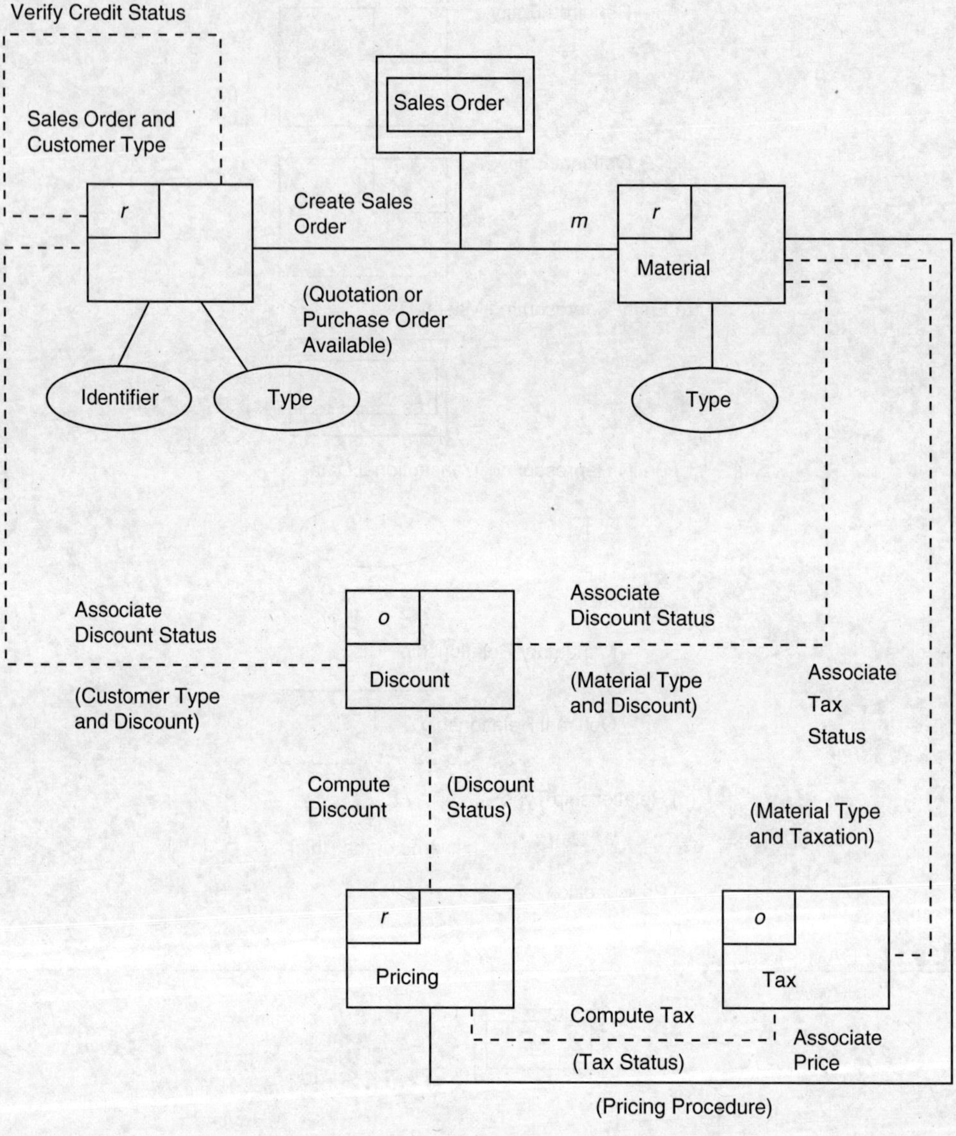

FIGURE 6.16 Sales Order Processes in DAMC

strategy. *Compute discount and compute tax* relationship between entities discount-pricing and tax-pricing is optional and depend upon *discount status* and *tax status,* respectively. The pricing procedure determines pricing of the material that uses entity pricing and material. Pricing uses entity discount and entity tax. More details of DAMC may be found in Negi and Bansal.[19]

CONCLUSION

The objective of this chapter has been to understand the RE phase of ERP project. The various ways of documenting requirements are learnt. One of the ways of documenting requirements is to use structured English. Small organization would generally use structured English for documenting their requirements. There are many formal ways of documenting the requirements. Event Process Chains by SAP, Object Process Model,[20] object-oriented modelling[21] and Data Activity Model for Configuration (DAMC)[22] are the ones which are discussed. There are many more modelling techniques which have not been discussed. The aim is to capture the requirements in sufficient details so that an appropriate ERP system can be selected.

CASE STUDY

Let us continue with RetailS and document their requirements. Recall that we have been working with RetailS in previous chapters. This is a retail company in Delhi, India. Here, we will look at the requirements of RetailS.

Business Processes of RetailS: The CMD of RetailS explained the business processes to us in detail and we have documented the processes. The objective of our interaction with the CMD was to understand the requirements and their concerns. Let us first understand the material that RetailS deals in. None of the material in which RetailS deals is manufactured by the company. The parameters associated with a product are just too many.

Just to get an idea, let us consider a metallic easy open can, one of the items that RetailS deals in. We have seen these cans used by Coke/Pepsi (RetailS may not be supplying cans to Coke/Pepsi). The parameters associated with these cans are as follows:

- Capacity
- Capacity unit
- Diameter of the can
- Height of the can
- Diameter of the top lid
- Diameter of the bottom lid
- Color of the can
- Color of the lid
- Color of the lacquer
- Text to be written on the lid

One way of representing data of a company is by using entity-relationship diagrams. These diagrams are taught in the course on database management course (refer to Bansal[23] for a brief introduction). Figure 6.17 shows the entities maintained by RetailS. RetailS maintains data about all its customers, suppliers, shipping agencies and items that it deals in. The entities are as follows:

- Customer
- Vendor
- Supplier
- Product
- Order

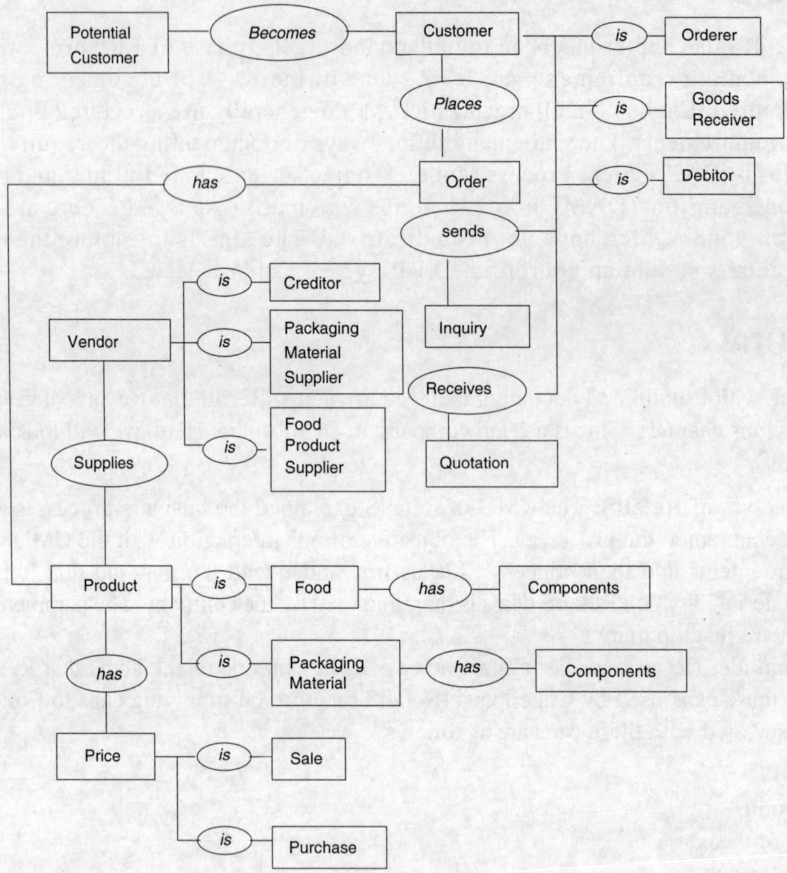

FIGURE 6.17 Entity-relationship Diagram for RetailS

Product entity has two specializations namely food and packaging material. Each of these has components which are different for each of them. A vendor plays different role such as creditor, packaging material supplier or food product supplier. For the reference of the staff and management, a price list is maintained consisting of sale price and purchase price. The prices are revised/validated every month. The top lids and bottom lids are separate components that may have their own specifications such as thickness, tab design, its location and style. Coming to the business processes, let us first look at the sales process. The salesman takes orders from a customer and then gets the material from a supplier directly shipped to the buyer. This seemingly simple process involves many steps and multiple outcomes for each step. Figure 6.18 shows simplified version of the process using EPC notation (from SAP). This process stepwise is mentioned below.

1. The salesman of RetailS may approach a potential buyer and ask their requirements. There are four possibilities:
   (i) The effort to contact may fail due to the change in contact details.

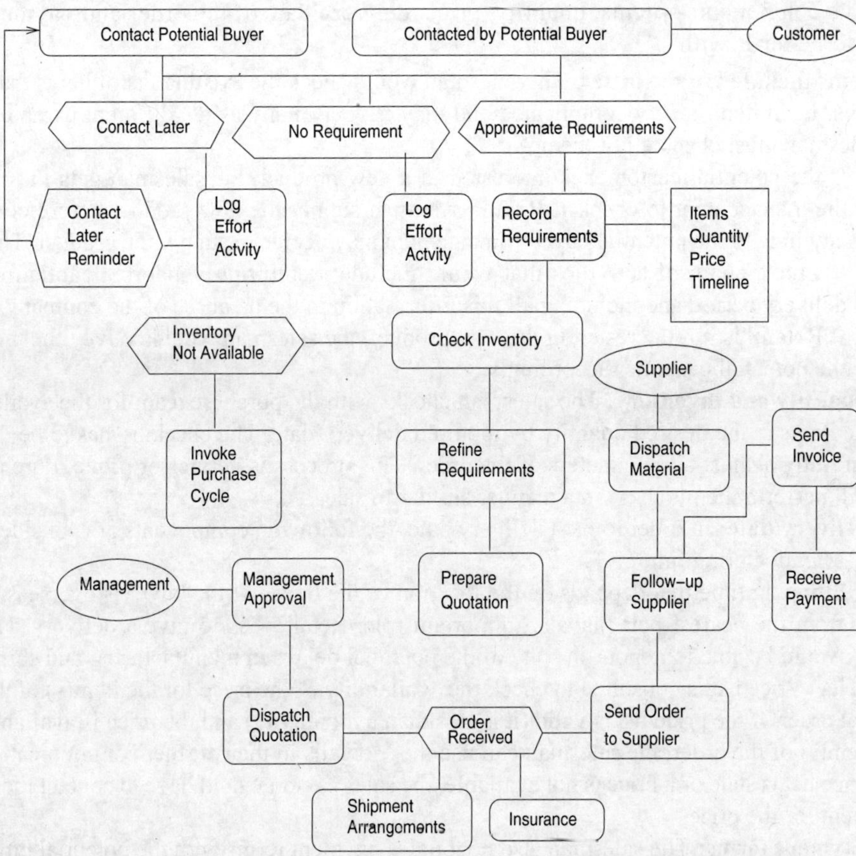

FIGURE 6.18 Sales Process for RetailS

(ii) The potential buyer may not have any requirements.

(iii) The potential buyer may ask the salesman to contact later.

(iv) If there is a requirement, they may give their approximate requirements in terms of products, price, quantity and timeline.

In case (i), the salesman would record his efforts in his log book and make another attempt to get the changed contact information. In case (ii), the salesman would record his efforts in his log book. The recording serves two purpose, one is no other sales person should contact them and the other tells the management about the activities of the sales staff.

In case (iii), the salesman would like to record the call and a reminder to himself to contact again. A mechanism is required to remind the sales person to contact the party again. It is worthwhile to point out that RetailS should contact the potential buyer as promised even if the sales person have left the organization or is on leave. Again, an ERP system would help sales staff to make the follow-up call.

In case (iv), he would like to record the details of the potential buyer along with the requirements and move on to Step 2.

2. All five components—items, quantity, price, delivery date of the order and payment terms need to be dealt with.
   - **Items included in the order:** The salesman would check the existing list of items that RetailS sells. Each item is very complicated and may have as many as ten different parameters. The salesman must check all of them.
     - If the potential customer is interested in a new product, the salesman gets in touch with the management to check if RetailS wants to supply the new product before committing anything to the potential buyer. Management may decide to supply the product. This would trigger a chain of activities that would include identifying vendors, negotiating prices, delivery period and including all this information in the database of the company.
     - If RetailS is not interested in the new product, the salesman would convey the message to the potential customer accordingly.
   - **Quantity and inventory:** The salesman checks with the purchase team for the availability of the items in the desired quantity by required delivery date. The checking has to be done very carefully against all parameters of the order. This process is very error prone. Purchase team will perform the purchase in a manner similar to sales.
   - **Delivery date:** In order to fix a delivery date, the following components are considered:
     - Manufacturing time.
     - Shipping time that depends on the location of the buyer. If the buyer is overseas, distance from the nearest port plays an important role. RetailS has to give a delivery date that it would be able to honour in spite of the potential delays in manufacturing and shipping.
   - **Price:** Price list is consulted to check the availability of the price for the item(s) of the potential order. If the price list is valid (it is less than a month old) and the price is available for the item(s) of the order, the salesman can use these details in their further communication. If the price list is stale or a price is not available, the sales person would have to contact the management for the price.
   - **Payment terms:** The salesman also negotiates payment terms with the potential buyer.
3. The salesman after obtaining all required information, records them, creates a quote and e-mails to the potential buyer. At present, RetailS has paper files for each customer containing all communications.
4. The salesman is expected to make follow-up calls to the potential customers and convert them into customers. When a salesman contacts a potential customer again, any of the four key components of the order may get modified including items, price, quantity or delivery date. The salesman may have to do another iteration of steps 3 and 4 before actually receiving an order.
5. The material is shipped directly to the customer through a shipping agency. The shipping agency is also contacted and space on the shipping vessel is reserved by the salesman. The terms and conditions are also negotiated by the salesman.
6. All material is insured before transporting.
7. As soon as a potential order is in view, the purchase team has to become active. The interaction of the purchase team with potential vendors is similar to the interaction of sales team with potential customers.

When we started talking to the CMD of RetailS, he voiced many of his concerns and his reasons for wanting to deploy an ERP system. We have mentioned some of his concerns while describing the process above and an overall picture of his concerns is given next.

Why RetailS Wanted ERP system?

- **Prices and their validity:** Associated with each item that RetailS deals in, there is a sale price. The management fixes prices for the known items and creates a price list. These prices are generally valid for a month. In certain cases, the prices may fluctuate in a positive or negative direction about which only the management knows. It is the responsibility of the management to update the price list. Since the management team consists of only three people and they are multi-tasking, it is not unusual for them to forget to update the price list. Sometimes, the monthly update of the price list is also not done. The sales staff may use the old list and cause loss to RetailS or overprice the customer that may result in loss of the customer or his goodwill or both.

  The sales price is dependent on the purchase price. The management negotiates the purchase price with vendor before creating the sales price list.

  The management wanted an IT system that will send a reminder to the management after a month to update the price list. The IT system should also prevent the sales staff to use a stale price.
- **Reduce errors:** Every order involves details that need to be carefully defined. There are multiple parameters associated with a product that RetailS deals in. A mistake or omission of one of the parameters may result in delay, cancellation or rejection of the entire order. IT system can force the staff to check every parameter.

  For instance, the payment terms have to be defined and agreed upon by RetailS and the customer. Any omission or a mistake may cause delay or confusion in the payments. IT system can help RetailS create a master list of possible payment terms to avoid any errors.
- RetailS needs to frequently follow up with their customers, vendors and shipping agents. A customer is contacted multiple times during the process of a sale that also requires staff to contact the vendors multiple times as well. IT system can generate a reminder to the concerned staff for a follow-up activity.

  An issue that management faces here is that the remaining sales team may not know about the call and others may also call the same potential buyer resulting in possible annoyance. An immediate solution is to divide the companies or zones among the sales staff. The solution suffers from usual load-balancing issues. The more reasonable solution is to have a real-time integrated platform where the call details and its outcome may be recorded for the sales team to see. This was one of the reasons, management wanted an ERP.
- **Trade secret:** RetailS succeeds in their business by identifying customers, providing them the items of required quality at agreed upon prices in a timely manner. All this is possible if the vendors supply them quality items at a reasonable cost and on agreed upon time. RetailS has to protect price information from their existing competition and from the potential competition that may even shoot up from within RetailS. The information should be available in a very selective manner to the employees. IT system can help RetailS to make only the required information available to an employee.
- **Reports:** IT systems can provide required reports to the management about the organization in real time in a desired format.

EXERCISES

Check Your Understanding

1. What do understand from the term *requirements engineering*? What are the stages preceding this phase in the life cycle of an ERP project?

2. What are the various ways with which a company may approach requirements engineering?
3. Why do we need to document the requirements and then manage these documents?
4. How can you capture requirements for an ERP system using structured English? Document sales process and requirements related to this process using structured English. Assume that the organization is a manufacturing organization and sells to their dealers in bulk only. List all the assumptions you make about the organization and its sales process.
5. Explain different components of EPC. Give an example for each component.
6. What are two different approaches to creating an object model? When will you use each of the approach?
7. Explain object process modelling technique. What are the main components of OPM. Create an object process model for scheduling production. You may have to make assumptions about how the production gets triggered. The choices may include inventory levels, sales orders, forecast or a combination of these.
8. Create a DAMC for delivering a sales order to the customer. The order is a bulk order and would be delivered by company's delivery vehicle to the customer. List any assumption that you may make about the process.

Apply Your Understanding

1. Study the available documents in your chosen organization if the documents are available and talk to people to check if the documented processes are followed in practice.
2. Document some of the processes of your organization in a formal way using the techniques that are discussed in this chapter using the existing documents as a reference. If the documents are not available, are incomplete, outdated or inconsistent, you may have to talk to the employees to understand business processes. What modelling technique did you use and why?
3. If your organization has already automated some of their business processes, find out all about requirements gathering and documentation.

ENDNOTES

1. M. Daneva, 'ERP Requirements Engineering Practice: Lessons Learned', in *IEEE Software* (2004), March/April, 26–33.
2. I. Sommerville, 'Software Construction by Configuration: Challenges for Software Engineering Research', in *Proceedings of the 21st IEEE International Conference on Software Maintenance* (2005).
3. P. Bollen, 'Enterprise Systems: Is There Still a Need for Requirements Determination?', in *Proceedings of the 6th Annual ISOnE World Conference* (Las Vegas, NV, 2007), April.
4. T. Curran, G. Keller and Andrew Ladd, *SAP R/3 Business Blueprint: Understanding the Business Process Reference Model*, Prentice Hall (1998).
5. A. Toffler, *Powershift,* New York: Bantam Books (1991).
6. Peter F. Drucker, 'The Coming of the New Organization', in *Harvard Business Review*, January–February, 1998.
7. James R. Rumbaugh et al., *Object-Oriented Modeling and Design, First Edition,* Prentice-Hall (1990).
8. Arnon Sturm, Dov Dori and Onn Shehory, 'Single-Model Method for Specifying Multi-Agent Systems', in *Proceedings of the Second International Conference on Autonomous Agents and Multi-Agent Systems* (AAMAS 2003) (Melbourne, Australia, 2003), July.

9. ibid.
10. J. Recker et al., 'Configurable Reference Modeling Languages', in P. Fettk and P. Loos (eds), *Reference Modeling for Business Systems Analysis*, Pennsylvania: Idea Group, Hershey (2006), 22–46.
11. M. Rosemann and G. Shanks, *Extension and Configuration of Reference Models for Enterprise Resource Planning Systems*, G. Finnie, D. Cecez-Kecmanovic and B. Lo. Coffs Harboour (eds), in Proceedings of the 12th Australian Conference on Information Systems (ACIS 2001), 2001, 537–46.
12. ibid.
13. J. Recker et al., 'Configurable Reference Modeling Languages', in P. Fettk and P. Loos (eds), *Reference Modeling for Business Systems Analysis*, Pennsylvania: Idea Group, Hershey (2006), 22–46.
14. H. Herbst, G. Knolmayer, T. Myrach and M. Schlesinger, 'The Specification of Business Rules: A Comparison of Selected Methodologies', in A. A. Verijn-Stuart and T. W. Olle (eds), *Methods and Associated Tools for the Information System Life Cycle*, Amsterdam et al.: Elsevier (1994), 29–46.
15. B. Chadha, G. Jazbutis, C. Wang and R. E. Fulton, 'An Appraisal of Modeling Tools and Methodologies for Integrated Manufacturing Information Systems', in Vijay Saxena (ed.), *Engineering Databases: An Enterprise Resource*, New York: ASME (1992).
16. H. Herbst, G. Knolmayer, T. Myrach and M. Schlesinger, 'The Specification of Business Rules: A Comparison of Selected Methodologies', in A. A. Verijn-Stuart and T. W. Olle (eds), Methods and *Associated Tools for the Information System Life Cycle*, Amsterdam et al.: Elsevier (1994), 29–46.
17. Il-Y. Song and K. Froehlich, 'Entity-Relationship Modeling', in *IEEE Potentials* (1994), 13(5), 29–34.
17. H. E. Eriksson and M. Penker, *Business Modeling with UML: Business Patterns at Work,* New York, USA: John Wiley & Sons, Inc., (2000).
19. Tripti Negi and Veena Bansal, 'Integrating Process and Data Models to Aid Configuration of ERP Packages', in *Business Information Systems* (Springer, 2009), 21, 228–39.
20. Arnon Sturm, Dov Dori and Onn Shehory, 'Single-Model Method for Specifying Multi-Agent Systems', in *Proceedings of the Second International Conference on Autonomous Agents and Multi-Agent Systems (AAMAS 2003)* (Melbourne, Australia, 2003), July.
21. James R. Rumbaugh, Michael R. Blaha, William Lorensen, Frederick Eddy and William Premerlani, *Object-Oriented Modeling and Design, First Edition*, Prentice-Hall, (1990).
22. Tripti Negi and Veena Bansal, 'Integrating Process and Data Models to Aid Configuration of ERP Packages', in *Business Information Systems* (Springer, 2009), 21, 228–39.
23. Veena Bansal, *Computing for Management*, Prentice Hall of India (2005).

chapter 7

Re-engineering

LEARNING OBJECTIVES

After reading this chapter, you will be able to understand:

- Business process re-engineering (BPR)
- IT-driven BPR and non-IT-driven BPR
- Characteristics of business processes
- Maturity levels of business processes
- Life cycle of BPR projects
- Life cycle of an IT-driven BPR project
- Mode of BPR projects

7.1 INTRODUCTION

Business process re-engineering[1] (BPR) is fundamental rethinking and radical redesign of business processes to bring about dramatic improvements in performance measured in terms of cost, quality, service and speed.

The definition assumes that the business processes have the scope for improvement. There are various reasons why the existing business processes seem to become inefficient over a period of time. If we look at the market and the way it his changed, we realize that the customer focus has increased dramatically. The processes that were focused on mass production render themselves inefficient and inappropriate. The definition gives an impression that the scope of BPR is restricted to improving business processes only. While improving the processes, the structure of the organization may also need changes to support redesigned processes or to reveal new design possibilities for processes.

As a small evidence of an inefficient process, one can visit the Web site of Indian airlines and check their list of frequently asked questions (FAQ). The following question that happens to be question 2 in the FAQ and its answer are quoted here verbatim:

> Question 2 Why we do not get incentives well in time earned through various schemes?
>
> Answer: Mandatory checks are carried out by the Finance Department before the dues are credited, steps are being taken for expeditiously crediting of incentives well in time.

The two types of BPR of different kinds with an example are explained below.

1. **IT-driven BPR:** An IT-driven BPR project focuses on integrating IT with business processes. The objective is to integrate business processes using IT. The integration and availability of information would improve decision-making ability of employees as the data will be available in real time. The delays and lead time are reduced by integrating the processes using IT. ERP systems are organization-wide information systems that can potentially integrate all business processes of the organization.

   Hammer[2] enumerates the following three principles for IT-driven BPR efforts.

   - Subsume information-processing work into the real work that produces the information.
   - Put the decision point where the work is performed and build control into the process. In other words, workers should be empowered to make the decision which implies that an organization should have workers who have knowledge of the organization and understand the role they play in the organization.
   - Capture information once and at the source.

   An order fulfillment for a manufacturing firm in West India used to take eight weeks which came down to eight days after they re-engineered their processes using IT. There are many cases in India parallel to MBL cases cited in Hammer and Champy.[3] A leasing and financing company in South India brought down its application processing time to one day from seven days.

2. **Non-IT-driven BPR:** Certain situations may demand redesigning business processes of the organization. Consider a situation where customers are not happy and many complaints are lodged. A shortcut is to create a position and install staff to handle customer grievances. It is an expensive solution but the easiest one to implement. Another course of action is to first identify the causes of dissatisfaction and then take necessary measures. The analysis may reveal problems with the product or service itself that may require fundamental changes in the existing processes. The focus is on redesigning the business processes. IT may not be the driving force for re-engineering, it may be a facilitator or enabler of changes.

   Indian firm manufactures consumer durable goods and markets them through door-to-door sales persons. These salesman book orders that are passed to the nearest godown through branch office. The goods are then delivered by installation and service team. The payment is collected by a salesman. A simple analysis makes the sequential nature of process clear. The customer has to deal with a salesman for placing their order, with an installation and service team and with a different salesman who comes to collect money. If there is a mismatch in the customer order and the goods, reconciliation would involve sales person, branch office and godown. The organization re-engineered its entire process. The branch office and its godown became single unit. The job profiles changed, salesman, installation guy and service man all merged into one sales executive who procured orders, delivered and installed the goods and collected payments. The sales executive were provided with hand-held computers which were used for order booking. In this case, the process has been radically changed, the job profile broadened and IT has become integral part of the business process.

   - Organize around outcomes, not tasks. Combine several jobs into one.
   - Have those who use the output of a process, perform the process. Work is performed where it makes the most sense.
   - Treat geographically dispersed resources as though they were centralized.
   - Link parallel activities instead of integrating their results. As a result, reconciliation is minimized.

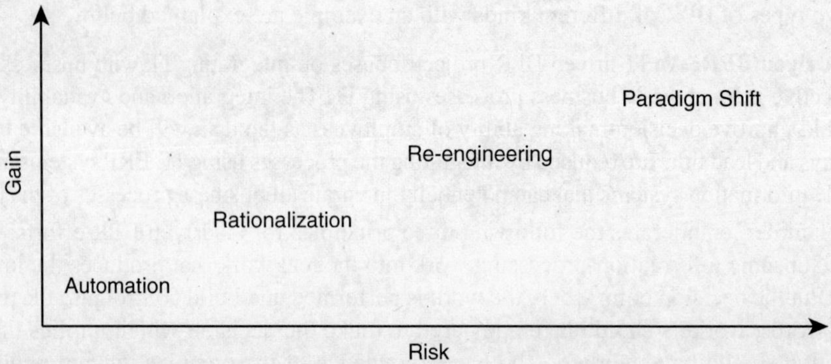

FIGURE 7.1 McFarlan Matrix Showing Four Dierent Activities Along with Associated Risk and Gain

BPR is considered a high-risk and a high-return activity. The McFarlan matrix as shown in Figure 7.1 has four activities, the risk associated with the activity on the horizontal axis and returns on the vertical axis. Automation is considered a low-risk and a low-gain activity. Rationalization that requires analysis followed by changes to the processes under consideration would yield better returns but involves little more risk than rationalization. Re-engineering is a high-risk and a high-gain activity as we will see in this chapter. Paradigm shift would involve major changes in the business or technology domain and is beyond the scope of this book.

Before attempting BPR, it is important to understand the business processes of an organization. In the next sections, an attempt to understand characteristics of business processes is made. If a process is inefficient, automating it will not make it efficient. If the processes are not coherently working towards achieving the organizational goal, making each process efficient will also not help. A BPR effort is initiated to look at the organization from structural, behavioural and process perspective.[4] In Section 7.3, we will learn about life cycle of a BPR project. ERP-driven BPR projects do not treat BPR as a separate project. We will highlight characteristics of an ERP driven BPR project in Section 7.4.

7.2 PROCESSES AND THEIR CHARACTERISTICS

Following characteristics will help us evaluate maturity of the business processes of an organization:

- A process requires a clearly defined owner who is responsible for its yield, cost, quality and schedule, and has authority to change or modify the process. However, it is not always easy to identify the owner of a process. Is department manager the business process owner (BPO) for the processes of his department? In a self-governing work group, who is BPO? We will need to, in any case, identify and establish BPO.
- Clearly defined boundaries of a process means that we can identify the beginning and end of a process. A well-managed process has clear boundaries. A process that modifies the data is referred to as transactional process and may not have clear boundaries.
- Capacity of a process is defined in terms of its output rate. Theoretical capacity of a process is usually more than its effective capacity. Factors such as equipment reliability, maintenance required and personnel factors including learning curve, illness and absenteeism affect the output rate of a process.
- Documentation of a process is also important. The document may describe the process in terms of process flowchart, assembly drawing, the operational steps or any of the representation as discussed

in Chapter 6. An organization may not have process documents or they may be obsolete. It is also possible that people at different level of hierarchy may have different view of the same process.

- **Control points:** A process must have control points established to manage the natural variations that occur in a process. The objective of the control points is to detect an unwanted change quickly and take corrective measures.
- **Effectiveness or ineffectiveness:** Ineffectiveness is easier to measure and generally used for measuring the effectiveness of a process. A process is ineffective if customers complain, output of the process has inconsistent quality or a corrective-action system is absent.
- **Efficiency:** It is defined as the ratio of the output and the input of a process. Inefficiency is easier to measure and identify. A process is inefficient if
  - Multiple off-line inspections are performed.
  - Redundant, unnecessary, non-value-added (rework/re-conciliation) activities are performed.
  - Supplier problems such as poor quality or late deliveries are reported.
  - Lot of corrective actions are performed such as rework and reconciliation.
  - The cost of value-added activities is excessive with respect to the competition.
- **Adaptability:** Adaptability is the ability of a process to adjust to the changes. A process is adaptable if the process can be changed to meet new requirements without significant modifications. An adaptable process may require some workflow change, personnel change or equipment change but the process remains largely intact.
- **Measurements:** A process must also be measurable through statistical measurement techniques. These measurements are to check various characteristics of the process and strive for continuous improvements. There are well-developed statistical techniques that can be employed to measure a process and its performance.
- Corrective actions are required to monitor and correct natural variation of a process, usually through internal feedback points. In a well-managed process, internal feedback points are established to monitor a process and take corrective action before sub-quality product is produced.

The above discussion is slightly oriented towards manufacturing processes. The service organizations and their processes have special features as described next.

7.2.1 Special Features of Processes of Service Organizations

A service organization is different from a manufacturing organization in many ways. For example, service is intangible. Service cannot be accumulated, since it is not an inventory item. Service industry is labour intensive, the role played by machines in manufacturing is played by people in the service industry. A manufacturing process has clearly defined owner, boundaries, input and output; whereas a service process may not have a clearly defined owner or boundaries. It may not be possible to establish control points for a service process. The corrective actions are usually reactive. The performance of a service process is hard to measure. Degree of customer contact also varies from being almost no contact (life insurance application processing) to close contact (dental care).

The maturity of a business process can be judged by looking at its various characteristics.

7.2.2 Process Evaluation

Lot of research has been done to judge the maturity level of business processes. The maturity levels defined by IBM, largely for manufacturing processes are mentioned below. IBM defines the following five levels of a process.

Level 5: A process at Level 5 exhibit the following properties:

- No designated owner.
- No process management.
- Process may not be effective.

Level 4: A process is at Level 4 when it exhibits the following properties:

- Process owner is identified and designated.
- The process is defined and documented.
- Control points within the process are present.
- Customer–supplier relationship and requirements that are internal as well as external to the process are established.
- Measurements of effectiveness and efficiency are identified and put in place to assess the process. Data collection process is in place to identify deficiencies, defects, rework, excess cost redundancies and supplier problems.
- A feedback mechanism is established for continuous quality improvement.

Level 3: A process at Level 3 exhibits all characteristics of a Level 4 process and the following additional features.

- Process-effectiveness measures show evidence that customer requirements are being met.
- In addition, the measurements should clearly show scope for further improvement. These improvements are required to progress to Level 2. Improvements needed to achieve Level 2 are identified and a plan is available to achieve the same.

Level 2:

- Major improvements planned at Level 3 have occurred.
- Positive results have been realized in terms of increased efficiency and effectiveness.
- The processes are flexible so that they can adapt to meet future demands.
- Efficiency measures must show continuous reduction in resources per unit of work.
- The process must be competitive both in terms of effectiveness and efficiency with respect to comparable process within the organization/industry.

Level 1:

- The process has been identified/benchmarked as a leader.
- The output must be primarily defect free.
- Minimum resources.
- Best of class, model process.

If the processes of an organization are not at Level 1 of maturity, it can re-engineer processes to make them Level 1. The objective of a non-IT-driven BPR project is broadly to improve business processes of the organization. Sometimes, an organization improves and evolves its business processes continuously but still the processes may become ineffective due to changes in the environment or introduction of a disruptive technology. BPR project may be initiated to get to Level 1 processes or to take a fresh look at the processes that in spite of being Level 1 seem to have become ineffective. One of the possibilities is misalignment between the business strategy of the organization and processes. The radical thinking or challenging the set ways of doing business becomes the keyword during a BPR project.

7.3 LIFE CYCLE OF A BPR PROJECT

BPR is a project that commences in phases and produces an output in each phase. A BPR project consists of the following stages:[5]

- Establishing the vision and objectives, the scope and mode of BPR
- Business modelling
- Business analysis
- Redesign
- Business transformation and continuous improvement

7.3.1 Establishing Vision, Objectives, Scope and Mode of BPR

This step involves identifying opportunities and business processes to be re-engineered. It is important to understand that a business process is not a function. BPR does not start by focusing on functions. It starts off by focusing on business processes. A change in a business process may also require changes in the structure of the organization. But BPR does not start off focusing on structural changes. The focus of a BPR project is also not downsizing, though it may happen as a result of changed business processes. BPR does not redefine the mission of the organization. BPR also does not focus on isolated manufacturing processes. BPR project may focus on customer satisfaction and during investigation may discover issues related to manufacturing. Scope of BPR is defined by executives who perceive the business as an integrated whole. The scope could be one of the following in the increasing order of scope and risk:

- A department
- Multiple departments
- Entire organization

The scope of the BPR project will clearly identify the business process that will be analysed and re-engineered.

Questionnaires, existing documents and semi-formal interviews may be used to collect the required information. The following activities are performed in this phase:

- Create a BPR team. Orient the process owner for re-engineering the process.
- Define key processes and preliminary re-engineering opportunity. Identify and gather the performance data for the processes. Benchmark the performance of the processes with the best in the industry. Some of required information may be available in the public domain while some may have to be purchased from the consulting companies that publish various survey reports. Some of the qualitative objective of a BPR project are the following:
  - Reduce cycle time of one or more cycles such as reduce time to market, provide quicker response to the customer.
  - Improve effectiveness of a process, e.g. deliver higher quality.
  - Reduce cost of a business process.
  - Eliminate non-mission activities from a business process.
  - Eliminate non-value add activities from a business process.
  - Convert the organization into a learning organization.
  - Enhance organizational flexibility and adaptability to change.
  - Enable business growth.
  - Enhance productivity.
  - Enhance profitability.
  - Enhance customer satisfaction.
  - Enhance competitiveness of the organization.

- Identify the parameters that will be used to measure the performance of re-engineered processes. The parameters must be quantitative and measurable. Some of the parameters may seem qualitative but with some efforts these can also be indirectly measured. As an example, customer satisfaction seems to be a qualitative parameter. The quantitative parameters that can capture customer satisfaction are number of complaints, turnaround time for a customer request. A BPR project must define objective of a BPR project in quantitative terms instead of qualitative terms. A quantitative objective can be measured and judged. For instance, the present response time to customer is six days and a possible target could be to reduce it to four days. This objective is measurable and verifiable. On the other hand, an objective of improving the average response time may mean different thing to different people and is not verifiable.
- Every process has a customer either internal or external to the organization. Identify the customers and the current mechanism for measuring customer satisfaction.

There are two possible modes of introducing changes: *radical* or *incremental*. The *incremental* mode aims to improve business processes in steps. The existing process is modelled and analysed for possible improvements. The improvements are introduced in steps causing minimum disruption. The risk is that the introduced change may not fit with the existing environment and may not sustain itself, eliminating non-value added activities. In the radical mode, the existing processes (also referred to as AS-IS processes) are ignored and the best practices are implemented. The impact on the organization may be to the extent that organizational structure is changed. The manpower is usually required to go through a training program.

7.3.2 Business Modelling

Some of the modelling techniques are learnt in Chapter 6. BPR would require modelling business processes and other characteristics of the process depending on the objective of the BPR.

Out of all the modelling techniques which were discussed in Chapter 6 and many more that exist in literature, one will have to choose appropriate modelling techniques. There are many integrated tools and environments for BPR projects. One may refer refer to Elzinga[6] for a collection of articles on tools, integrated environments and methodologies.[7–10]

If incremental mode is used, the existing processes and organizational structure will be modelled. If a radical mode is to be adapted, the focus is on to-be process or future business process and structure.

The incremental mode[11] is a bottom-up approach that advocates modelling the existing processes to gain understanding, and then streamlining them appropriately to meet the strategic objectives. The focus is on changing the AS-IS processes by identifying opportunities for improving them.

The radical mode originally prescribed in Hammer, Champy and Stanton[12–14] is a top-down approach, which suggests that the BPR team should focus on determining how the strategic objectives of the organization can be met without letting its thinking be constrained by the existing process. The emphasis is on the to-be process.

7.3.3 Business Analysis

Analysis: The models are analysed to answer why and what-if questions. The challenge is for every existing process to understand the scope for efficiency and effectiveness. The objective is to develop future solutions. The analysis may focus on different aspects of the processes. We have listed 10 different characteristics of a process in Section 7.2 that can be used for analysing a process. The analysis would provide insight into the process and lead to redesign of the process. There is an array of techniques that have been developed and used to analyse business processes. Articles by Glykas and Valiris[15] and Mayer and DeWitte[16] have explored analysis in detail. Some of these articles are case based where they explore BPR of a particular company. It is beyond the scope of this book to discuss various analysis techniques. One may refer to books on BPR by Elzinga, Gulledge and Lee[17] and Hammer and Champy[18] for further details. The idea is to collect process metrics from the business models. These metrics give a thorough knowledge of the process and used for benchmarking against the best in the industry. Some of the examples are mentioned below and an attempt was not made to be exhaustive.

Equivalent salary analysis: The objective of this analysis is to find out cost per employee of an activity. A business process modelled and data on the salary of each person associated with the process is collected. The salary figure can be adjusted for people who may be part time employed on the process. Sum the total salary and divide it by total number of full time employees to get average salary of a person associated with the process. This figure can then be used to check if it is high against the industry standards. If it turns out to be high, one has to look for reasons. The reasons may be the following

- People are underutilized
- Process is inefficient
- Lack of automation
- People with higher skillset are employed.

On the other hand, if the average salary turns out to be low, it may indicate that the process is not considered important in the organization or skill level is low. In an example analysis,[19] it was found that the average salary of an employee in IT department is much lower as compared to the industry standards. Equipped with this information, the BPR team investigated further to learn that the company has not paid attention to automation. A seemingly simple data such as average salary in IT department may provide important insight into the processes of the organization. The information that average salary is high or low for a particular process is useful information that must be complimented by process analysis before a solution is proposed. Cycle time of the process, control structure and value add of each function/activity may have to be done to redesign a process.[20]

Activity analysis: The objective is to analyse value of an activity or a process to the customer and to the organization. If the focus is customer, it is called value-added analysis and if the focus is organizational goal, the analysis is referred to as mission/non-mission activity analysis. In either case, business model is created with all constituent processes and activities.

Business model should be clear to both—model creators and the BPR team. This is a difficult task because end-users and modellers use different terminology and their objective in modelling the organization may not be the same. However, if the model is not understood by the end-users, they will not be able to validate the model and it may not be true representation of the organization.

If in spite of best efforts of the model creators, the model does not pass the test of clarity,[21] the organization structure may have problems. Probably, the activities are being performed by an inappropriate department or are replicated unnecessarily.

Each process and activity is challenged with why it is being done? and what if we do away with it, or move to another department or outsource it.

If too many specific or specialized resources and activities are part of the model, one has to question existence of specialized activities and resources. If an organization has too many specific resources, people in the organization with specific skillset will be required who may not be used for performing other tasks. Specific objects are the resources that cannot be reallocated as resources for performing other tasks. Specific skillset or specific resources may translate into less freedom to choose from the available manpower or may lead to vendor locking for specific resources.

In this section, few ways of analysing an organization have been discussed. The key idea is to get a handle on the organization, its components, its structure and its activities though modelling and then work towards improvement.

7.3.4 Redesign

Finally, the new processes are designed and deployed. IT may be used extensively to redesign the processes. The new business processes may also require changes in the structure of the organization. The new structure also has to design and details have to be worked out.

7.3.5 Business Transformation and Continuous Improvement

The changed business processes and structure are finally deployed. The measurements are done on a continuous basis to check the performance. BPR is a continuous process at least in terms of incremental changes that must be introduced on a regular basis.

7.4 LIFE CYCLE OF AN IT-DRIVEN BPR PROJECT

ERP-driven BPR focuses on re-engineering its processes by adapting the processes built into the ERP system. ERP system has the following three characteristics that make it a suitable candidate for a BPR project:[22]

- Its scope
- Configurability
- Integrativeness

An ERP system can potentially cover all departments and their functions. It can be extended to cover the external agencies such as customers, suppliers and vendors. The scope of an ERP project decides the processes that will be covered during the ERP implementation. Will the processes improve and become world class or Level 1 as defined earlier? ERP vendors claim that they have incorporated world class processes in their software. One of the reasons for implementing an ERP is to improve business processes and their flexibility. Coming to configuration, it does two things:

- Define the business processes.
- Define the structure of the organization.

During the configuration, one of the options from various available options for a process are selected. These decisions are equivalent of redesigning and deploying the re-engineered business processes. A company looks for an ERP system that would require minimum changes to its existing processes. If a company has changed and evolved its business processes and structure to keep itself at Level 1, deployment of an ERP system would integrate the business in a seamless manner without requiring much change. If the company has not evolved, ERP system would introduce many changes in its business processes and bring them to Level 1.

An ERP system has all the data in a single database. Not everyone can be given full rights (read, modify and create) to all the data. Who gets what access rights and to what data will have to be decided by the management. This decision indirectly creates the structure of the organization. The span and layers of management will get defined through the access rights.

An ERP-driven BPR project need not treat BPR as a separate project.

In the next section, some of the examples to get to the essence of re-engineering and its different flavours of it are explained.

7.5 RE-ENGINEERING EXAMPLES

MBL:[23] An insurance company processed an application using 30 discreet steps, involving 19 people which were spanned over five departments. The steps were performed in a sequential manner. Turn-around time for an application was average 15 days. As mentioned earlier, there are three options:

- Automation
- Rationalization
- Re-engineering

Automation would not help here as the total time spent on an application is 17 minutes that needs no further reduction. Automation would have been done via a workflow system. Number of steps would have remained the same and confusion for the customer would have been reduced a little. No rationalization is required either as there are no bottlenecks. The only option is to re-engineer. First option is to look at the industry to find a better process. It turns out that everyone in the industry was following the same approach. The sequential approach to doing jobs and narrow job definitions have their origin into mass manufacturing based on economies of scale as competitive strategy. The economic scenario changed and the focus is changed to customer. A radical new system that made a customer responsible for an application and customer was introduced. The job definitions changed dramatically as one would have to perform all the steps. The number of steps would reduce as some of the steps were to facilitate communication with the next person in the sequence. Expert systems and database system made the new system feasible. The structure of the insurance handling department would have changed dramatically.

It is possible that the company added, modified and refined their process on a continuous basis and it was a Level 1 process. But the environment changed and a new radical thinking only could have rendered the new process. A model of an AS-IS process would make the sequential nature of the process clear. But only the principles of re-engineering would have triggered the thinking in the right direction–why are we doing, what we are doing and what if we do away with a step and introduce new steps. This example brings out the essence of re-engineering. An existing process cannot evolve after a point and a radically different process is required.

Nestle:[24] The article focuses on management issues involved in an ERP project. But it mentions at least one problem that the company was facing—not being able to consolidate its data across departments and sister organizations. The problem got solved by deploying an ERP system that puts all the data into one database and provides interface for accessing consolidated data. Nestle went no further than doing an ERP-driven BPR. ERP brought changes to its procurement process. Nestle implemented SAP and adapted their processes. The modelling of AS-IS processes was done only to select a closest fitting ERP solution. All the issues discussed in the case are related to managing an ERP project. The change management is also related to ERP project. BPR is not an independent project.

Ford-Mazda Case:[25] Mazda employed handful of people to handle their accounts payable. Their strategy was to place an order, receive goods only if it matches the order and then pay according to the order. This strategy is known as a two-way match. Ford used a three-way match where the goods received could differ from the order placed and then a three-way match among order placed, goods received and invoice received had to be done that also required reconciliation. Ford needed hundreds of people for accounts payable. Ford considered rationalization but they found Mazda's process to be Level 1 process in the industry and adapted it. This is a case of re-engineering where a reference process was available. There will be an impact on the procurement process and an indirect impact will be reduction in the headcount of people in accounts payable department. The suppliers will be impacted, they can supply only full order and exactly what has been ordered. Ford could afford to make this change in their policy towards their suppliers but a small manufacturer may not be in a similar position with respect to his suppliers.

Hansen Case:[26] Hansen is not the true name of the company. It is a manufacturing company whose production, sales and distribution is distributed over various geographical locations. The company decided to do a BPR project followed by an ERP project. The BPR team consisting of 16 members and a consultant, after a year of effort, suggested over 80 reorganizations. While these suggestions were being deployed, SAP R/3 implementation started. The suggestions made by BPR team were again analysed and adapted to work with SAP. The suggestions made by BPR team centred around integration and centralization. Main feature of SAP R/3 is also integration.

CONCLUSION

BPR and its life cycle are discussed in this chapter. BPR involves looking at the business process of an organization closely. In order to understand and attempt BPR, one needs to understand the characteristics of processes. Section 7.2 talks about processes and their characteristics in detail. If processes of an organization are mature and well documented, it is easy to analyse them. However, if the processes are not documented, BPR becomes much more challenging. The processes of an organization are modelled using some standard techniques that were described in Chapter 6. Models are then analysed for improvement by looking at them from different perspectives. BPR may be either ERP driven or non-ERP driven. ERP-driven BPR counts on the processes of ERP system for improvements in the business processes and integration. There are two different modes for introducing the changes identified during the analysis, namely radical and incremental. Based on the characteristics of the organization, one of the two modes is selected.

CASE STUDY

RetailS is a young organization and their processes are very simple. Their main objective was to automate the processes and there was no perceived need for re-engineering. We did look at purchase process of an organization that was known to take a considerable long time. It was checked with users of the process and found that a purchase after getting initiated could take upto three months before a purchase order is issued. The objective was to improve the process. It all started by studying the existing process and it was found that no manual or document are available for the process being followed. The process

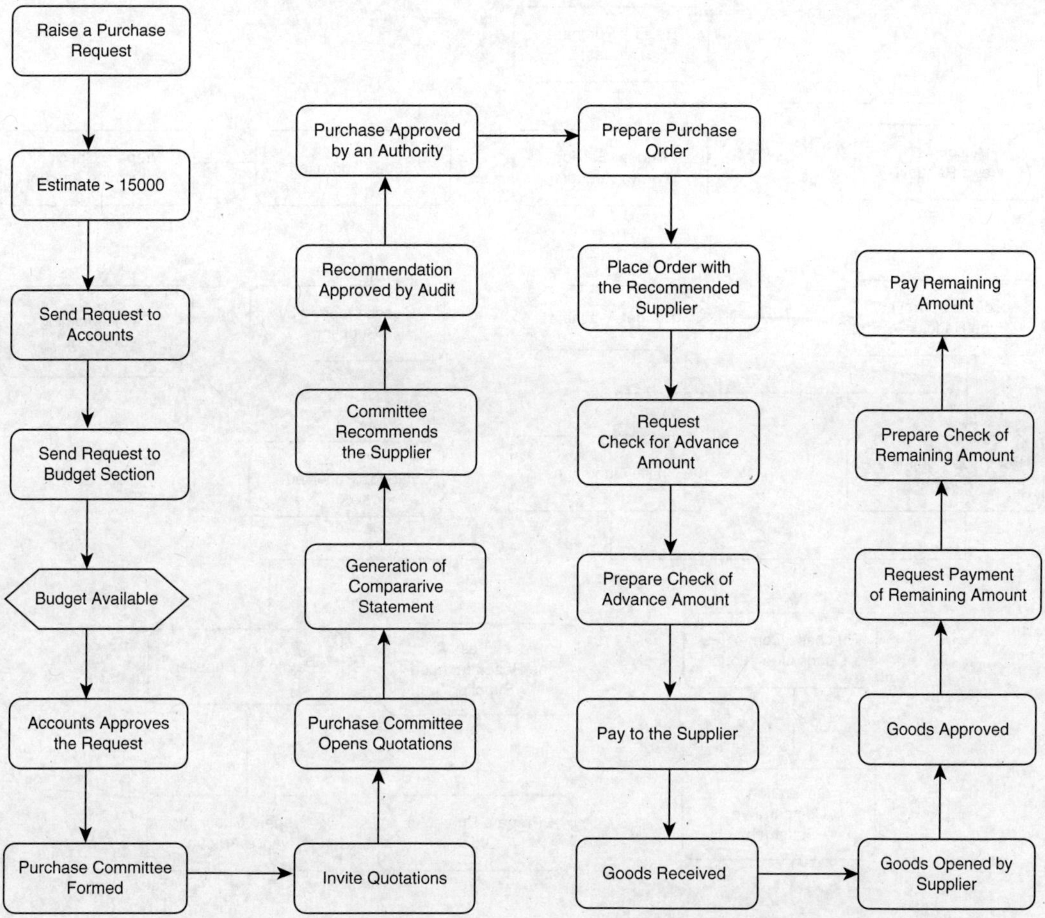

FIGURE 7.2 Purchase Process of an Organization That was Considered for Re-engineering

has been communicated from person to person in bits and pieces. A purchase involves five different units of the organization—accounts, budget, approving authority, audit and unit of the person who initiates the purchase. In the absence of formal documentation, roles and processes followed in a department are communicated to re-engineering team by their department heads, since no one was able to explain the full process. The team consolidated the information gathered and created the AS-IS process that is shown in Figure 7.2.

A careful look at the process revealed that the process has too many sequential steps. The process came into existence when the entire system was paper-file based and there was no automation. The organization itself was small and not too many purchases were done under the pressure of time. The scenario has now changed. There is lot of automation and data is accessible to all units involved in the purchase in real time. The team was told that the steps are all necessary as they are approved by

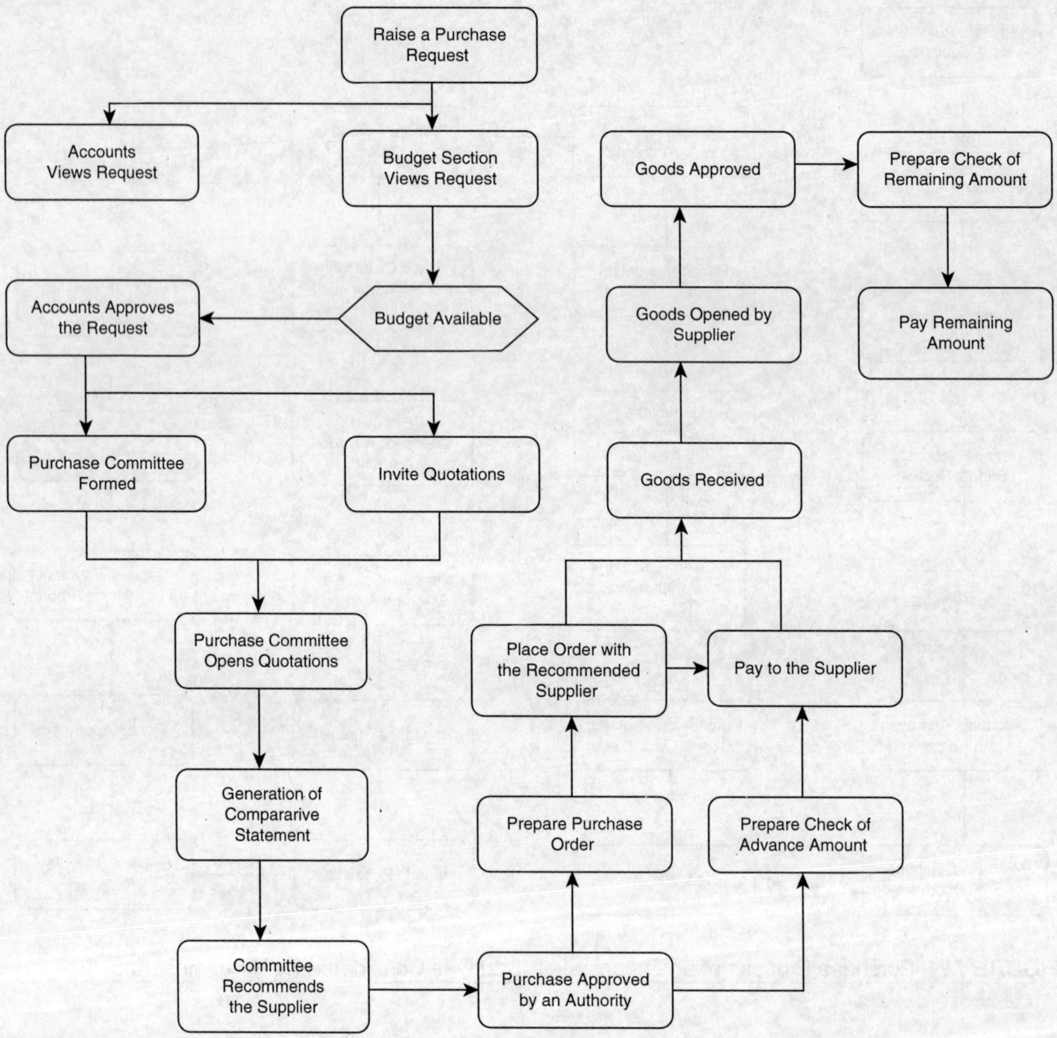

FIGURE 7.3 Purchase Process of an Organization after Re-engineering

the audit at the organizational level as well as at the country level. The team focused on paralleling the process. The resultant process is shown in Figure 7.3. The process has all the essentials steps but has now become parallel. As soon as the data required for a step becomes available, the step is carried out. The number of sequential steps have reduced from 24 to 15, a reduction of almost 36 per cent. This is an example of non-IT-driven re-engineering where IT has facilitated the new process. The data becomes available to concerned units because of IT.

EXERCISES

Check Your Understanding

1. What is the objective of business process re-engineering? Describe BPR and its life cycle.
2. Contrast and compare IT-driven and non-IT-driven business process re-engineering.
3. Describe characteristics of a process that are relevant for business process re-engineering.
4. Compare and contrast the characteristics of the processes at Level 1 and Level 5.
5. What are the principles for BPR efforts?

Apply Your Understanding

1. What is the relationship between process maturity levels and likely level of resistance discussed in Chapter 4 that will be offered by employees to a BPR project?
2. Pick a process that you think has problem or you have been a customer of the process and faced problems. Model the process and analyse it for problems. Also suggest an improved version.
3. Pick 5 to 10 activities that are performed in your organization. Analyse these activities for value addition to the organization.

ENDNOTES

1. Michael Hammer, 'Reengineering Work: Don't Automate, Obliterate', in *Harvard Business Review*, (1990), July–August.
2. M. Hammer and J. Champy, *Re-engineering the Corporation: A Manifesto for Business Revolution,* London: Nicholas Brealey Publishing.
3. ibid.
4. M. Glykas and G. Valiris, 'ARMA: A Multi-disciplinary Approach to BPR', in *Knowledge and Process Management* (1999), 6(4), 213–26.
5. ibid.
6. D. Jack Elzinga, Thomas R. Gulledge and Chung-Yee Lee, *Business Process Engineering: Advancing the State of the Art,* Springer (1999).
7. A. W. Scheer and Th. Allweyer, 'From Re-engineering to Continuous Process Adaptation', in D. Jack Elzinga, Thomas R. Gulledge, Chung-Yee Lee, *Business Process Engineering: Advancing the State of the Art*, Springer (1999).
8. Mathias Kirchmer, 'Market- and Product-Oriented Design of Business Processes', in D. Jack Elzinga, Thomas R. Gulledge and Chung-Yee Lee (eds), *Business Process Engineering: Advancing the State of the Art*, Springer (1999).
9. Richard J. Mayer and Paula S. DeWitte, 'Delivering Results: Evolving BPR from Art to Engineering', in D. Jack Elzinga, Thomas R. Gulledge and Chung-Yee Lee (eds), *Business Process Engineering: Advancing the State of the Art*, Springer (1999).
10. Mathias Kirchmer, 'Market-and Product-Oriented Design of Business Processes', in D. Jack Elzinga, Thomas R. Gulledge, Chung-Yee Lee, *Business Process Engineering: Advancing the State of the Art,* Springer (1999).
11. H. J. Harrington, *Business Process Improvement: The Breakthrough Strategy for Total Quality, Productivity and Competitiveness,* New York, NY: McGraw-Hill.
12. M. Hammer and J. Champy, *Re-engineering the Corporation: A Manifesto for Business Revolution,* London: Nicholas Brealey Publishing.

13. Michael Hammer, 'Reengineering Work: Don't Automate, Obliterate', in *Harvard Business Review* (1990), July–August.
14. M. Hammer and S. Stanton, 'How Process Enterprises Really Work', in *Harvard Business Review* (1999), 77(6), 108–18.
15. M. Glykas and G. Valiris, 'ARMA: A Multi-disciplinary Approach to BPR', in *Knowledge and Process Management* (1999), 6(4), 213–26.
16. Richard J. Mayer and Paula S. DeWitte,. 'Delivering Results: Evolving BPR from Art to Engineering', in D. Jack Elzinga, Thomas R. Gulledge and Chung-Yee Lee, *Business Process Engineering: Advancing the State of the Art*, Springer (1999).
17. D. Jack Elzinga, Thomas R. Gulledge and Chung-Yee Lee, *Business Process Engineering: Advancing the State of the Art,* Springer (1999).
18. M. Hammer and J. Champy, *Re-engineering the Corporation: A Manifesto for Business Revolution,* London: Nicholas Brealey Publishing.
19. M. Glykas and G. Valiris, 'ARMA: A Multi-disciplinary Approach to BPR', in *Knowledge and Process Management* (1999), 6(4), 213–26.
20. ibid.
21. S. Ip and T. Holden, 'A Knowledge-based Technique for the Process Modelling of Information Systems: The Object Life-cycle Diagram', in P. Loucopoulos (ed.), *Proceedings of the 4th Conference in Advanced Information Systems Engineering,* Manchester: Springer-Verlag (1992).
22. C. Koch, 'BPR and ERP: Realising a Vision of Process with IT', in *Business Process Management Journal* (2001), 7(3), 258–65.
23. M. Hammer and J. Champy, *Re-engineering the Corporation: A Manifesto for Business Revolution,* London: Nicholas Brealey Publishing.
24. Case: *Nestle's Enterprise Resource Planning (ERP) Odyssey*, http://www.cio.com/article/31066/Nestl_eacute_s Enterprise_Resource_Planning_ERP O
25. Adapted from M. Hammer and J. Champy, *Re-engineering the Corporation: A Manifesto for Business Revolution,* London: Nicholas Brealey Publishing.
26. Adapted from C. Koch, 'BPR and ERP: Realising a Vision of Process with IT', in *Business Process Management Journal* (2001), 7(3), 258–65.

chapter

8

ERP Selection

LEARNING OBJECTIVES

After reading this chapter, you will be able to understand:

- Importance of selecting the right ERP system
- Selection team
- Parameters for ERP selection
- ERP selection process

8.1 INTRODUCTION

The focus of this chapter is selection of enterprise resource planning solution—the phase that follows requirement engineering phase in the life cycle of an ERP implementation. The output of the requirements engineering phase is available in the form of business blueprint containing requirements. Based on the requirements, the selection of an appropriate ERP system is made by a selection team. The selection process includes negotiation and contract with the software vendor and implementation partner. Most of the ERP vendors do not implement their ERP system themselves, they outsource this activity to their certified implementation partners. Negotiations have to be done with both ERP vendor as well as implementation partner.

Given the considerable financial investment, and potential risks and benefits, the importance of selecting an appropriate ERP system cannot be over emphasized. ERP evolved from MRP/MRP-II keeping manufacturing industry at the centre. Existing commercial packages have further evolved according to the needs of their target industry and industry segment. Thus, no single ERP software can meet all functional and business requirements of a company. It is important to choose an ERP software that meets most of the requirements, and a cooperative vendor that will help the company manage the balance requirements either through customization or business process re-engineering. A company must avoid getting carried away by ERP vendor hype or by competitors' selection. The vendor makes every effort to convince an organization to sell their products. There are many ERP packages available in the market and each one of them claims to be different. The difference may come from the industry focus or features supported or both by the ERP package. Each company is unique in terms of its strategies, objectives and requirements. ERP system implementation has great impact on the business processes often coupled with business process re-engineering. A company must understand implications of implementing ERP for their business. The selection process should be guided by the goals and competitive strategy of the organization so that the selected ERP system is aligned with the objectives of the organization.

The selection of the most appropriate ERP solution is a semi-structured process. There is no formal procedure that can be followed. It is a challenge to select the most appropriate ERP package.

In Section 8.6, various parameters that may be considered while selecting an ERP solution are discussed. The selection team may take anywhere from two to six months for selecting an ERP system. The constitution of the selection team is discussed in Section 8.2. Analytical hierarchy process for choosing the right set of parameters amongst all possible parameters and ordering them is discussed in Section 8.9. A similar process may be adopted for vendor and implementation partner selection.

8.2 ERP SYSTEM SELECTION TEAM

A team is required to collect relevant information about ERP systems and to evaluate them on selection parameters. The team first selects and prioritizes the selection parameters which are then used for selecting a fitting ERP system. There are three different ways to form a team:

- Top management and external consultants are the members of the selection team. The participation of functional heads from within the organization is minimal. Such a team selection works best when in-house capability for making major IT procurement decisions does not exist.
- An organization may have a selection process in place and decision makers may include functional unit heads and few senior level managers. A mature organization will usually have systems and processes in place for various activities. In some organizations, ERP project is treated as an IT project and the selection is made by information officer with or without the help of a consultant.
- A democratic way of making a decision is to include all stakeholders or their representatives in the selection team. The chances of making right selection and success of subsequent ERP implementation increases if the stakeholders are directly or indirectly involved, right from the beginning. The involvement enhances awareness and consequently the motivation of employees. A selection team consist of representatives of different user departments, chief information officer and senior manager.

The middle and top management may work together to form a selection team. The team generally would consist of 4 to 10 persons. But the selection team consisting of as many as 60 persons for a large organization is not unusual. ERP selection is a planned and budgeted activity. The selection process may take two to six months to complete. The selection team gathers information about ERP solutions available in the market. One can buy relevant studies done by benchmarking companies or analyse prototypes. Smaller companies mail their requirements in the form of a questionnaire to various ERP solution providers and analyse their responses. A small number of bidders are asked to make presentations where the selection team can ask further questions. Small organizations tend to use an informal method to analyse the information gathered and to arrive at a decision. Large organizations use more formal methods such as scoring and ranking method, 0–1 goal programming or analytical hierarchy process (AHP). Let us look at the parameters first, AHP and its application for selecting ERP system will be discussed later.

8.3 ERP SOLUTION AND VENDOR SELECTION

The selection process involves the following steps:

1. Gather information about the vendors and their products using available channels and resources
2. Preliminary filtering
   - Demonstration by the vendors
   - Filtering using high level parameters
3. Decide selection parameters
4. Prepare and release RFP (request for proposal) using the business blueprint prepared during the requirements engineering phase
5. Analyse and select the vendor
   - Evaluate vendor's ERP system on certain paramaters
   - Analysis of financial terms and conditions
   - Detailed demonstration by the vendors

We will discuss each of these steps in detail in the following sections.

8.4 INFORMATION GATHERING

Information about the ERP solutions and vendors is available from different sources.[1] One can analyse the prototypes and demonstration versions that are available. Many consultancy companies study ERP solutions and release reports every year. These reports are expensive but very rich in contents. One can buy these reports for information. The vendors can be invited to make presentations. IT magazines, exhibitions and Internet sites also provide information about ERP solutions and vendors. If there is no inhouse IT competence, a consultant can be hired to gather information about ERP solutions.

8.5 PRELIMINARY FILTERING

The preliminary filtering or first level of filtering can be done on few high level parameters. Some of parameters that have been cited in literature are listed in Table 8.1

TABLE 8.1 High Level Parameters That Can Be Used for Initial Filtering of the Vendors[2]

Parameter	What Parameter Means to the Client?
Vendor size and presence	Has vendor supplied ERP solutions to the organization similar in size and scope to our company and does the vendor have presence in our geographical area?
Cost	Does the range of cost of ERP suits us?
Industry	Does the vendor have a solution for our specific industry?
Technology	Does the ERP run on our choice of platform (hardware, OS, database etc.)
Add-on software	Does vendor supplies add-on software such as SCM, CRM or does the solution integrates with add-on solutions?
Stability of vendor and their solutions	How is the financial performance of the vendor for last two years and how frequently the software is updated?

After the preliminary filtering, there are two ways of selecting a vendor:

- Competitive bidding
- Two-phase acquisition

In competitive bidding, the vendors bid and the most competitive one is awarded the contract provided he fulfills the requirements. In two-phase acquisition, the seleted bidders are asked to do some additional work on which they are evaluated and awarded the contract. ERP vendors are generally selected through competitive bidding only.

8.6 PARAMETERS FOR ERP SELECTION

Following factors are considered important for ERP selection:

1. **Business process support or functionality:** An important criterion used in selecting an ERP system is the ERP fit[3] with current business processes. An ERP system must support business processes of the organization. In fact, this is one of the most critical requirements. A good match would support more than 90 per cent of the business processes without requiring any change in the processes. The following factors capture the process fit:

   - The organizational processes flow
   - The business practices
   - The organizational processes

   ERP system must support all business processes, business practices and process flow.

   Process fit of an ERP may be less in Asia because the reference process models are influenced by European and American industries. The implementation partners suggest that the company should change their processes according to the chosen ERP system. The researchers and many client companies maintain that the ERP software should change to fit. In any case, a company would like to pick an ERP solution that will require them to change a little. Apart from business processes, one should also look for *data* and *user interface* fit.

2. **Data fit:** There are three functions associated with the data—creation, storage and usage. The users who create the data and use the data are the end-users of the data. There are certain properties associated with the data that are important for the end-users. These are as follows:

   - The name and meaning of data items used in the company (i.e. an sales order sheet, sales report).
   - The form and format of data items of documents.
   - The output data items of the documents.
   - The input data items of the documents.

   The name and meaning of data items used in the company should remain same. A sales order should not become proforma invoice or a product should not become an item. These changes may confuse the employees. Similarly, data fields within sales order should also not change to something different. The form and format of data items of documents should also remain the same.

3. **User interface fit:** User interface has three following components:

   - User interface structures.
   - User capabilities required to use interface of the ERP.
   - Sufficient user interface to meet the business needs of the company.

The user interface should offer sufficient functionality to meet the business needs of the company. The look and feel of the user interface should remain just about the same. The structure of the user interface should not change much. User capabilities required to use the interface of the ERP should remain at almost the same level.

If ERP solution does not fit well, significant effort may be required to either adapt ERP or the organization. Many interesting examples of misfit are cited in the literature.[4] The names in most ERP systems are entered in the western format as first name, middle name and last name. Now think of South Indian and Chinese names. One time, a new American student in the class asked me, 'Tell me your first name or last name or whatever it is'. Some companies enter the entire name as first name. The implications far reaching, names are usually sorted on either last name or first name. The output in this case will not be sorted either way. How about searching? It is left it to the reader to think about the searching. Every system has some mechanism to uniquely identify people, objects and transactions. A system may define a logical bank account and it may interface with the actual bank. If ERP system insists on using auto-generated numbers, bank interface may not work anymore. Access to ERP system is controlled for security against intentional and unintentional threats. Many ERP vendors give access to named users and charge license fee. A user who needs limited rights to limited data costs money to the company. Sharing password is not a good idea because then the accountability becomes an issue. An employee who is needed just to view the data also costs to the company, which is not something any company likes. As an example, an organization that has over 5,000 users always need one more type of reports. The IT staff spends considerable time to get the data from the system and format it in the required format. These reports are a major concern and it has now been acknowledged by ERP vendors. Many of the ERP systems provide capability to create report by dragging and dropping data items.

An ERP solution that fits well would result in the following:

- Lower resistance from the users
- Reduced training needs
- Less organizational adaptation

An organization would undertake an exercise that is referred to as gap analysis for figuring out the gap between the process, data and user interface requirements and ERP offering. Gap analysis is discussed in Section 8.8.

4. **Implementation time:** Small organizations prefer to buy an ERP solution that would take only couple of months to implement. However, for large organizations, implementation time runs in tens of months. Implementation time of an ERP package depends on the following parameters:
   - *Number of sites where ERP has to be implemented:* If an organization has offices or manufacturing facilities at multiple locations across the country, considerably more effort would be required in comparison to the organization having only one site. The implementation effort would be even more if an organization is spread across countries, as ERP system would be configured for handling different regulatory rules, fiscal years and languages.
   - *Number of modules or functions to be implemented:* ERP systems support almost all processes in all functional units of organization, but an organization has an option of selecting processes for implementation. The more processes and functions an organization implements, longer it will take.

- *Maturity level of organizations:* As mentioned in Chapter 1, IT systems have been developed and deployed in organizations in phases where phases progressed through transaction processing systems, management information systems, decision information systems and organization systems. Each advanced phase integrates IT more closely with the organization. An organization that has been using information systems in the past will take less time than an organization with less exposure and experience with information systems. Implementation time also depends on the maturity of processes of the organization (refer to Chapter 7). Organizational readiness (refer to Chapter 4) to implement ERP system also has also an impact on the implementation time.
- *Customization:* Small organizations prefer an ERP solution that would require no customization as customization adds to the implementation time. Certain amount of customization may be required if the organization is reluctant to re-engineer its processes or feels that their processes are better which often times happen in large organization. Customization increases implementation time of an ERP system.

5. **Total cost:** An ERP implementation is an expensive project (refer to Chapter 3). For a small organization, cost is an important factor in selecting an ERP system. Large organizations are somewhat more relaxed about this parameter. AHP model and to assign weight to various parameters will also be discussed later.
6. **Platform independence:** For large organizations, platform (operating system and hardware) independence may be important. Their manpower and existing infrastructure including servers and operating systems may be diverse. It may be better to buy an ERP system that will run on multiple operating systems and hardwares. Platform independence may save company considerable initial cost in infrastructure and training. Getting vendor-locked is another issue that larger organizations like to avoid. As an example, China has started training their people in Linux because the government did not want to depend on MS Windows as it is an American company and changed political situation may prevent free access to American products.

   Small and medium organizations work with small cash flow and they like to use their existing IT infrastructure to save switching cost and avoid excessive training. A company will have to assess their situation and then decide how important platform independence is for them. AHP, which will help decision makers to quantitatively decide relative importance of parameters is also discussed later.
7. **Process improvement:** An organization starts small that subsequently grows in a sizeable organization. The organization and its processes grow in somewhat ad hoc manner leading to inefficient processes. Many organizations expect an ERP system to bring in best practices to improve their processes. Organizations of all sizes consider ERP system implementation an opportunity to improve their processes. Most of ERP vendors continue to improve the processes implemented by ERP systems through research and releasing new versions accordingly.
8. **Reliability:** For engineering purposes, reliability is defined as the probability that a system will perform its intended function during a specified period of time under stated conditions. It is hard to judge reliability of an ERP package. One may try to gather information from references provided by the vendor and relevant studies from benchmarking agencies. A mature system is often more reliable than a new system as reliability of a software system improves as it matures. A reliable system is stable and performs its functions as expected with negligible down time. In case of

failure, the system should recover quickly to a consistent state using data recovery mechanism. An enterprise system must be available 24 hours, 7 days a week (popularly written as 24 × 7). A system that handles customer orders or production schedules need to be much more reliable than say a payroll system. Depending on the planned functionality to be implemented, a company may decide its reliability requirements.

9. **Flexibility and scalability:** ERP system, once implemented, becomes an integral part of the organization, and a long-term relationship develops with the vendor. As the organization evolves, its IT requirements also change. ERP system should provide a mechanism (such as EXIT points of SAP) for integrating other applications. The ERP system itself should also evolve and newer version should become available. The ERP should be upgradeable and easy to integrate with other systems such as electronic data interchange (EDI, refer to Chapter 10). An ERP system should evolve as the organization evolves and should not in any way hamper growth of the organization. An organization may expand by starting operations at additional sites and increasing volume of business. ERP system should be able to scale up.
10. **User friendliness:** It has been established (refer to Technology Acceptance Model (TAM) and Extended Technology Acceptance Model (ETAM)[5,6]) that if a system is user friendly, the employees of the organization would accept the system easily without offering much resistance. Users should not require extensive training for using the system, a brief training session of a week or so is acceptable though. User friendliness is very subjective. A system that seems user friendly to the employees of an IT savvy organization may not get same response from the employees of another organization. ERP system providing a user interface that looks and feels similar to current systems may score high on user friendliness parameter.
11. **Market position of the vendor:** Market position of the vendor is also a concern for organizations. If vendor is strong and has successfully implemented ERP systems in the past, the organization will feel more confident about the vendor. A strong vendor is unlikely to go out of business leaving its clients without any support and future updates. If an ERP is popular, finding trained manpower may be easy, most of the critical points in its implementation would be known, cost and implementation time will be easy to estimate through benchmarking. One may expect continuous improvement in the software and release of newer versions to incorporate any changes in the regulations from a strong vendor.

Most of the parameters that have been compiled by researchers and documented were explained. An organization may come up with additional parameters such as capability to develop inhouse modules and integrate with ERP system.

8.7 PREPARE AND RELEASE REQUEST FOR PROPOSAL (RFP)

If the client has decided to carry out requirements engineering phase without the help of vendor as discussed in Section 6.1, the requirements become part of the RFP. In case the client has decided not to carry out an independent requirements engineering phase, high level requirements will be included in the RFP. A sample RFP is shown in the following sections where only the high level requirements have been enumerated.

TIM MANUFACTURING
DELHI

Proposal request
for procuring and implementing an appropriate
ERP system
for TIM MANUFACTURING

1 INTRODUCTION

1.1 Objective

TIM Manufacturing Delhi (hereinafter referred to as **TMD**) intends to implement ERP System in the organization in a phased manner consisting of two phases to be completed in tandem.

The organization is currently small in size but will be growing in the coming years. Presently there are about 200 employees. An ERP solution is required which is economical and can be upgraded in the coming years to meet the increasing requirements. The main goal is to have complete automation and move towards paperless organization.

TMD requests proposals for supply, installation and commissioning of ERP solution described in the attached specifications by interested parties (hereinafter known as "the vendor"). Prices quoted shall be all-inclusive and represent procurement and complete implementation at TMD site as per the specifications included in this document. The vendor shall be responsible for all parts, labour, and all other associated apparatus necessary to completely procure, configure, test, deploy and acceptance by TMD, as per the specifications given in this document.

1.2 Schedule of Events

The following is the required schedule of events for this project. The schedule may change depending on the results of the responses and a final schedule will be established prior to contracting with the successful vendor.

Event	Date
Release of RFP	Day 1
Pre bid meeting and demonstration by the vendors	Day 8
Response from bidders	Day 15
Opening of technical bids	Day 20
Evaluation of responses and further inquiry required, if any	Day 27

Opening of financial bids	Day 32
Contract award	Day 42
Project commencement	Day 57
Project Phase I complete	Day 177 (4 months)
Testing, exploring and bug fixing (if any)	Day 210
Warranty including support	Throughout the implementation and 12 months from the date of successful commissioning of the module in any phase.
AMC	Three years after completion of warranty period

2 TERMS AND CONDITIONS

2.1 Response Submission

It is a two-bid (Envelope 1 and Envelop 2) system. Both the envelopes will be sealed separately and will be enclosed in one main envelope subscribing on it as below:

MAIN ENVELOPE

Responses to this RFP should be submitted in a sealed envelope (containing Envelope 1 and Envelope 2). It is the sole responsibility of the respondents to ensure that their responses arrive in a timely manner. TMD reserves the right to reject all late arrivals. The vendor must submit both the technical and financial proposal latest by ……………..till 3:00 pm.

To
ERP Project Manager
TMD, New Delhi

Envelope 1 (Subscribing Technical Bid)

The technical proposal should detail the technical specifications of the proposed solution, compliance to the specifications of various modules detailed in the RFP, implementation plan, post implementation warranty and support plan along with the checklist for technical bid supporting documents such as registration certificates (Income tax PAN No, service tax, sales tax certificate etc.), EMD, bidders profile. Any other relevant paper which a bidder feels necessary along with the terms and conditions duly signed and accepted by the bidder.

Envelope 2 (Subscribing Financial Bid)

The financial proposal should give detailed breakup of price of various modules and associated price of implementation and post implementation warranty/ support and AMC period in the proforma enclosed.

2.2 Costs Associated with Preparation of the Vendor's Response

TMD will not be liable for any cost incurred by the respondents in preparing responses to this RFP or negotiations associated with award of a contract.

2.3 Onsite Study for Effort Estimation

Onsite study will be permitted for one week after release of RFP, at TMD for the purpose of effort estimation, and receiving questions from the vendors that intend to respond to this RFP. Attendance at this onsite study is optional.

2.4 Proposal Binding Period

Prices quoted in the vendor's response for all labour and materials will remain in effect for a period of at least 240 days from the issuance date of the vendor's response.

2.5 Omissions

Omission in the proposal of any provision herein described shall not be construed as to relieve the vendor of any responsibility or obligation requisite to the complete and satisfactory delivery, operation, and support of any and all equipment or services.

2.6 Payment Conditions

Payment shall be made upon acceptance of the job by TMD. The software systems will be deemed acceptable when the vendor delivers to TMD:

- ERP (functionality described in Section 4) package implemented and functional.
- All deliverables including source code, documents reflecting the latest software architecture, configuration and description.
- Other

Acceptance will be deemed *in full* upon receipt by the vendor of a Notice of Acceptance issued by TMD upon full implementation of the Terms and Conditions and Technical Specifications of the Contract. Upon receipt of the Notice of Acceptance, the vendor shall notify TMD in writing of a release of all liens for all materials and services associated with this project.

Schedule of payments:

1. 20 per cent of the total cost (the license fee and implementation cost) will be paid on commencement of project.
2. 40 per cent after successful installation and running, and acceptance of the system of phase one modules.
3. 40 per cent after successful installation and running, and acceptance of the system of phase two modules.

2.7 Warranty and Support

The software systems specified and furnished shall be fully guaranteed and supported by the vendor for 12 months after implementation against any defects. Defects which may occur as the result of faulty code within the warranty period after implementation and acceptance by TMD shall be corrected by the vendor at no additional cost to TMD. The vendor shall promptly, at no cost to TMD, correct or re-perform (including modifications or additions as necessary) any nonconforming or defective work within the warranty period after completion of the project of which the work is a part.

The vendor will provide support through call to ensure the smooth running of the system.

The period of the vendor's warranty for any items herein are not exclusive remedies, and TMD has recourse to any warranties of additional scope given by the vendor to TMD and all other remedies available at law or in equity. The vendor's warranties shall commence with acceptance of the work in full.

The bidder shall do the preventive maintenance once a quarter for upkeep of the application running. This schedule shall have to be adhered to strictly by him.

2.8 AMC (Annual Maintenance Contract)

Subsequent to warranty period, AMC terms and conditions shall be mentioned in the tender. The payment during AMC period will be paid on half-yearly basis after completion of service period. The organization reserves the right either to avail AMC from the vendor or otherwise.

2.9 Acceptance and Title

Acceptance will be at TMD and upon successful implementation. If the services supplied to TMD are found to be defective or do not conform to the specifications, TMD reserves the right to cancel the contract upon written notice to the vendor and return work-products at the vendor's expense, based upon the terms of the Contract.

TMD shall at all times have access to the work wherever it is in preparation or progress, and the Vendor shall provide proper facilities for such access and for inspection

2.10 Price Quotations

Price quotations are to include the furnishing of ERP solution (functionality and other project details given in Section 4), its implementation, data migration, maintenance, training; its source code, manuals, tools, and the provision of all labour and services necessary or proper for the completion of the work. TMD will not be liable for any costs beyond those proposed herein and awarded. The Vendor shall include all applicable sales, consumer, use, and other similar taxes in the price quotations. The taxes and other charges if any is to be mentioned specifically, otherwise the rates will treated as inclusive of all.

The price quotation should give complete breakup functionality-wise cost including the cost of the software licenses, cost of configuration and free warranty and warranty support for 12 months after rollover and AMC for a further period of three years after completion of warranty period.

In case of discrepancy in computed proposal prices, the lowest combined value of individual units costs shall prevail.

The Vendor may also include a time and materials quotation in their bid.

2.11 Price Stability

Contract prices and discounts shall be fixed at the time of contract approval by TMD and the vendor. In the event of price changes, replacement equipment shall be purchased at the lower or then current market price. In no case shall a price higher than contract price be paid for equipment proposed.

In the event that TMD desires to purchase equipment or services not contained in the contract, future purchases will be determined using The vendor-specified discount rate in the proposal from the manufacturer's suggested retail price as of the date of the order.

In no case shall the price exceed the favoured vendor prices.

2.12 Project Team Composition

The composition of the project team assigned by the vendor to TMD projects will be reviewed and approved by TMD. The vendor will be required to submit resumes of prospective team members for review by TMD.

The vendor must have experienced project managers, leaders, database administrators and developers on staff. The project shall be staffed at all times by a project manager and project leaders who, in the role of lead persons, will be able to provide leadership and technical resources for the remaining team members on the project.

If, in the opinion of TMD, any team member does not possess adequate qualifications to participate in the project, TMD reserves the right to require the vendor to assign a team member who, in TMD's opinion, possesses the necessary skills and experience required for this project.

2.12.1 Project Manager

The vendor will provide a full-time, project manager who will act as a single point of contact for all activities regarding this project. The project manager will be totally responsible for all aspects of the work and shall have the authority to make immediate decisions regarding configuration work.

The experience and background of the Project Manager should be between 6–8 years.

2.12.2 Project Leaders

The vendor will assign project/module leaders. The background/experience for project/module leader should be of minimum 4–6 in the required field.

2.12.3 Developers and Implementors

At least 70 per cent of the configuration team, assigned to the TMD project, should have at least one year of vendor's ERP software configuration experience. The vendor will guarantee that the TMD project will not be used as a training ground for fresh engineers hired by the vendor.

2.12.4 Database Administrator

The vendor must have a Database Administrator (DBA) on staff, who will be responsible for the database creation for this project. The DBA must have sufficient experience in this type of project as to be able to lend adequate technical support for deployment, during the warranty period, and during any extended warranty periods or maintenance contracts.

2.13 Changes in Team

After project initiation, the Vendor *cannot* pull out team members from the TMD project team unless (a) they leave the company or (b) TMD requests for a change. In case of (a), the vendor will inform TMD in writing and submit documentary evidence of the person resigning from the vendor company.

Any new team member will be allowed to join the TMD project team only after the background has been reviewed and approved by TMD. Should any team member assigned to the project change during the project life cycle, the vendor must submit a resume of the new team member assigned for review by TMD. The experience and background specifications (given above) hold for any changes in team.

2.14 The Vendor Qualifications

2.14.1 Experience

The selected vendor shall be fully capable and experienced in deployment of the software systems specified. To ensure the system has continued support, TMD will contract only with vendors having a successful history of software configuration, installation, service, and support. During the evaluation process, TMD may, with full cooperation of the vendors, visit the vendors' places of business, observe operations, and inspect records.

2.14.2 References

TMD may, with full cooperation of the vendors, visit client installations to observe operations and consult with references. Specified visits and discussion shall be arranged through the vendors; however, the vendor personnel shall not be present during discussions with references. The vendor must provide a reference accounts at which similar work, both in scope and design, have been completed by the vendor within the last two (2) years.

2.15 Codes, Standards and Ordinances

Software related to accounting work shall conform to the latest rules, regulations, procedures and standards declared by the Central Auditor General, and all local codes and ordinances, as applicable. All software functions must conform to the IT Act, wherever applicable. The software design should be such that it is given acceptance by the MP/Central Audit.

2.16 Performance and Payment Bonding

Within two (2) working days after notice of award, the vendor is required to have a valid Performance and Payment Bond in the form of Bank Guarantee in force covering the work performed up to the acceptance by TMD. The amount of Bond will be based upon the cost of implementation.

2.17 Bid Evaluation Criteria

Apart from the pricing, bids will be evaluated based on the following criteria:

- Fit of ERP solution and its components
- Compliance with bid documents
- Completeness of bid
- Qualifications and experience
- Domain experience and background
- Level of tailoring of development implementation process to suit TMD needs.
- Client references

2.18 Right to Reject

TMD reserves the right to reject all bids. Responses should be submitted initially with the most favourable terms that the vendor can propose.

3. PROJECT DETAILS

3.1 Onsite/Offsite

TMD would prefer maximum part of the project to be executed onsite. The parts which ***must be*** carried out by the company onsite are: requirements study and configuration. The company must maintain presence of its key configuration team members during Acceptance Testing also.

During onsite implementation/configuration period, TMD will provide office space for the team members including amenities.

3.2 Reporting

The vendor will submit a status report on the progress of the project on a weekly basis to the Project Manager in TMD. The template for the status report must be approved by TMD. During onsite phases, the project team of the vendor will meet the project monitoring team of TMD on a weekly basis for project reviews. The status report may be the starting point for discussion during weekly project review meetings.

The vendor will be required to make technical presentations to give a report on the progress, any problems encountered and their resolution, any deviations from the project plan/schedule, planned activities and their schedule, and any pending issues. Any feedback given during the presentation will be incorporated in the relevant plan/document, and a follow-up presentation made, if required.

3.3 Configuration Process

TMD expects that the vendor will use a configuration process which is more suited to manufacturing organization.

- The requirements study and analysis must be allocated appropriate resources so that the study is carried out thoroughly and extensively.
- At least two cycles of acceptance testing will be required – one by the in-house team and one by the end-users.

3.4 Configuration Management

TMD expects that the vendor will have appropriate tool-based configuration management in place to manage the project of TMD.

3.5 Deliverables

The following deliverables are expected by TMD from the vendor:

- Installation scripts including scripts for creation of hard data.
- User manuals
- Technical documentation including functional description of the system
- Source code
- Application software executables working
- Documents produced in each phase as follows:

Phase	Documents
Analysis and requirements study	▪ Requirement specifications ▪ Acceptance test plan ▪ Acceptance test cases
Implementation and configuration	▪ Functional description of the system ▪ System test plan ▪ System test cases
System testing	▪ System testing results
Acceptance testing and user training	▪ Deployment details ▪ Training manuals

3.6 Standards

TMD expects that the vendor will use standards, especially for configuration and user-interface, which will be used throughout.

Checklists for reviewing user interfaces must be developed and used by the vendor.

3.7 Integration Issues

The vendor will identify and provide integration of new software with existing software or system, if any, wherever required. Information regarding existing software will be provided to the vendor by TMD when requested by the vendor or otherwise.

3.8 Data Migration and Retrospective Conversion

The vendor will be responsible for migrating all required data from databases of legacy software, if any, to the database for new software. The migration should be done through scripts and should be a repeatable exercise, as it may be carried out for acceptance testing and later again for final implementation. The new software and legacy software will run in parallel for a period of time before use of legacy software is stopped completely.

For modules where no legacy software is available, need for retrospective conversion of information has to be identified by the vendor. The vendor must include any special programs or screen interfaces that may be required for entry of retrospective data, in the software design. TMD will be responsible for any data entry required for retrospective conversion.

3.9 TMD Involvement

TMD will assign a project manager and a tester. The project manager will be the single-point contact for the project.

All major decisions must be made with the involvement and agreement of the TMD project team. At no time must the vendor hold back any information related to the TMD project and system, which is requested for by the TMD project team. It is the responsibility of the Vendor to ensure that the TMD project team has complete information on the software and system so that, after the warranty period, the TMD project team is fully capable of maintaining and enhancing the software system.

The TMD Project team will participates in reviews of all documents and will have approval authority.

3.9.1 Requirements Gathering Period

The TMD project team will fully participate in all activities of the requirements study and configuration period. The TMD team will be responsible for validating the outcome of the requirements study done by the vendor. TMD will fully participate in the configuration of the system and the database creation, and review and approve the outcome of the design.

3.9.2 Configuration and Implementation Period

The vendor must keep the TMD project team fully informed and involved during configuration and implementation period of all technical details on the software, including information on configuration, software structure, techniques used, and any major or minor decisions made regarding the software configuration and implementation.

3.9.3 System Testing

In case resources are available, TMD may like to run a system test cycle after the vendor has performed system testing. The vendor has to make the system test plan and cases used by it for system testing available to TMD. Any defects found by the TMD project team during system testing must be removed by the Vendor.

3.9.4 Acceptance and User Training Period

TMD project team would like to run at least two cycles of acceptance testing and will fully participate in implementation efforts by the vendor. It will aid the vendor in ensuring that the software developed by the vendor is tested and the end-users are trained to use it effectively and efficiently.

4. INTEGRATION, SECURITY AND BACKUP

- It should be possible to build the ERP modules into a fully integrated system and various modules shall be totally interlinked. As far as possible, system shall remove duplication of work. Every module shall be provided with user login and password security.
- ERP modules should support multi-user, multi counter network with 100 per cent protection against unauthorized access. Every user shall have login name and password for every module he wants to work. System administrator shall be in a position to give access to limited menus: sub menus to a user. Powerful backup and recovery procedures must be available and must ensure 100 per cent security of data and smooth functioning of the system. This shall is a time tested ERP and must support smart card/RFID. The smart cards/RFID may be purchased from other agency at later date. Smart card/RFID vendor will provide SDK (System Development Kit) for the interface. The successful bidder will be required to interface the smart card/RFID system with the ERP developed.
- The vendor will identify and provide integration of new software with existing software or system, if any, wherever required. Information regarding existing software will be provided to the vendor by TMD when requested by the vendor or otherwise.
- No unauthorized access to modules and it should be possible to integrated Active Directory and LDAP.
- Facility shall be provided for system administrator for creation of desired number of users for various modules. To different user, depending upon his level and work done by him, various privileges can be given by system administrator. He can give access to specific menus and submenus to a user. All the transactions such as data entry/modification shall be stored with user names so

that accountability of user is possible. IP address-based protection shall be given for more critical applications. Normally administrative activities such as payroll processing, service record entries, fees collection, etc are to be performed from specific computers. To such users, IP address-based protections may be provided. So, such crucial transactions can be entered through specific nodes only. Well-established backup and security procedures shall be defined. Backup must be automatic. Practically there shall be no chance of data loss.

- The exact data security and backup arrangements shall be worked out after system studies and total network study by the successful bidder. Following sections define software requirements of various modules.
- Bidder may give a graphic outline of the deployment architecture of the ERP system

5. PERFORMA FOR FINANCIAL/PRICE BID

S No	Description	Cost (INR)	
		License Fee	Implementation cost
1	**Module**		
	I. Material management (MM) (Phase 1)		
	II. Sales and distribution (SD) (Phase 1)		
	III. Financial accounting (FI) (Phase 1)		
	IV. Production planning (PP) (Phase 2)		
	V. Quality management (QM) (Phase 2)		
	VI. Controlling (CO) (Phase 2)		
3	Technological planning		
4	Servers		
5	Database management server		
6	Additional hardware		
7	Additional software		
8	Data migration		
9	Training		
10	AMC charges		
	I. Year 1		
	II. Year 2		
	III. Year 3		
11	Any other charges		
12	Total		

6. IMPLEMENTATION STRATEGY

The overall project will be implemented in two phases. The modules to be implemented in Phase I are:

- Material management (MM)
  - Purchasing
  - Inventory management
  - Materials requirements planning
  - Valuation
  - Product catalogue
- Sales and distribution (SD)
  - Sales
  - Billing
  - Credit management
  - Transport and shipping
  - Sales information system
- Financial accounting
  - General ledger (GL)
  - Accounts receivable (AR)
  - Accounts payable (AP)
  - Legal consolidation (LC)
  - Accounting information system.

Phase II modules are:

- Production planning (PP)
  - Sales and operations planning
  - Master planning
  - Capacity requirements planning
  - Production orders
  - Product costing
  - Material requirements planning
- Controlling (CO)
  - Cost element accounting
  - Cost centre accounting
  - Activity-based accounting
  - Profit centre accounting
  - Profitability analysis
  - Product cost controlling

8.8 GAP ANALYSIS

The objective of gap analysis activity is to learn the offering of an ERP system and to assess the gap between the offering and the requirements of the organization. As mentioned earlier, three to four ERP systems are considered thoroughly. An initial filtering may be done using some gross features. The gap analysis will involve the vendor as well as the selection team. There are two ways to perform the gap analysis:

ERP			
S.No	**Activity/Event**	**Support**	**Customization**
1	Contacted by Potential Customer		√
2	Log Effort		√
3	Contact Later Reminder	√	
4	Record Request	√	
5	Check Inventory	√	√
6	Refine Requirements	√	
7	Dispatch Material		√
8	Follow-up Supplier	√	
9	Prepate Quotation	√	
10	Management Approval	√	√
11	Dispatch Quotation	√	
12	Sales Order to Supplier		√
13	Shipment Arrangement		√

FIGURE 8.1 Gap Analysis Report for Sales Process of RetailS

- Vendor may be asked to make a presentation of their ERP system. The vendor may also make a prototype available, that one can experiment with. The selection team may ask questions, and based on the answers of the vendor, gap is established.
- Vendor may be provided with a detailed document of requirement and the vendor submits a response to all requirements.

In both the cases, the choices for a response include full support, will require minor changes and customization. After checking for all requirements, the team may declare that the ERP system supports 80 per cent of the requirements, 10 per cent requirements would need a change in the ERP system and the remaining 10 per cent requirements can be handled by changing the requirements. The gap analysis report is shown in Figure 8.1. This is a planned activity for which budget, resources and time is allocated. For RetailS, sales process is used as shown in Figure 6.18 of Chapter 6 as a reference. The ERP system that KN—a company, had was evaluated. KN is a company that provides ERP solutions for small companies. The sales process as a reference was used and the product that KN demonstrated to us was evaluated.

8.9 AHP FOR ERP SELECTION

A model based on Analytic Hierarchy Process (AHP)[7] enables a decision maker to express a problem seemingly requiring qualitative judgement as a hierarchy and make a quantitative decision. AHP transforms a subjective problem into an objective one. AHP has been applied to decision making in many diverse domains. A hierarchy is created by putting the objective or the decision at Level 1. For choosing an appropriate ERP system, the objective may be stated as *Select the most suitable ERP system,*[8] sub-objectives are placed at Level 2 of hierarchy. An ERP system is supplied by the vendor and implemented by one of the implementation partners of the vendor. The sub-objectives are to pick the most suitable ERP system (or vendor) and implementation partner. These two items are available at Level 2. At Level 3, parameters that were discussed earlier for selecting ERP system are placed. The parameters for selecting an implementation partner are not yet explained. The components of parameters included at Level 3 are placed at Level 4. For example, component of the cost parameter are infrastructure cost, software cost, license cost and consultancy cost. It is not necessary to have components for every parameter. Level 4 could be empty for some of the parameters.

Coming back to picking up a good ERP implementation partner, the most appropriate partner may not be the one who has the highest market share or who has largest clientele. It may be the one for whom customer is important and will pay enough attention to customer's project in a productive manner. The parameters for selecting appropriate implementation partner are listed below. The selection committee would hold multiple meetings to discuss and select the parameters that are important for the organization. During discussions and meetings, some team members may talk about high-level objectives and some may quickly jump to the parameters and sub-parameters. All these are required to be put into a hierarchy. Building a hierarchy is an iterative process as well as art. If the team is not satisfied with the hierarchy, one can modify till most of the team members are satisfied. It may not be possible to satisfy all team members.

Let us say in a meeting, the following parameters/objectives etc. were discussed:

Cost	Implementation time
No customization	No process modification
Platform independence	Maintenance
Running Cost	Consultancy cost
Software cost	Hardware cost
Infrastructure cost	Training required
Availability of trained manpower	Payment terms
Total cost	Total time
Functionality	Flexibility
Reliability	

Some of the team members would quickly get into drilling down and ask questions such as 'how do we test flexibility of a system?' or 'what is the cost of the ERP system?' Some of the questions can be easily answered while many will have no clear answer. Here are some other questions that may surface during deliberations:

- *Is the ERP designed to work with RDBMS:* Most of the big ERP systems require RDBMS at the backend. One may like to find out what RDBMS will be required. This is also a direct cost factor and may be added at Level 4 as a component of the *cost* or as a parameter under *flexibility*.
- *Uploading the legacy data:* One will have to upload legacy data into the database. The legacy data may need cleaning and conversion before it can be uploaded into the database. This activity progresses in parallel and does not add to the overall time of the project. This parameter may be added as a component of the *cost*.
- *Material requirement planning (MRP):* There are whole lot parameters that go into deciding material requirements and there are lot many MRP algorithms. It is required to find out that MRP

solution integrated into the ERP solution matches the expectation. This is a Level 4 parameter that belongs to functionality fit.

- *Security:* Security is a major concern and becomes more important after ERP implementation as the entire data of the company is in a centralized database. It is necessary to find out the security layers incorporated into the software. This is also a Level 4 parameter that belongs to functional fit.
- *Support:* Is implementation partner located in your town? It will be difficult to get required support from a remote location. This may again be a Level 4 parameter under *Technical Support* at Level 3 that, in turn, is under sub-objective *Select Appropriate Vendor* at Level 2.
- *Vendor experience:* Has the vendor implemented modules that your organization needs earlier? One may not want to become training ground for the vendor. Hence it is essential to check IT/ERP experience of vendor. The implementation time will decrease if the vendor has implemented a similar system elsewhere. This seems like a Level 4 parameter under *Technical Support* at Level 3 or under *Good Reputation*.
- *Availability of the product:* Is the product ready and available for immediate delivery? What is the level of maturity of the product? Such a situation may arise if there has been a change in the governing rules and vendors are modifying their software. There could be a change in the technology leading to a similar situation. Government of India has introduced value added tax (VAT) and all ERP softwares had to be touched to incorporate changed tax rules. This could be a parameter at Level 4 under *Implementation Time*.
- *Does the software maintain an audit trail of all the transactions?* All financial transactions must leave an audit trail. The auditor should be able to check the time of transaction, the person who made the transactions in addition to the transaction details. If a change is made in the transaction, the earlier document is not changed instead a new document is created referring to the earlier document. This parameter may be a Level 4 parameter under *Functional Fit* at Level 3.
- *Database size:* Will ERP system support the data through its database system? Performance and scalability becomes, important as the size of the data grows. This may be a parameter under *Scalability*.
- *Objective:* Will ERP help the organization to achieve its business objective? For example, will ERP help in reducing lead times of the selected business processes? This parameter may find place under *Functionality*.
- *Some more parameters:* There are some parameters that may be discussed during the selection process. The selection team may come up with concerns such as:
  - Hardware support
  - Upgrade support for the software
  - Documentation
  - Web-enabled access
  - Will the software be implemented in modules?
  - Will the software be purchased in modules?
  - Year-ending accounting
  - Posting of transaction online
  - Business rules
  - Data entry screens
  - Report generation
  - Master data preparation
  - Is the customization cost included in the ERP cost?

The objectives, sub-objectives, parameters and sub-parameters are all put in a hierarchy. The team can collectively work in deciding the levels of the hierarchy. But generally 4 levels are sufficient. There are some hierarchies that have been prepared by the researchers and if any of these appeal to the team possibly with some modification, the hierarchy can be used.[9] One hierarchy is shown in Figure 8.2 that includes objectives, sub-objectives, parameters and sub-parameters which are discussed above.

AHP is used for making two decisions:

- Compute relative importance of parameters based on the input from the ERP selection team.
- Compute relative performance of ERP systems under consideration based on the important parameters identified in previous step.

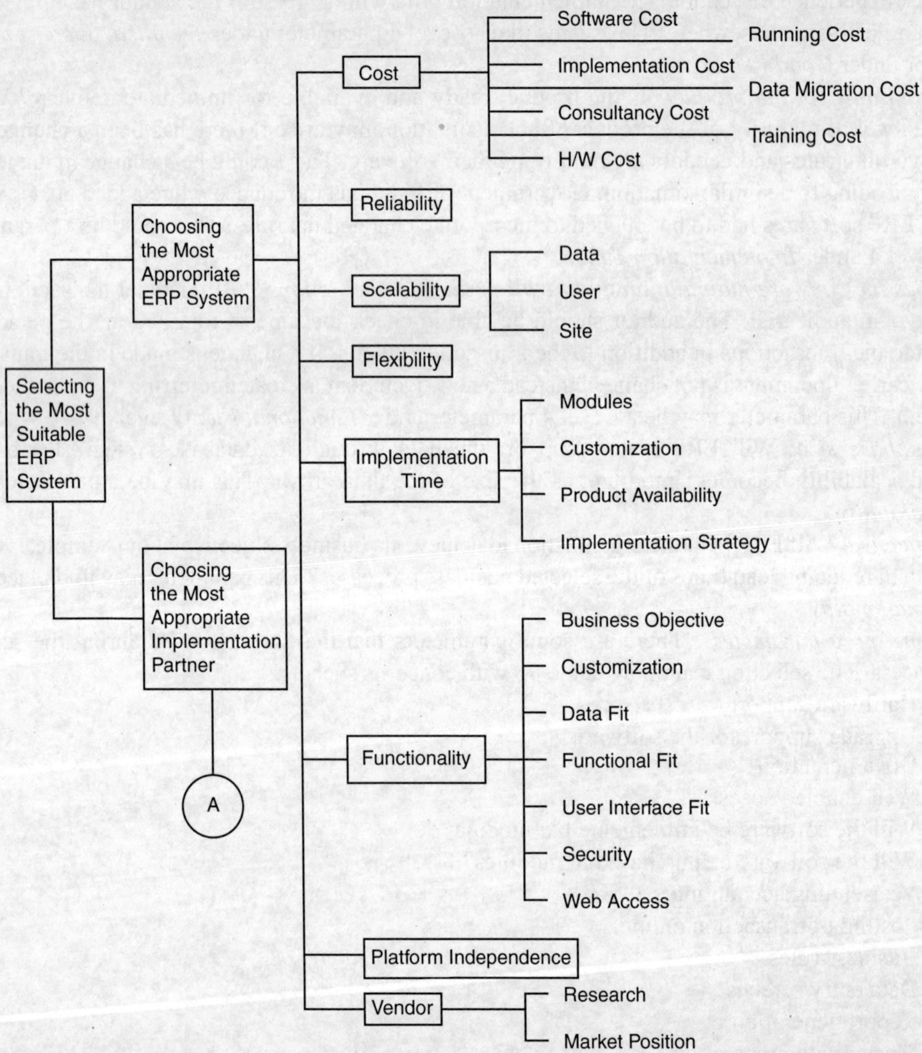

FIGURE 8.2 Hierarchy Built—Based on Objectives, Sub-objectives, Parameters and Sub-parameters

The process is same for making these decisions (Figure 8.2). There are eight parameters at Level 3—cost, reliability, scalability, flexibility, implementation time, functionality, platform independence and vendor. The objective is to figure out relative importance of these parameters.

The process of making the decision consists of the following five steps.

Step 1

Create a matrix for level 3 parameters as shown in Table 8.2. The team makes pair-wise comparison to answer questions of the form—what is the relative importance of $Parameter_i$ with respect to $Parameter_j$? We can use a scale of 1 to 5 (1 to 9 or 1 to 3), where relative importance of 1 means that both parameters are equally important and 5 means that $Parameter_i$ is five times more important than $Parameter_j$. We will prepare matrices for each level of hierarchy and make pair-wise comparisons for each level. Every member of the team will fill up these matrices.

TABLE 8.2 Matrix for Pair-wise Comparison of the Parameters

	$Parameter_1$	$Parameter_2$	......	$Parameter_n$
$Parameter_1$				
$Parameter_2$				
....				
$Parameter_n$				

Example for Step 1

For the hierarchy shown in Figure 8.2, the matrix as shown in Table 8.3 will be created for deciding relative importance of the parameters.

TABLE 8.3 Pair-wise Comparison of the Parameters Filled by One Team Member

	Cost	Functionality	Reliability	Time	Platform	Vendor	Flexibility	Scalability
Cost	1	1/9	3	1/7	3	5	1	3
Functionality	9	1	5	2	7	1	9	3
Reliability	1/3	1/5	1	1/3	5	3	4	2
Time	7	1/2	3	1	7	3	4	5
Platform	1/3	1/7	1/5	1/7	1	1	1/3	2
Vendor	1/5	1	1/3	1/3	1	1	3	5
Flexibility	1	1/9	1/4	1/4	3	1/3	1	3
Scalability	1/3	1/3	1/2	1/5	1/2	1/2	1/3	1

All people responsible for making the selection decision will have to fill the matrix according to the relative importance of the criteria using a scale of one to nine.

Step 2

One can use software like Expert Choice[10] to analyse the data. At the end of analysis, we will get a vector giving us relative importance of parameters. The parameters that turn out to be relatively less important can be ignored from further consideration to reduce the number of parameters. Let us call this vector:

$$W: < w_1, w_2, w_3, \ldots, w_n >,$$

where w_i is the relative importance or weight of parameter *i*.

Expert Choice is available as trial version that one can download and run a Level 3 hierarchy with three participants. This software also checks for consistency of the responses. A response will be inconsistent if a respondent says, A is three times more important than B, B is two times more important than C and C is three times more important than A where A, B and C are the parameters being compared. Such responses are ignored from further consideration.

Example for Step 2

For the matrix of Table 8.3, the following vectors are ortained:

$$< \textit{Cost, Functionality, Reliability, Time, Platform Independence, Vendor, Flexibility, Scalability} >$$
$$\leq .119, .327, .10, .242, .035, .091, .052, .033 >$$

We can evaluate ERP solutions on top five parameters—functionality, time, cost, reliability and vendor, and ignore the remaining parameters.

Step 3 and Example for Step 3

After discovering relative importance of the parameters, we evaluate ERP solution under consideration on the selected parameters. We create one matrix for each parameter as shown in tables 8.4 to 8.8. We compare every pair of ERP solutions on each parameter and fill the matrices. We would answer questions such as: Does ERP solution A meet our requirements better than ERP solution B? Does solution A more reliable than solution B?

TABLE 8.4 Pair-wise Comparison of ERP Solutions A, B, C and D on Functionality

Pair-wise	**ERP$_A$**	**ERP$_B$**	**ERP$_C$**	**ERP$_D$**
ERP$_A$	1	2.0	7.0	7.0
ERP$_B$	1/2	1	7.0	7.0
ERP$_C$	1/7	1/7	1	1
ERP$_D$	1/7	1/7	1/7	1

TABLE 8.5 Pair-wise Comparison of ERP Solutions A, B, C and D on Reliability

Pair-wise	**ERP$_A$**	**ERP$_B$**	**ERP$_C$**	**ERP$_D$**
ERP$_A$	1	1	3	3
ERP$_B$	1	1	3	3
ERP$_C$	1/3	1/3	1	1
ERP$_D$	1/3	1/3	1	1

TABLE 8.6 Pair-wise Compare of ERP Solutions A, B, C and D on Cost

Pair-wise	ERP_A	ERP_B	ERP_C	ERP_D
ERP_A	1	5	5	6
ERP_B	1/4	1	3	6
ERP_C	1/5	1/3	1	6
ERP_D	1/6	1/6	1	1

TABLE 8.7 Pair-wise Comparison of ERP Solutions A, B, C and D on Implementation Time

	ERP_A	ERP_B	ERP_C	ERP_D
ERP_A	1	3	4	5
ERP_B	1/3	1	4	5
ERP_C	1/4	1/4	1	2
ERP_D	1/5	1/5	1/2	1

TABLE 8.8 Pair-wise Comparison of ERP Solutions A, B, C and D on Vendor

	ERP_A	ERP_B	ERP_C	ERP_D
ERP_A	1	5	7	9
ERP_B	1/5	1	4	6
ERP_C	1/7	1/4	1	2
ERP_D	1/9	1/6	1/2	1

Step 4

After we have filled all these matrices, we will run them through Expert Choice and get one vector for each parameter that gives relative score of each ERP solution on each parameter. Now we have relative score of each parameter for each ERP solution:

$$\text{Param}_1\text{:} < \text{score\_}ERP_A\text{, score } \text{ERP}_B\text{, ... , score\_ERP}_D >$$
$$\text{Param}_2\text{:} < \text{score\_ERP}_A\text{, score } \text{ERP}_B\text{, ... , score\_ERP}_D >$$
$$\text{Param}_3\text{:} < \text{score\_ERP}_A\text{, score\_ERP}_B\text{, ... , score\_ERP}_D >$$
$$\text{Param}_4\text{:} < \text{score\_ERP}_A\text{, score\_ERP}_B\text{, ... , score\_ERP}_D >$$
$$\text{Param}_5\text{:} < \text{score\_ERP}_A\text{, score\_ERP}_B\text{, ... , score\_ERP}_D >$$

Example for Step 4

We compared ERP_A, ERP_B, ERP_C and ERP_D as shown in tables 8.4 and 8.8 on five parameters. When we solve these matrices using Expert Choice, we get ratings of each ERP solution on all five parameters as shown in Table 8.9.

TABLE 8.9 Rating of Each ERP System on All Five Parameters

	ERP_A	ERP_B	ERP_C	ERP_D
Functionality	0.516	0.363	0.061	0.061
Reliability	0.375	0.375	0.125	0.125
Cost	0.056	0.131	0.353	0.460
Time	0.069	0.121	0.316	0.495
Vendor	0.653	0.225	0.076	0.047

Step 5

We can now consolidate the scores by multiplying weight of each parameter with score of ERP and add them as follows:

$$\text{Overall score of } ERP_A = 15 \text{ weight of Parameter}_i * \text{ score of } ERP_A \text{ for Parameter}_i$$
$$\text{Overall score of } ERP_B = 15 \text{ weight of Parameter}_i * \text{ score of } ERP_B \text{ for Parameter}_i$$
$$\text{Overall score of } ERP_C = 15 \text{ weight of Parameter}_i * \text{ score of } ERP_c \text{ for Parameter}_i$$
$$\text{Overall score of } ERP_D = 15 \text{ weight of Parameter}_i * \text{ score of } ERP_D \text{ for Parameter}_i$$

Example for Step 5

For the above weights and scores, the final vector turns out to be

$$ERP_A = 0.327 * 0.516 + .1*0.375 + 0.119* 0.056 + 0.242*0.069 + 0.091*0.653 = 0.289$$
$$ERP_B = 0.327 * 0.363 + .1*0.375 + 0.119* 0.131 + 0.242*0.121 + 0.091*0.225 = 0.221$$
$$ERP_C = 0.327 * 0.061 + .1*0.125 + 0.119* 0.353 + 0.242*0.316 + 0.091*0.076 = 0.158$$
$$ERP_D = 0.327 * 0.061 + .1*0.125 + 0.119* 0.46 + 0.242*0.495 + 0.091*0.047 = 0.211$$
$$< ERP_A, ERP_B, ERP_C, ERP_D >=< 0.289, 0.221, 0.158, 0.211 >$$

ERP_A is the preferred solution based on five parameters and their weights with ERP_B the second choice.

We can use the same process for selecting important sub-parameters for functionality, cost and implementation time. The same process applied to the hierarchy shown in Figure 8.3 would rank the implementation partners.

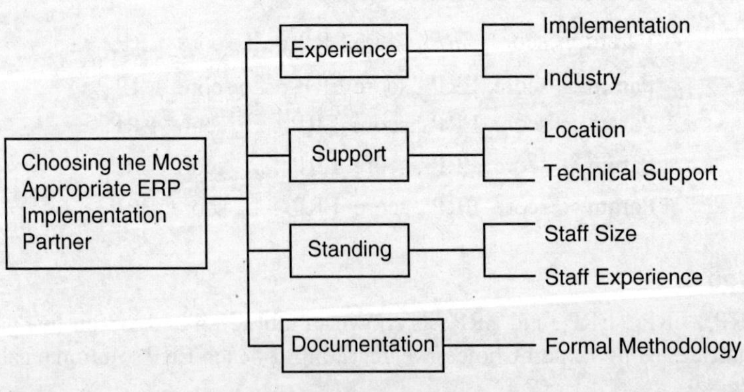

FIGURE 8.3 Hierarchy Built—Based on Objectives, Sub-objectives, Parameters and Sub-parameters

CONCLUSION

ERP selection is a planned and budgeted activity in an ERP project. A team is constituted by the management consisting of generally 6 to 10 people. The job of the selection team is to identify parameters that are important for the organization. The objective is to select an appropriate ERP system for the organization. The constitution of the selection team and their role in selecting an ERP system were discussed. It is possible that too many parameters are mentioned by the team initially. The team can use Analytical Hierarchy Process (AHP) to learn the relative importance of the parameters (and sub-parameters). Smaller number of important parameters are then used to evaluate ERP systems under consideration in an objective manner using AHP.

CASE STUDY

Let us observe the selection process that we followed for RetailS. You would recall that RetailS is a small retail company and we have been working with company right from the beginning of the book. The main concerns of the company were the following:

1. Cost should be between ₹4,00,000 to ₹5,00,000.
2. Implementation time should be six months or so.
3. No process change.

Since it is a small company, solutions such SAP or Oracle were not feasible as they are unnecessarily bulky and expensive for RetailS. These concerns ruled out any of the standard package. We then started looking at the custom made solutions. The process started with vendor selection.

Vendor Selection

There are three different channels to locate a vendor:

- Search engines such as Google
- Business directories and Yellow pages
- Personal contact

Search engine and business directories gave us more than 50 potential ERP vendors. We went to the Web sites and based on the look and feel, and the last update, we shortlisted about 15 companies to contact. Some of the companies could not be contacted because either their phone number was stale or the company did not exist anymore. Some of the Web sites overclaimed their expertise and they were dropped from further consideration after first interaction. We were looking for a company based in Delhi (NCR) region. If a company did not have presence in NCR, it was also dropped. We managed to get a list of about six companies to interact with us. We made appointment and waited anxiously on each appointment for the company representative. To our utter surprise, each one of them was late for their appointments. Since these appointments were spread over a week and all these companies were in NCR region, we failed to find any valid reason. Moreover, their representatives turned up without any preparation. None of our questions were answered. The whole experience was very disappointing and we decided to try the next channel—personal contact.

We approached our friends and colleagues for finding an ERP vendor. We quickly zeroed upon two companies, both were located in NCR region. We made appointment with one of the company and the guy arrived about 45 minutes late. This was the first meeting that was organized at RetailS and CMD of RetailS was present. He questioned the company representative and objected to his latecoming. His response was very annoying and we dropped his company. We then moved onto our last option—let us call this company KN and its CMD Mr Tiwari (not his real name). Mr Tiwari also arrived late but by now, we all had lowered our expectations and decided to impress upon him to be on time from next time onwards.

First interaction with Mr Tiwari was reasonable and we all felt that we can work with him. His team members were just about average or below average from our expectation. Mr Tiwari showed us his product that they delivered to another client. His claim was that he can quickly adapt the existing system to suit requirements of RetailS. After two meetings, the terms and conditions of the contract were finalized and a time line for various phases that were in accordance to the schedule we had in mind. Everything got formalized and a contract between RetailS and LN was signed. The signing amount was paid to KN right away.

EXERCISES

Check Your Understanding

1. Give some good reasons for allocating time and budget for ERP selection activity.
2. What will be the constitution of a selection team of medium size manufacturing enterprise?
3. List seven parameters that you think are important and should be considered while selecting an ERP system. Explain each of these parameters briefly.
4. Briefly explain AHP for making an ERP selection decision. You may use an example for clarity.

Apply Your Understanding

1. Create a selection team for the organization that you chose in the beginning. Justify the constitution of the team that you created.
2. Use AHP matrix to collect data on the relative importance of the parameters that you identified in question. You may request 10 to 15 of your classmates for filling the matrices. Run the collected data through Expert Choice to identify the four most important parameters.
3. In Chapter 1, you chose an organization to work with. If the company has already implemented an ERP system or any other large information system, learn who made the selection and how? What were the parameters that were considered important? If your organization has not deployed any major information system, try to find out how major procurement decisions are made?

ENDNOTES

1. E. Bernroider and Stefan Koch, ERP Selection Process in Midsize and Large Organisations, in *Business Process Management Journal* (2001), 7(3), 251–257
2. C. Wei and M. J. Wang, A Comprehensive Framework for Selecting an ERP System, in *International Journal of Project Management* (2004), 22, 161–169.
3. Y. V. Everdingen et al., 'ERP Adoption by European Midsize Companies', in *Communications of the ACM* (2000), 43(4), April, 27–31.
4. C. Soh, S. S. Kien and J. Tay-Yap, 'Cultural Fits and Misfits: Is ERP a Universal Solution?', in *Communications of the ACM* (2000), 43(3), 47–51.

5. F. D. Davis, 'Perceived Usefulness, Perceived Ease of Use, and User Acceptance of Information Technology' in MIS Quarterly (1989), 13(3), 319–39.
6. Kwasi Amoako-Gyampah and A. F. Salam, 'An Extention of the Technology Acceptance Model in an ERP Implementation Environment', in *Information and Management* (2004), 41, 731–45.
7. T. L. Saaty, *The Analytic Hierarchy Process,* NY: McGraw Hill (1980).
8. Chun-Chin Wei et al., 'An AHP-based Approach to ERP System Selection', in *International Journal of Production Economics* (2005), 96, 47–62.
9. ibid.
10. *Expert Choice*, www.expertchoice.com

chapter 9

Managing an ERP Project

LEARNING OBJECTIVES

After reading this chapter, you will be able to understand:

- Management of ERP projects
- Multidimensionality of success of an ERP project
- Critical success factors (CSF) for an ERP project
- Management of risks associated with an ERP project
- Measurement for performance of an ERP project

9.1 INTRODUCTION

An ERP project has to be managed like any other project. In Chapter 2, all the phases of an ERP project are enumerated. The project plan is created, after a selection of the ERP solution has been made and an implementation partner has been selected. Generally, the implementation partner would bring in an implementation methodology to manage the project. The methodology would serve as a guide on dividing the project into tasks and sub-tasks. SAP calls its methodology *ASAP*. Oracle calls its methodology *Application Implementation Methodology (AIM)*. People Soft calls their methodology *Compass*. The objective of each of these methodologies is to divide ERP project into phases and enumerate tasks to be performed in each phase as well deliverables. The idea is to ensure that no task is missed or delayed. They all will use a project management tool to manage the project. There are many project management tools in the market. A project management tool will allow the following:

- Create tasks.
- Allocate resources to each task.
- Define a start and finish date for each task.
- Define interdependence of tasks.
- Set milestones.
- Set deliverables.

- Track progress of each task.
- Raise alarms if there is a deviation.

Once the project commences, the progress can be measured by entering the percentage of the completed task. If big tasks have been appropriately broken down into sub-tasks then monitoring the progress becomes simple. The system can check the tasks that are lagging behind the schedule, and raise alerts. The project management system can be configured to send email alerts to the project manager and the persons allocated to the task. The plan must contain tasks to be done by vendor, implementation partner and the team of the client or host or implementing organization. Milestones are the checkpoints for assessing the health of the project. The project manager can watch every milestone and take corrective actions, if required. Weekly or biweekly milestones are often used. The objective is to complete the project on time and within allotted budget. However, an ERP project may complete on-time and within budget but still may not be considered success if it fails to deliver the set objectives. The success and the failure of ERP projects are discussed in following sections.

9.2 SUCCESS OF AN ERP SYSTEM IS MULTI-DIMENSIONAL

Let us start with what is success, and what is failure? One simple answer is that if people do not fail then they are successful. The only trouble with this answer is that there is need to define failure. It seems that it is required to define either success or failure in order to proceed. An ERP project is considered a failure due to one or more of the following reasons:

1. Cost overrun
2. Schedule overrun
3. System performance deficit
4. Failure to achieve the expected benefits
5. Organization misfit of ERP
6. Low alignment of ERP with business strategy
7. ERP does not meet organization requirements in terms of data, processes or user interface

First two factors pertain to ERP implementation project failure whereas the remaining factors would surface after the system goes live and people start using it. Factors 3 to 7 would impact effectiveness of ERP system.

Some cases where ERP implementation failed that have been reported in the media are mentioned below.

W. L. Gore and Associates were very upset with People Soft Inc., ERP vendor as well as consultants Deloitte & Touche in October 1997. The system went live but it was faulty. Gore and Associates claim that during the installation, Deloitte & Touche consultants called People Soft's customer service hotline for help. Gore expected the consultants to be expert of People Soft as they were certified by People Soft.[1] Gore claims that the installation was a total disaster.

Anderson Consulting and SAP America were held responsible by **FoxMeyer Drug Co.** for pushing them to bankruptcy in 1998. The system went live but the implementation could not handle the huge volume of transactions and had integration problems. The details of the case may be found at Buxbaum.[2] The SAP project has been analysed by experts and it turns out that SAP project was not aligned to FoxMeyer's business strategy. The project also failed due to a very tight schedule that did not permit proper configuration and testing.[2]

The state of Ohio on behalf of Cleveland State University is suing People Soft for $510 million, they have also included Kaludis Consulting Group in their law suit who helped them select and implement the People Soft application.[3] The system did not work as it was full of bugs and required a huge number of fixes. The university faced difficulty in collecting dues and lost $5 million as it could not collect dues from the students. University is also unhappy about the hardware it had to buy for the new system.

Hershey filed a law suit against ERP vendor SAP AG R/3 in 1999. IBM was their lead consultant. The SAP R/3 implementation was full of bugs and Hershey's inventory went up by 29 per cent from the previous year.[4] But it seems everyone involved learnt from the experience, and in 2002 Hershey upgraded their SAP without hitches. This time, they completed the project within 20 per cent budget under-run. They made 30 improvements to their core business processes within 60 days of going live. There are Web sites quoting various ERP failures.

Each of the failure mentioned so far was considered failure for different and multiple reasons. Simple criteria such as cost over-run or time delays do not work in case of an ERP project. Let us consider cost over-run. It can be checked if an ERP project has over-run its allocated budget only if an accurate reference budget is available. The current state of affairs is very dismal with no mechanism to accurately estimate ERP budget. Most of the projects are estimated by benchmarking them with an earlier implementation. As mentioned in Section 3.3 of Chapter 3, there are direct costs involved that one can estimate but the indirect cost and ongoing cost also makeup for a major share in the total cost. One can compromise on the required customization to keep the cost under check and on schedule. Will such an implementation be called a success?

ERP implementation is an ongoing project and even after it goes live, it is not necessary that the project is over. So, it is hard to declare an ERP project a failure or a success just because it went live or did not go live on the designated date.

As far as the performance is concerned, it can be measured after at least six months or longer after the implementation is over. There is a systematic way of measuring the performance of an ERP system through a balanced scorecard.[5] Balanced scorecard and its application to ERP system performance measure is explained in Section 9.5.

ERP projects are prone to problems such as organizational misfit, misalignment with business strategy and user expectation. If the ERP system does not meet the requirements of the organization, either the system is changed or the business processes are changed. In either case, the changes may add to the chances of failure.

The companies in late 1990s, went for ERP implementation to solve Y2K problem without realizing the complexity of the system. The infrastructure, expertise and mindset were not ready for a complex system like ERP. For instance, Hershey Foods started SAP R/3 implementation with an original schedule of 48 months. The company then forced the implementation to complete in 30 months. They forgot that an ERP project cannot be rushed up from 48 months to 30 months. The system went live on almost the designated date with all sorts of integration problem. Was it a success? As it is known that it was a total failure.

The implementation process often times ignores the *people* dimension. People issues are addressed in Chapter 4. The management needs to support the project, training program and understanding towards employees who are somewhat uncertain or shaky in the beginning. If the mandate to implement ERP came from the top management, then the user commitment, involvement and sense of ownership may reduce even further. In an organization, technology, task, people and structure are interrelated.[6] A change to one component necessarily implies change to other components. An ERP system brings direct changes to technology as the legacy systems are dumped and client/server architecture, web-based access and central database are implemented. Tasks or processes, of course, affected as the present business

TABLE 9.1 Most Often Cited Reasons for ERP Implementation Project Failure

Reason	%
Poor communication between relevant parties	57%
Lack of planning of scheduling, resources and activities	39%
No quality control	34%
Milestones not being set	29%
Inadequate co-ordination of resources	26%
Costs getting out of hand (it is a symptom not a cause)	20%
Mismanagement of progress (overlaps with poor communication)	17%
Overall poor management	13%
Suppliers skills overstretched	12%
Supplier under-resourced	11%

processes are replaced by the best practices implemented by the ERP software. The technology and process together almost dissolve the existing functional boundaries and makes the organization much flatter. A comprehensive framework which incorporates various dimensions into account for measuring performance of an ERP project while it is being implemented and after it becomes operational is required. One such framework called balanced scorecard is discussed in Section 9.5.

An informal survey conducted over 80 organizations by Robbins-Gioia Survey[7] in year 2001 discovered that 51 per cent respondents viewed their ERP implementation as unsuccessful and 46 per cent felt that the ERP system was not being used effectively. The next section talks about a list of reasons for a few successfully implemented systems and some who did not see the success. Some of these reasons are manifestation of bigger issues. In the next section, critical success factors that have been identified in the literature are enumerated.

9.3 CRITICAL SUCCESS FACTORS

Various critical success factors (CSFs) have been identified in the literature. CSFs are the factors that are considered vital for the success of an ERP project. If addressed, CSFs improve the chances for success of an ERP project significantly. CSFs have been divided into strategic and tactical factors. The groups were further divided into strategic, tactical, operational, organizational and technological. CSFs can also be looked at from the perspective of stakeholders. In an ERP project, end users and the management are the main stakeholders. Various perspective with which CSFs have been studies are summarized in Table 9.2. People have also categorized CSFs for each phase of an ERP project. As we discussed in Chapter 2, following are the phases of an ERP project:

1. Project preparation
2. Requirements engineering
3. ERP solution selection
4. Technical planning
5. Change management and training
6. Implementation and deployment planning
7. Configuration

Table 9.2 Various Perspectives and Views Used for Analysing CSFs of ERP Projects

Perspective	Views
Geographical	Global–national
Industry	Small–large
Economy	Developed–developing
Stakeholder	End user-management
Ownership	Public–private
Management	Technological–tactical–strategic–operational-organizational

8. Custom coding
9. Final preparation
10. Go live

We will look at CSFs applicable to each phase in this section. The maximum number of CSFs identified are 94 that have been put in 15 categories.[8]

- Careful selection of ERP package and implementation partner.
- Clear goals and objectives.
- Project management.
- Interdepartmental communication and co-operation.
- Training and change management.
- Project team competence.
- Top management support
- Vendor support
- Organizational characteristics
- ERP system
- User involvement
- Project monitoring
- Environment
- Implementation strategy
- Software development

In the literature, these phases have been combined into the following three phases specifically for analysing relevance of CSFs:

- Planning phase that consists of the following phases
  - Project preparation
  - Requirements engineering
  - ERP solution selection
  - Technical planning
  - Training
- Implementation phase that consists of the following phases
- Implementation and deployment planning

- Configuration
- Custom coding
- Final preparation

- Stabilization phase that consists of the following phase
  - Go live

Change management is an activity that spans all phases of the project. Incidentally all CSFs are relevant to all three phases of an ERP project. Description of each CSF will make this point clear.

All these factors are explained below in detail.

- **Careful selection of ERP package and implementation partner:** Chapter 8 discusses vendor support and package selection. An ERP vendor's motive is to close a deal as soon as possible. The aim should be to make sure to get it done rightly. Too often, companies jump right in to a project without validating the vendor's understanding of business requirements or their project plan. The more time spent ensures these things are done rightly at the beginning of the project, if less time is spent then fixing problems will take more time later on. A wrong selection of an ERP system would require customization or excessive changes in the business processes. The cost and time may just turn the project into a failure. In the extreme case, the ERP system may not meet the requirements of the organization and the project may have to be abandoned after spending considerable time and money.
- **Clear goals and objectives:** This is arguably one of the most important factors. It is easy to see that many big companies are running SAP or Oracle, but it is hard to consider that maybe one may not require an ERP system. Perhaps process improvement, organizational redesign or targeted best-of-breed technology will meet business objectives at a lower cost and more effectively. By clearly understanding the business objectives and what one is trying to accomplish with an ERP system, one should be able to make a more appropriate decision on which route to take, which may or may not involve ERP.
- **Project management:** The project management includes proper project planning and its execution. If the team is competent, they will plan the project properly so that there is no fire fighting. All the possible risks must be enumerated and resolved before the project commences. The risk mitigation and management is discussed in Section 9.4. Milestones should be set, proper utilization and co-ordination of resources should be ensured, communication to the all concerned must happen through a formal channel in a timely manner and the progress should be measured. The project management team must be able to pick the early signs of problems and resolve the problems to keep the project on track. A careful selection of project management tools and techniques is critical to the success of the ERP project.
- **Top management support:** Importance of top management support to a project cannot be overemphasized. The energy in the project percolates from the top. The top management allocates budget and resources to the project. An ERP project is a business project. The top management will have to resolve business and people issues. Support from a CIO or IT Director is fine, but it is not enough. The top management creates the project team who run the project. It is the top management that decides the fate of the project by creating a strong and committed ERP team.
- **Interdepartmental communication and co-operation:** An ERP project involves and impacts all functional areas of the organization. It is essential that everyone identifies with the ERP project right from the beginning. ETAM model is discussed in Section 4.4.1 of Chapter 4 that shows the importance of communication and its positive impact on the acceptance of the system. The project management team must create formal channels for communication about the project. People should be informed and not left guessing about the project. The team must also keep the top management informed about the project. The project team must keep itself aware of the expectations of all the groups. Awareness at all levels is required for managing the change as well as project successfully.

- **Project team competence:** The project is run and managed by the project team. The team is responsible for the success of the project. They can ensure that none of the factors that have been mentioned in the last section for failures go out of control. If the team is competent, they will not miss out on critical aspects of an ERP project management. They would focus on quality, co-ordination and measurements to ensure the success of the project.
- **Ensure adequate training and change management:** ERP system has to be learnt and it takes some amount of efforts to use the system effectively. It is important to plan training sessions as part of the project planning. The budget and resources must be allocated to the training program. Before the project commences, all stakeholders need to be involved to win their commitment and support. As discussed in Chapter 4, a change management plan is required to support people to adapt to new ways. Spending time and money on training and change management, is crucial to the success of any ERP project.
- **Vendor support:** Vendor should proactively learn the business processes of the organization to map the processes and suggest industry's best practices. Vendor should work closely with the client to plan the project and to enhance the chances of success of the ERP project. Trained manpower with sufficient domain knowledge and appropriate tools are essential to the success of the project. The vendor becomes a part of the team at very early stages in the project. A client may involve the vendor right from the stage of requirements specifications till the very last stage of the project. Vendor is responsible for mapping the processes, configuring the system, deploying and providing the support. Vendor support is critical for the success of the project.
- **Organizational characteristics:** We have discussed organizational characteristics in Chapter 4, Chapter 5 and Chapter 7. An organization whose processes are at Level 1 as defined by IBM (refer to Section 7.2.2 of Chapter 7) is considered a mature organization. It is easier to map business processes of a mature organization to that of an ERP system. Other characteristics of organization such as freedom to each stakeholder to communicate his views goes in favour of ERP project.
- **ERP system:** This factor refers to the capability of the chosen ERP system. The selection team and the selection process for ERP system may be excellent but the system selected will be one that is available in the market and even the best available system may be not be a good fit to the organizational needs. The system may require customization, may have reliability issues etc. It is important to identify shortcomings of the system during planning phase and address the issues. The earlier the issues are addressed, the less expensive it would be.
- **User involvement:** Stages theory (refer to Section 1.7 of Chapter 1) can be used to assess user's ability to use advanced level of information systems. If an organization has successfully implemented information system in the past, users will be receptive of the ERP system. If the system has users buy-in, the chances of success go up many folds. The team from the client side should have thorough knowledge of business processes.
- **Project monitoring:** We have talked about competence of the project team as one of the CSFs and project management as another CSF. A team that is not directly involved in the implementation of the project, should monitor the progress of the project and assess success of the project. The team will have to define quantitative success parameters and parameters for monitoring progress of the project. The objective is to pick early signals of slippage and take measures.
- **Environment:** This CSF refers to the environment in which organization operates and the environment in which ERP system has to operate. The market may present new opportunities as a result of deployment of ERP system such as integration of suppliers and customers leading to better supply chain management. The system may provide some level of differentiation to the organization. ERP system may need support from the environment within the organization.
- **Implementation strategy:** Implementation strategy encompasses the high-level decision that are taken throughout the project. Designating a champion, creating a vision for the project, creating a

policy for resource allocation and empowering the team are all part of the implementation strategy. A suitable set of decisions at the high level is an important CSF.

- **Software development:** Most of the organizations have legacy systems and third party solutions that are integrated with the ERP system. This integration requires careful planning of the architecture and then putting all the components together. The team should be knowledgeable and equipped to use advanced tools for achieving the integration.

These critical success factors would help a project team to focus on the key factors to enhance chances of success of an ERP project. The team can identify all the critical factors and assess if the team and the organization are ready to handle the situation, if something goes wrong. The risk mitigation and management plan which is discussed in the following section is to identify all that can go wrong and prepare for it.

9.4 RISK ASSOCIATED WITH AN ERP PROJECT

A risk can be defined as the threat or probability that an action or event will adversely affect the project. The impact of a risk could be negligible—leading to minor inconvenience, marginal—leading to degradation of secondary mission, critical—leading to serious threat to primary objective or catastrophic leading to failure of primary mission. The objective of the project team should be to identify all critical and catastrophic threats to the project and deal with them proactively. There are three quantities associated with a risk:

Event	Associated Probability	Associated Cost	Exposure
E_1	P_1	C_1	$P_1 \times C_1$
E_2	P_2	C_2	$P_2 \times C_2$
E_3	P_3	C_3	$P_3 \times C_3$

In case event E_1 occurs, it will adversely affect the ERP implementation and, in turn, the organization. The likelihood of event E_1 occurring is P_1 and the cost associated with the event is C_1. One can make a list of events that are likely to have an adverse impact on the project, likelihood and cost associated with them. Each of the factors that have been listed in the previous section may pose a threat in multiple ways.

For instance, poor selection of the ERP packages is a major source of risk. The impact of wrong selection would be either excessive customization or major changes required in the business processes. The team leader can do risk analysis and prepare mitigation and management plan. The team need to assess probability P_1 associated with the event—how likely are we to make a wrong selection? The team may involve the ERP team or business process owners to get a better estimate of the probability. The team also needs to estimate the cost of wrong selection. Let us take the figures from the Dell ERP implementation case that was estimated to cost \$150 million, but was abandoned after spending \$115 million. Let us use \$115 million as the cost associated with the wrong selection in our risk analysis. In practice, the associated cost will be estimated. It is assumed that the probability of picking the wrong ERP solution has been estimated to be 0.6. The risk analysis is mentioned below:

Probability of wrong selection, P_1	0.6
Cost	\$115 million

Risk exposure = 0.6 × \$115 m = \$69 million

The figure of $69 million implies that it is a very expensive risk. It is better to safeguard the project against wrong selection. The impact of this risk is critical to catastrophic and will render the project useless. The next step is to mitigate the risk by reducing the associated probability and/or cost. The risk may occur due to one or more of the following reasons:

- Selection team not appropriate.
- Selection process not right.
- Budget is not adequate.
- Time allocated is not adequate.

The mitigation plan would be to allocate sufficient budget and time to the selection process. The selection team is properly constituted and the process itself should be capable of selecting the right product. The mitigation plan aims to reduce the risk exposure by reducing the probability of the risk. The team knowing that wrong selection has been identified as a major risk may opt for a two stage selection process where a prototype is evaluated first or may do a pilot project. The risk management plan aims to contain the risk exposure once the risk has occurred. In this case, the management plan would be to explore business processes that may be changed to adapt to the ERP system or the ERP modules that may need changes. The management plan includes an assessment of the feasibility of the changes, estimates of the cost, time, and the resources required for handling the risk. In case of Dell, if the risk had been identified and its exposure estimated, the management plan would have suggested a phased approach to ERP implementation to contain the exposure.

All possible risks can be analysed the same way. Or one can use AHP for prioritizing the risks and their exposure. AHP is discussed in Chapter 8. The risks with exposure more than the threshold decided by the management need to be addressed by creating mitigation and management plan. Since the resources are limited and not all risks would materialize, therefore, prioritization of risks would enable proper resource allocation to the risk management activity.

The risk identification, mitigation and management planning is an integral part of the ERP project management. There are risks that are specific to an ERP project and these are listed in the previous section. There are risks associated with any project whose major part is software and there are risks associated with any project. The project team must consider all these risks. Some common risks are security, attrition, change in business environment and technology obsolescence.

Table 9.3 lists major risks associated with an ERP project. The risks have been divided into three groups that we have already discussed.

These factors can also be categorized in three different classes: project governance, change management; and technological, processes and people issues. The risks associated with each class are the following:

Project governance

- Management support
- Implementation strategy
- Project team competence
- Consulting

Change management

- Ineffective communication system
- Low user involvement
- Ineffective project management techniques

Table 9.3 Risks Associated with an ERP Project

Risk associated with every project	■ Low user involvement ■ Poor project team skills ■ Low top management support ■ Poor project monitoring ■ Ineffective project management techniques ■ Scarcity of resources ■ Changing external environment ■ Attrition
Risk associated with a technology project	■ Inadequate management of IT issues ■ Scope creep ■ Volatile IT system ■ Instable vendor ■ Implementation strategy
Risk associated with an ERP project	■ Inadequate selection ■ Ineffective communication system ■ Inadequate change management ■ Ineffective vendor and consultant ■ Inadequate training ■ Inadequate business process reengineering ■ Inappropriate implementation strategy ■ Complexity of the ERP system ■ Inadequate legacy system management

- Inadequate change management
- Inadequate selection

Technological, processes and people issues

- Complexity of the ERP system
- Inadequate business process re-engineering
- Ineffective vendor
- Inadequate legacy system management
- Poor project monitoring
- Scarcity of resources
- Changing external environment
- Attrition
- Inadequate training

We have discussed these issues throughout the book. An important observation worth making is that these risks are not independent. For instance, if project team is not competent, the selection, project monitoring, user involvement, project communication and many more risks will become more probable.[9]

As already discussed is the previous section, success of an ERP project is complex to measure. Success of an ERP project means different things to different people. In order to capture everyone's perspective, balanced scorecard can be used.

9.5 MEASURING PERFORMANCE OF ERP SYSTEM USING BALANCED SCORECARD

Balanced Scorecard[10] (BSC) is a strategic planning and management framework. BSC is also discussed in detail in Chapter 5. BSC includes four perspectives for measuring the performance of an organization. BSC has been (Rosemann and Wiese)[11] adapted to measure performance of an ERP system after it becomes operational. In order to measure the performance from a particular perspective, the following can be figured out.

- **Objectives:** What is the objective?
- **Measures:** What variables will be measured to assess if the organization has achieved the objective?
- **Targets:** What are the target values for variables being measured? The parameters that are decided to measure will have initial values and need to set target values. The objectives translate into these target quantitative values. The key indicators should be easy to quantify. Moreover, the data required to be collected should be readily available. Heterogeneous groups should be able to interpret the data easily and the interpretations should be non ambiguous. There are some basic qualities that data must possess such as reliability, relevancy and accuracy.

If quantitative targets had been set before the project commences, success of the project by looking at the discrepancy between the targets and actuals can be measured. The four perspectives are namely financial perspective, implementation team perspective, end-user perspective and organizational perspective. They are discussed below in detail.

- **Financial perspective:** The objective is to complete the project within allocated budget. All expenses associated with the project should be measured. The target value of the budget is set in the beginning when the project is started. If the actual expenditure is close to the target value, the project is a success, financially. If actual cost is less in comparison to the budgeted cost, one needs to find out the reason. The expenses are recorded in a detailed manner. There could be some heads where under-spending has happened. If training is one of them, it may indicate that training was not done to the extent planned or the estimates were not higher. If the training cost has been more than budgeted, it could mean that the budget estimate was not right or more training effort was required than estimated. If consultancy cost has escalated, it may mean that the core competence expected from internal team is less than what was estimated. It could also mean that the amount of customization done has been more than expected. One can look at the different cost heads such as hardware, software and consulting. These measurements could provide lots of insight into the health of the project.
- **Internal process perspective:** The objective from internal process perspective is set while scoping the project such as integration of processes, bringing the transactions into ERP system and removal of bottlenecks. The objectives for implementing an ERP system were discussed in Chapter 3. It is also mentioned that the objective has to be defined quantitatively. For this perspective, the focus will be on the strategic objective. The objective may be to integrate all business units. The variables to be measured may include number of business processes to be covered by the ERP system, number of existing processes that have been discarded and number of processes that have been adapted from the ERP system. These variables will be measured to check the performance of the ERP system from internal processes perspective. If the measured figures are close to the targets or exceed the targets, the project has done well. If the targets could not be achieved, the reasons for the discrepancy would have to be identified.

– **Lower coverage:** Lower coverage would happen if the ERP system was not able to support the processes as expected. A lower number of the processes that were to be adapted from the ERP system than expected may indicate resistance for the change or misjudgement on the part of the implementation team.
– **End-user perspective:** The end-users of the system are the employees of the organization and indirect users are the customers of the organization. Operational benefits are what end-users will see. Objectives from end users perspective may include reduction in a particular cycle time, number of transactions that may be performed per unit time or number of problems in order processing. If the system has been configured properly and the users have been trained properly, variables associated with end-users would give a clear indication.
– **Preparedness for future:** There are three distinct parameters to judge the preparedness for the future. The manpower has to trained, the system has to support the business in the future, and the vendor has to update its ERP system to take care of the future changes in the business environment. The objectives could be set as—train people according to industry standard to make the organization largely independent of the consultants. One needs to set target and measured amount of customization. If large amount of customization has taken place, ERP system may not be able to evolve. It is a strong indicator for the organization to start looking for an alternative. The frequency of new release would indicate preparedness of the vendor to support the organization in the future as well.

Balanced scorecards can be created in tandem. A high-level scorecard may be created for the project manager and then specific cards can be created for each team member. The objectives for technical team would be different from that of business process owners. But all these scorecards put together would measure the success of the project on all four axes. It will enable us to capture various aspects of success of an ERP project.

High-level scorecards have also been created as shown in Figures 9.1 to 9.4. One should be able to create scorecard for people at every level. The average values would be obtained by consolidating the data from scorecards at the next level of hierarchy.

Financial Perspective		
Objective: Complete the Project Within the Budget		
Variable	**Target (INR)**	**Actual (INR)**
Hardware	75,000	
Consultancy	1,50,000	
Training	65,000	
License	1,25,000	
Project Team	60,000	
Miscellaneous	10,000	

FIGURE 9.1 Balance Scorecard for Measuring Success of an ERP Implementation Project from Financial Perspective

End-user Perspective		
Objective: Improve Operational Efficiency		
Variable	**Target**	**Actual**
Average Time for Completing a Transaction Average Number of Problems in Completing a Transaction Average Time for Obtaining a Report Average Number of User Complaints Average Cycle Time for Accounts Receivable		

FIGURE 9.2 Balance Scorecard for Measuring Success of an ERP Implementation Project from End-user Perspective

Internal Process Perspective		
Objective: Integrate and Improve Processes		
Variable	**Target**	**Actual**
Number of Processes Integrated Number of Processes Adapted from ERP System Number of Processes Abandoned Number of Bottlenecks Removed Number of Business Transaction Covered Average Workload of a User System Availability		

FIGURE 9.3 Balance Scorecard for Measuring Success of an ERP Implementation Project from Internal Process Perspective

Preparedness for Future Perspective		
Objective: Make the Organization Ready for Future		
Variable	**Target**	**Actual**
Training Hours per End User Training Hours per Developer Average Consultancy for a Module Number of New Release of ERP per Year Number of Modules Customized		

FIGURE 9.4 Balance Scorecard for Measuring Success of an ERP Implementation Project from Future Perspective

CONCLUSION

ERP project is like any other project that must be managed. There are many project management tools that are available in the market and extensively used for managing a project. A project management tool will allow us to create a project plan by defining tasks and sub-tasks, and to allocate resources to these tasks. One can do critical path analysis to identify the tasks that can delay the entire project and plan to pay extra attention to these tasks. As the tasks get completed, people would enter the details in, and it is recorded by the project management tool. Any deviation will trigger an action for the project manager. The division of the project into tasks and sub-tasks is guided by the ERP vendor methodology. Each vendor has a methodology that has been developed and refined, based on their experience with ERP projects. The objective is always to complete the project within budget and on time.

The success of an ERP project is judged from multiple perspectives. An ERP project that completes within allocated budget and time may fall short of the user expectations or may be just too difficult to use. The system may just not deliver the benefit the organization expected from the system and hence may be a failure in spite having been completed on time and within budget. There are many cases reported in the literature about the failure of ERP projects. Wrong ERP package selection, wrong implementation partner, not paying enough attention to people issues or wrong technology selection are some of the top reasons for failures. In order to avoid a failure, the project team should identify major risks for their project and prepare a mitigation and management plan.

Balanced scorecard is used for assessing the performance of an ERP project after the system goes live. The performance has to be measured from financial perspective, end-user perspective, internal process perspective and future preparedness perspective.

EXERCISES

Check Your Understanding

1. What does the statement, 'ERP project has to be managed like any other project' means to you? How will you manage an ERP project?
2. Why does success of an ERP system depends on multiple factors? What are important factors for measuring success of an ERP system?
3. What are the critical success factors for an ERP project? Explain each factor briefly.
4. What is a risk? Why should the risk mitigation and management is required for an ERP project?
5. How can one use a balanced scorecard to measure success of an ERP project after it has gone live? Prepare a scorecard for a person who handles sales order in the organization.

Apply Your Understanding

1. You have been working with an organization from the beginning of this book. Identify an information system that has been deployed recently.
   - (a) Find out the factors that were important for the success of the system. Is the system considered a success?
   - (b) What were the risks associated with the project? Was there a mitigation and management plan?
   - (c) Find out the measurements that were taken during the project. How were these measurements used?

ENDNOTES

1. Kim Girard and Melanie Austria Farmer, *Business Software Firms Sued Over Implementation*, http://news.cnet.com/Business-software-firms-sued-over-implementation/2100-1001 3-232404.html (2011) November.
2. For more details on the project refer to Peter Buxbaum, *Lawsuit Against an ERP Consulting Firm Could Signal More Litigation for the Industry*, http://www.techrepublic.com/article/lawsuit-against-an-erpconsulting-firm-could-signal-more-litigation-for-the-industry/5033891 (2011), November.
3. Keith Regan, *PeopleSoft Sued for 'Faulty' ERP Rollout*, http://www.technewsworld.com/story/33273.html?wlc=1252431233 (2011), November.
4. Todd R. Weiss, *Hershey Upgrades R/3 ERP System Without Hitches*, http://www.computerworld.com/s/article/74008/Hershey Upgrades R 3 ERP System (2011), November.
5. M. Rosemann and Jens Wiese, 'Measuring the Performance of ERP Software: A Balanced Scorecard Approach,' in *Proceeding 10th Australian Conference on Information Systems* (1999), 773–84.
6. G. Stewart et al., 'Organizational Readiness for ERP Implementation,' in *Americas Conference on Information Systems* (2000), 966–71.
7. Project failure: *The Robbins-Gioia Survey (2001)*, http://www.systemsstudynotes.com/2010/04/project-failure-robbinsgioia-survey.html
8. L. Shaul and Doron Tauber, CSFs Along ERP Life-cycle in SMEs: A Field Study, in *Industrial Management and Data System*, 112(3), pp. 360-84.
9. D. Aloini, R. Dulmin and V. Mininno, Risk assessment in ERP projects, in *Information Systems*, 37 pp. 183–99 (2012)
10. R. Kaplan and D. Norton, *The Balanced Scorecard: Translating Vision into Action,* Boston: Harvard Business School Press (1996).
11. M. Rosemann and Jens Wiese, 'Measuring the Performance of ERP Software—A Balanced Scorecard Approach,' in *Proceedings of 10th Australian Conference on Information Systems* (1999), 773–84.

chapter 10

ERP and Related Technologies

LEARNING OBJECTIVES

After reading this chapter, you will be able to understand:

- Electronic Data Interchange (EDI)
- Supply Chain Management (SCM)
- Customer Relationship Management (CRM)
- Data warehouse
- Data mining

10.1 INTRODUCTION

ERP integrates business of an organization through a centralized database. The organizational data and transaction data are stored in the database. This data is a rich source of information. There are many software tools that would process the data and discover useful patterns. These techniques are referred to as *data mining*. The data from an ERP system may not be directly usable by data mining tools. The data may have to be pre-processed and made ready for data mining. A data warehouse is created from the ERP data that makes the data ready for data mining. An organization needs to interact with their suppliers for obtaining the raw material or semi-finished goods. They also need to interact with their retailers and dealers. These interactions may happen using EDI technology. Supply chain management (SCM) refers to managing suppliers and retailers. Customers are the reason why a business exists. The focus has changed from providing customer a product to providing a service built around the product. Customer relationship management (CRM) is the technology that helps an organization to manage its customers. CRM and SCM both integrate with ERP system and are collectively referred to as ERP-II. In this chapter, the technologies which are related to ERP technology are discussed.

10.2 ELECTRONIC DATA INTERCHANGE

Electronic data interchange (EDI) is structured data interchange between two applications running on two different computers that may be heterogeneous and belong to two different organizations. The sender may not know the application used by the receiver and the exact nature of the application. The sender will not have any control on the application running on the receiver's site. The structure of the data that is interchanged through EDI is predefined and agreed upon by the two communicating applications. EDI is used for communicating documents such as invoices, purchase orders, shipping requests and acknowledgements. The advantages of EDI are as follows:

- Data is entered only once and then transmitted in a directly usable form to the recipient whose information system may be very different from the sender's system.
- EDI reduces cycle time as data is transmitted in real time.
- EDI reduces paper work as documents arrive in electronic and usable form.
- The number of errors and chances of errors also gets reduced as data is entered only once.
- An indirect advantage of EDI is that both parties (sender/recipient) adapt standards for their documents.
- All above advantages together provide competitive advantage to both organizations involved.

10.2.1 EDI Standards

There are two popular EDI standards:

- ANSI X.12 or ASC X12
- EDIFACT International EDI OLE standard

Digital interchange of data that does not use either of these protocols is generally not treated as EDI. There are many other protocols such as XML, HTML and FTP for data interchange that are not treated as EDI. X12 and EDIFACT protocols occupy the application layer in TCP/IP protocol suite just like FTP, telnet, ping and SMTP. EDI protocol ensures peer-to-peer communication, reformatting the data if required (ASCII to EBCDIC for example), encrypt (decrypt) the data for security and perform error checking. E-mail is not treated as EDI as the data interchanged via e-mail is unstructured. Figure 10.1 is a simple depiction of EDI. There is a sender (who would be a receiver for other transactions) and a receiver (who would be a sender for other transactions). Both would install EDI system at their end that support agreed upon EDI protocol. EDI system interfaces with applications and network layer of TCP/IP. The application handovers the data to the EDI system. EDI system change the data in the format required by the corresponding EDI at receiver's end, perform the required encryption and other transformation to the data for communicating with transport layer (assuming that the communication is being done over TCP/IP which is the case most of the time). The data then travels to the receiver where transport layer handovers the data to the EDI system. EDI perform decryption and other required transformation to the data to make it suitable for the application. The data is finally handed over to the application. There is virtual communication between both applications shown with a broken line arrow in Figure 10.1. Virtual communication also takes place between both EDI systems. Such virtual communication is also termed as peer-to-peer communication.

ANSI X 12 Accredited Standards Committee (ASC) X12 was created by the American National Standards Institute (ANSI) in 1979 to develop what is now known as EDI standards. The protocol created by ASC is termed as ASC X 12 or simply X 12 or alternately ANSI X12. ASC X 12 has a set of over 300 transactions (documents) defined to transmit 300 different documents. The ASC members meet regularly to update X 12 transaction suite.

Electronic Data Interchange for Administration, Commerce and Transport (EDIFACT) is the international EDI standard developed under United Nation Economic Commission for Europe in 1986–87. The maintenance work and further developments of this standard is done through the United Nations Centre for Trade Facilitation and Electronic Business (UN/CEFACT) under the UN Economic Commission for Europe in the Finance Domain working group UN CEFACT TBG5. EDIFACT has been adopted by the International Organization for Standardisation (ISO) as the ISO standard ISO 9735. EDIFACT has a collection of 200 transactions/messages.

10.2.2 EDI Architecture

There are different ways with which EDI can be implemented. One is to install EDI in the organization, and the party with whom the organization communicates will also installs the system at their organization. The situation is shown in Figure 10.1. Another option is to avail EDI as a service from a vendor with whom one would communicate using e-mail (Figure 10.2). The party that one would communicate with, has EDI installed at their organization. The EDI system running at the provider's site would receive the documents via e-mail, extract the data from the document, put the data in the format that the receiving party expects, and then deliver the data to the receiving party. The reverse will be done to facilitate communication in the other direction. Third option is that both communicating parties avail EDI as a service from the vendors. The EDI service would then extract and convert the data to the desired format so that the communicating applications can use them without any human intervention. In the current scenario, EDI is becoming less popular and communication through Web sites over Internet is gaining popularity.

10.3 SUPPLY CHAIN MANAGEMENT

Supply chain management (SCM) is concerned with an efficient integration of suppliers, factories, warehouses, distributors and retailers so that the merchandise is produced and distributed in the following way:

- In the right quantity.
- To the right location.
- At the right time.

The objective is to satisfy customers' requirements at minimum cost. SCM systems focus on reducing lead time, redundant effort and inventory for minimizing the cost. All these efforts are required because production rate, demand and location of the demand for a product changes dynamically. All of the

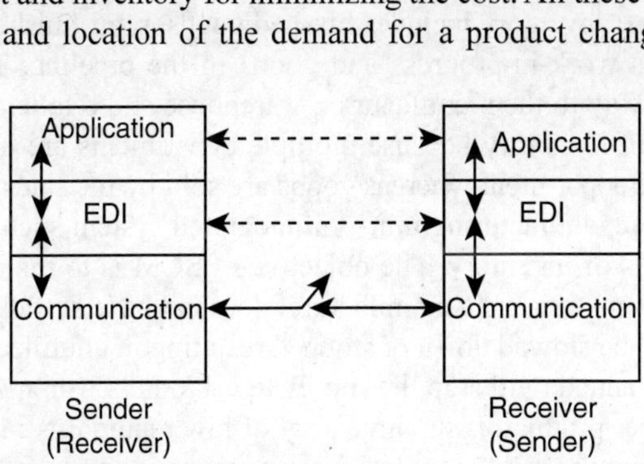

FIGURE 10.1 Generic EDI Architecture

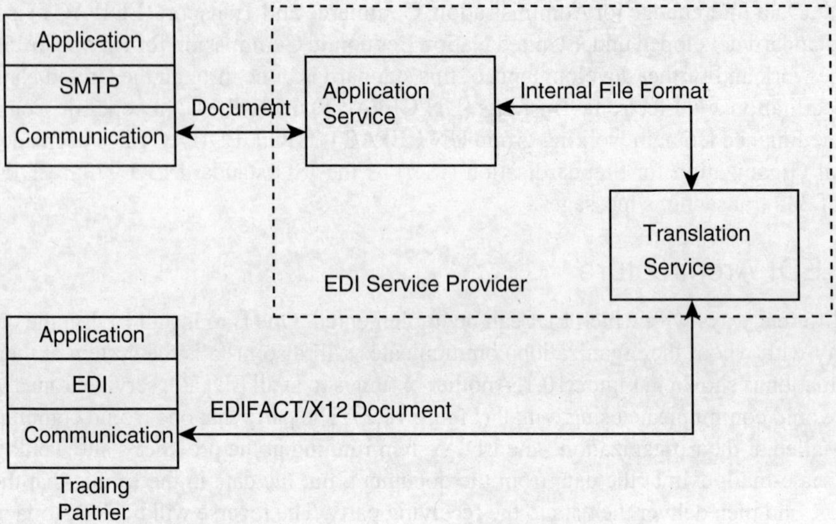

FIGURE 10.2 Architecture, When EDI is Provided as a Service by a Vendor

advanced strategies for SCM focus on global optimization and on managing uncertainty. Figure 10.3 shows the agencies involved in a supply chain. Suppliers of raw material and semi-finished products, manufacturer, wholesalers and retailers are all part of the supply chain. The raw material and semi-finished products flow to the manufacturer and the finished products flow downstream to the customers. The information about the demand, flows in the opposite direction to the flow of goods. It is simple to see that money flows in the direction opposite to the flow of goods. A manufacturer may obtain goods from various suppliers and may store the goods in multiple warehouses, a wholesaler may be served by more than one warehouse, and a retailer may also be served by multiple wholesalers. At each stage, there may be some amount of delay involved. The demand that is communicated by the retailer to the manufacturer or anticipated by the manufacturer based on the historical data may be different from the actual demand. In order to meet the customer demand while keeping the cost under control, a SCM system must handle the following key issues.

- **Inventory management:** Inventory includes finished goods, semi-finished goods and raw material. Inventory also includes work-in-progress and goods in the pipeline. The goods in the pipeline include goods on their way to the manufacturer, warehouse and retailer. It is a challenging task to know the exact levels of inventory because multiple departments are involved. The procurement is done by the purchase department whereas goods are sold by the sales department. The work-in-progress happens in the manufacturing unit. An integrated system such as ERP makes it possible to know the exact levels of inventory. The objective of SCM is to maintain appropriate levels of inventory. Consider raw material, if a manufacturer does not have sufficient raw material available, production may have to be slowed down or stopped resulting in unutilized manufacturing capacity. Production, less than planned, will stop the supply to customers who may either start complaining or may switch to another product. If the inventory of raw material is more than required, the carrying cost of raw material adds to the cost of the product resulting in reduced project margins. The objective is to achieve appropriate levels of inventory.

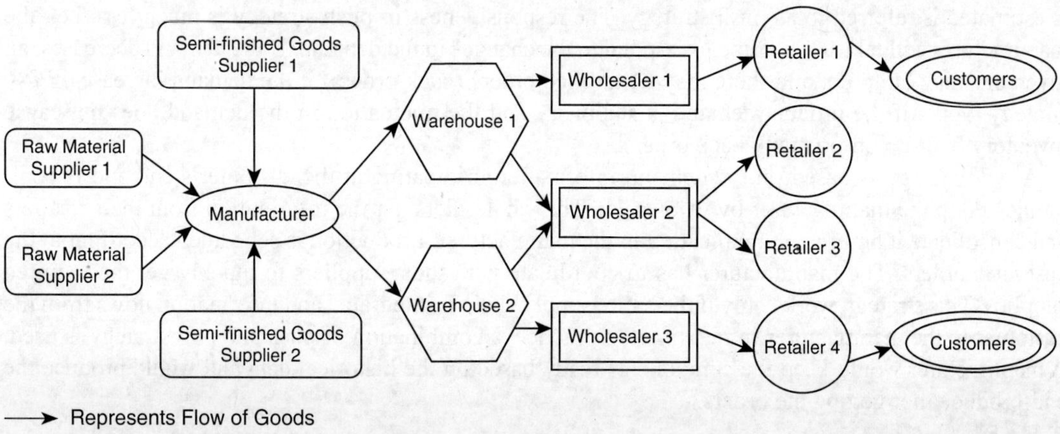

FIGURE 10.3 Agencies Involved in a Supply Chain [Flow of Money is in the Reverse Direction (not Shown in the Figure]

- **Facility location:** Facilities include the manufacturing facility, distribution centres, retailers and warehouses. Locations of facilities have a bearing on the cost of transportation and manufacturing. Transportation cost is kept under control by economies of scale, i.e., the transportation cost is less when more is transported. If an organization has too many warehouses, then the cost of transportation to the warehouse and from warehouse to the retailer or the customer may become too high. The cost of the warehouse and their maintenance will also be prohibitive. The same argument holds true for manufacturing facility and distribution centres. The objective is to locate facilities at optimal locations. As the demand and supply both are uncertain, it is not possible to even define the optimal locations for various facilities. But if an organization has an ERP system, the past data can be utilized to estimate demand and used for better decision making.
- **Forecasting:** Can we predict the demand? If we know the demand, we can work towards matching the supply with demand, by adjusting manufacturing schedules and quantity.

The demand is generated by the customers, i.e., communicated to the manufacturers by retailers through wholesalers. Customers do not come to the retailers to first announce their demands and then come later to pick up the product. The retailer has to anticipate and communicate the demand early enough to get the supply to meet the actual demand. One way is to use the past data to predict the future demand. Other method is to take average of the past data. The parameters involved are the time duration over which the average is taken and the weight assigned to the past data. The recent data may be assigned more weight than the older data. There are forecasting tools based on simulation, statistical analysis and artificial intelligence. These tools forecast and adapt the parameters to reduce the error in the actual demand and the forecast. The difference between the forecast and the actual demand would never be zero. Bursty demand during festival seasons and low demand during monsoon must be accounted for. There are other factors that will make a perfect match impossible—inexact data about inventory, pending orders, uncertainty in lead time, transportation time and availability of raw material.

There are many tools that implement various methods to forecast the demand. ERP systems provide these tools. One can also buy standalone forecasting software tools. The strategy when demand is estimated is referred to as push strategy. The responsiveness in push strategy is much less, i.e., the manufacturer will take a long time to respond to the changes in the demand. If the demand decreases, an inventory may build up; and there may be unfilled orders (back orders) if the demand increases. *Push* strategy works if the product demand is stationary and the fluctuation in the demand does not cause inventory built-up or too many back orders.

A *pull* strategy is based on the demand information originating at the customer's end and is communicated to the manufacturer by wholesaler. The wholesalers get the information from their retailers and consolidate it before communicating to the manufacturer. Production is scheduled according to the customer orders. The manufacturer has to coordinate with their suppliers to quickly get the required supplies. This strategy works only if the entire supply chain is integrated and information flows from the customer to the manufacturer in real time. In practice, a combination of push and pull strategy is used. A manufacturer would keep the components ready based on the historical data and would produce the end-product after getting the orders.

10.3.1 Role of IT in SCM

Figure 10.3 shows all the agencies involved in the supply chain of a manufacturing organization. The figure also shows the material flow among various agencies. The information flows in the reverse direction of the material flow. The role of IT in managing flow of goods and information is discussed in this section.

EDI is discussed in Section 10.2 that is used for information interchange between two parties when both use different systems. EDI would help supplier receive orders from the manufacturer in real time. The distributors and retailers can also use EDI to communicate with manufacturers and with each other. Another option would be to use web-based services to let the supplier see the purchase orders and update the status of the order. A similar interface can be provided for the customers where they can upload their orders, and manufacturer and other concerned parties get to see the orders.

Global Positioning System (GPS) can be used to track the location of goods while in transit. The GPS system can be integrated with the ERP system of the manufacturing organization and other agencies. The sales department will use this information to answer queries regarding the status of their orders. The procurement department of the manufacturer would know the location of the raw material.

RFID is another technology that can help the SCM. When the goods enter the manufacturer's premises that have RFID tags associated with them, the data gets entered into the ERP system automatically without anyone having to enter the data manually. Same way, when goods arrive at the warehouse or retailers premises, the data about the material would become part of their information system automatically.

ERP system would help the manufacturer in keeping track of the inventory and customer orders. An ERP system would also help the manufacturer in forecasting the demand based on the historical data. The performance of the forecasting algorithm can also be checked against the actual demand, and the parameters of the algorithm may be adjusted for better performance.

Warehouse Management Systems (WMS) is another IT system that can be used to manage a warehouse better. A WMS provide functions for controlling storage and material movement in the warehouse. WMS is also part of large ERP systems. One can define logical storage locations for storing the material and goods. The material can be reserved for picking up later for delivery through WMS. Once the material is removed from the warehouse, the corresponding data in the ERP system is modified.

There are specific software solutions for transportation planning, inventory positioning and load planning. These are decisions made at tactical levels. Such solutions would integrate with ERP system and get the data which are used for analysis and decision making.

It remains a challenge for most of the organizations to seamlessly integrate the suppliers, wholesalers and retailers and to maintain accurate data across entire supply chain in real time. Every software adds to the cost, and overheads to the system. But the SCM systems have considerably reduced the lead time for pull-based supply chains from 90 days to 3 days in last 50 years.

10.4 CUSTOMER RELATIONSHIP MANAGEMENT

An organization deals with a potential customer (marketing), a customer (sales) and an existing customer (after sales). The objective of marketing department is to turn a potential customer into a customer. The sales department would like to serve the customer to their satisfaction. A company can serve its customers better by knowing them and their requirements. A customer expects a product that meet their requirements in terms of functionality and quality. A customer would like to find the product on the shelf when they go for shopping of the product or would like the product to be delivered to them in a timely manner. If a product requires after sales service, customer expects the company to honour its service level agreement (SLA) and provide service within agreed time. CRM refers to IT solutions that cover all these activities of the organization. CRM covers end-to-end customer interface with the company. CRM plays different roles for a customer, marketing team, sales team and after sales service team. The management would also like to get reports through its CRM system for strategic planning. The roles of CRM from different perspectives are described below.

Customer's perspective: CRM provides an interface to the company. A company aims to achieve the following through its CRM system.

- To provide information about the product and services through a Web site.
- To provide web interface to the customer for placing and tracking an order.
- To provide a web interface for lodging a complain.
- For customer support.

Marketing team's perspective: Marketing force of a company would like to use CRM to answer the following questions:

- Who should we target as potential customers?
- How should we reach out to potential customers?
- How successful our efforts have been?
- Are our efforts cost effective?

Sales force perspective

- Orders that have been received.
- Status of the orders.

After sales service team's perspective

- What are the complaints?
- What is the status of complaints?
- What is the schedule of after-sales services?

Management's perspective

- Who are our loyal customers?
- Who are our major customers?

CRM would only be able to answer all these questions if the sales data is entered into the CRM system. Let us consider a manufacturer who sells its products through retailers. The order details would provide only retailers data and not the customer data. If the manufacturer wants to get customer data, a CRM is required that would capture the required information about the customers from the point of sale (POS). It is not hard to see though that this level of integration would be difficult to achieve. Each retailer may use the manufacturer's system directly or installs a system that provides data to the manufacturer. In both the cases, the reliance on the communication network is heavy. The security and privacy issues also surface in the first case. In the latter case, retailers wish to share the data and the data compatibility are the issues to be dealt with. Customers may not always be willing to provide their details.

If manufacturer sells through wholesalers, there is no way to get customer data from sales orders.

Why would manufacturer ask the above questions? If loyal and major customers are known, certain schemes may be launched for these customers. It is well established that retaining a loyal customer is much less expensive than acquiring a new customer. All the questions that are raised so far can provide valuable information to the middle- and the high-level management. They can use this information to adapt their business strategy. The management can get a consolidate picture from CRM and analyse their performance. Some of the sample questions that may help the management are the following:

- What are the characteristics of our customers?
- Are there certain types of customers who stay away from us?
- Are there certain types of customers who are price sensitive?
- Are there certain products that customers with specific characteristics buy?
- Can we adapt our marketing strategy to reach out to more customers?
- Do we need to move from mass marketing to individual marketing?
- Is our marketing strategy cost effective?
- Has the customer characteristics changed in last one year?
- Should we expect change in customer characteristic in next six months?

These questions can be answered by data mining the customer data and specify the purchase they made. The organization may adapt their business strategy based on the answer to these questions.

10.5 DATA WAREHOUSE

A data warehouse is subject-oriented, integrated, time-variant and *non-volatile collection of data used in support of management decision-making process.*[1] Data stored in a data warehouse is used by knowledge workers for strategic decision making.

Data warehouse is used to organize data in terms of subjects such as customer or product (subject oriented). Recall that the database associated with an ERP system stores operational and transactional data of company's ongoing operations. Data mart is a specialized version of data warehouse where data is stored for a specific purpose. One can create multiple data marts from a data warehouse and a union of many data marts would result in a data warehouse. The data for data warehouse may come from company's database, external sources such as competitor's reports, marketing agency's reports which is then integrated and kept in the data warehouse (integrated). The data in the data warehouse is associated with time, and as the new data is brought in, the old data is archived (time-variant). Consequently, one can ask questions such as what was the sale of item-A during first quarter in the north zone in year 2010. The data once put in the data warehouse is never modified (read only) that makes the data non-volatile.

The data may be removed after it has attained certain pre-specified age. For instance, the data older than four years may be deleted from the warehouse and new data may be brought in. The grain size may be a month or three months.

The relational database management systems record organizational transactions whereas data warehouse supports and facilitate management-level decision making. Data warehouse is created to facilitate and support management level decisions that are based on historical data. For instance, management may decide to analyse sales data of the organization. It is not hard to see that historical data spanning over from few months to few years would be required. Management would like tools that are easy to use and virtually require no training to render the required data in required format. A data warehouse is characterized by the following:

- The data warehouse is for strategic decision making.
- The warehouse data is integrated.
- The warehouse contains historical data over long time horizon.
- The warehouse data is oriented around various subjects.
- The warehouse data is mainly read-only with periodic batch updates from operational data sources.
- The data warehouse contains data with several levels of details such as current details data, old detail data, lightly summarized data and highly summarized data.
- The data warehouse is characterized by and optimized for read-only transactions.
- One of the popular architecture for data warehouse is a three-tier architecture.
- The applications that run on a data warehouse include OLAP, data mining tools and query tools.

Let us look at the architecture of a data warehouse.

10.5.1 Architecture of Data Warehouse

The most popular architecture for a data warehouse consists of three layers referred to as three-tier architecture. The layers are as follows:

- Application layer
- OLAP server
- Data warehouse

The architecture is shown in Figure 10.4. The figure shows only the data flow from lower layers to higher layers.

The application layer consists of application tools that are categorized as follows:

- Data mining tools
- OLAP tools
- Query tools
- Graphic tools

Data mining tools are discussed in Section 10.6. OLAP supports roll up and drill down operations for providing consolidated view and detailed view of the data, respectively. For example, one may have a view that shows sales data for each zone, each quarter and each product category. A drill-down view may show data for each product in selected category or for each month in selected quarter. The data may be shown as a labelled cube or a table.

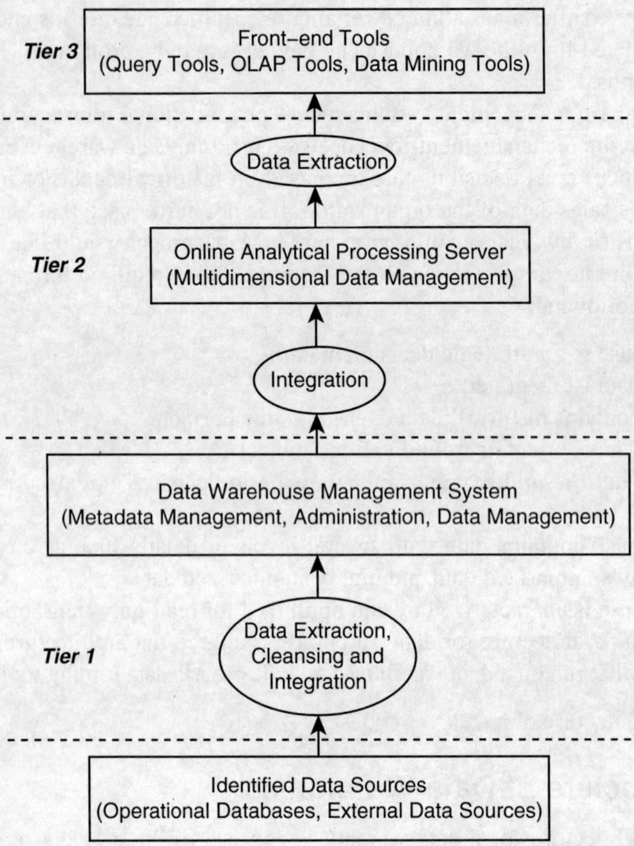

FIGURE 10.4 Three-tier Architecture for Data Warehouse

OLAP server receive requests and provides multidimensional data to the application layer tools. OLAP server is optimized to answer queries using multidimensional data. OLAP server extracts data from the layer below, aggregates it and organizes it to optimally answer the queries expected from the application layer.

The data warehouse layer is responsible for extracting, cleaning and integrating the data from the layer below. The data in this layer is generally stored in RDBMS. This layer is also responsible for retiring the old data and bringing in the new data.

10.5.2 Process of Creating a Data Warehouse

The steps involved in the data warehouse design are the following:

- **Identify data sources and data acquisition policy:** The data for data warehouse may come from company's database, external sources such as competitor's reports, marketing agency's reports which is then integrated and kept in the data warehouse. The decision about the sources should be

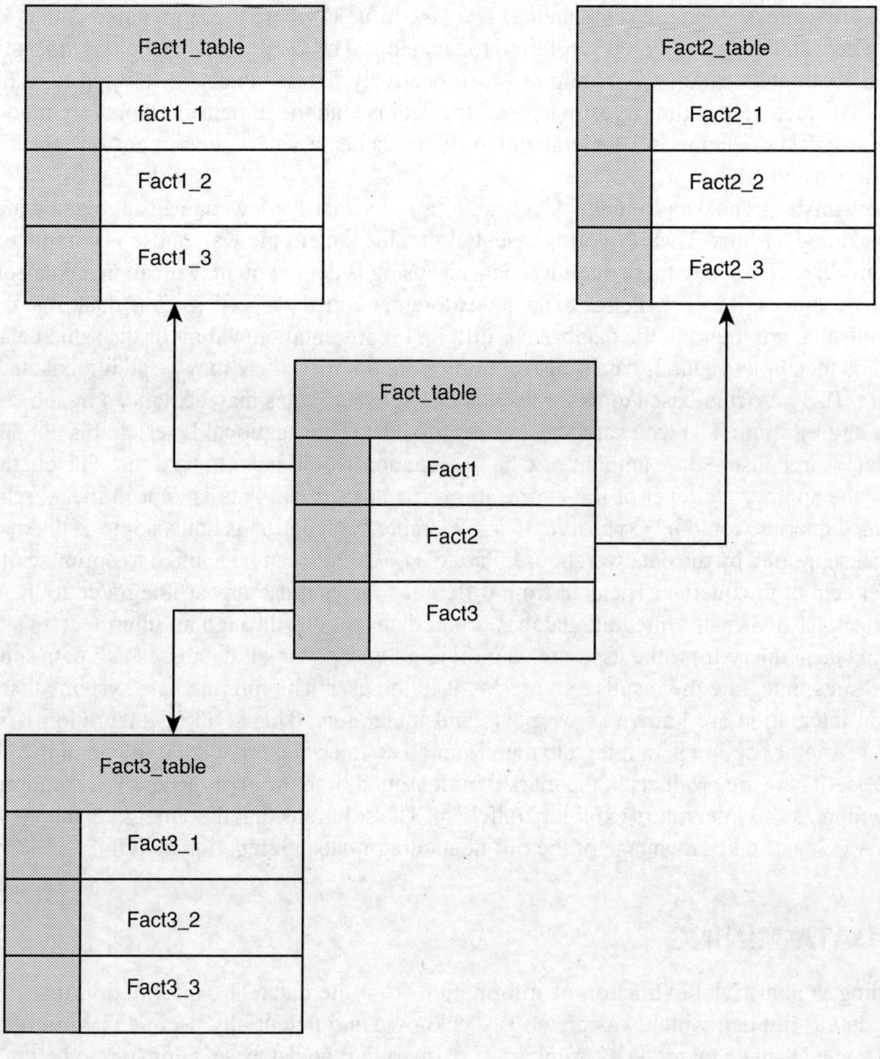

Figure 10.5: Star Schema for Data Warehouse

made, based on the requirements. The person/team/department responsible for providing the data should also be identified and told about the data required. The frequency for receiving the data and the medium for the data should also be decided and communicated.

- **Data warehouse design:** Data warehouse has to be designed in just the same way a relational database system is designed to meet the objective of the system. The following two schema are used for representing data in a warehouse:
  - Star Schema
  - Snow Flakes Schema

Figure 10.5 shows a generic star schema. The *fact_table* is where the aggregated data is kept. This table where all the data is stored is referred to fact table. The *fact1_table* and *fact2_table* store information about the attributes *fact1* and *fact2*, respectively. These tables are referred to as dimension tables. The fact table is the largest where all the data is, and the dimension tables are much smaller. The snow flakes schema is a generalization of star schema where the dimension tables may also have dimension tables.

- **Data cleansing:** The data from the data warehouse is primarily viewed in an aggregated manner and for making decisions. Therefore, it is essential that the data in the warehouse is complete, accurate and error free. To ensure these qualities, data cleansing is done. You may recall that data comes from different sources. It is a challenge to achieve aforementioned properties of the data. Just think of all the nulls that are found in the database or different representation/coding of the same data, missing data and incomplete data. If data is also coming from flat files, there may be additional challenges to handle. There are rule-based tools for data cleansing where rules may be defined by the users.
- **Data aggregation:** The data sources have detailed data (transactional level) that is not appropriate for data warehouse. Some amount of data aggregation would have to be done. The challenge is to know the appropriate level of the aggregation. If transactional data is kept in the warehouse, aggregated queries would be expensive. If considerable aggregation is done, some of the queries may not get supported by the data warehouse. Pareto's 80/20 rule can be applied to optimize the data for 80 per cent of the queries. The data from different sources must appear integrated to the user. One approach is to virtually integrate databases and data sources through an intermediate system that would take a query from the user, create individual queries for all databases and data sources, collect results, integrate the results and present it to the user. The intermediate systems that facilitate virtual integration are known as wrappers and integrators. This style of integration is very inefficient. Another option is to integrate data from all sources and organize it in one unified relational database. There are products in the market built around both the approaches. The solutions built on the wrappers and integrators exploit parallelism. The solutions that first integrate, then populate the data warehouse take advantage of the offline nature of data aggregation activity.

10.6 DATA MINING

Data mining is non-trivial extraction of information from the data. The information that is extracted from the data is implicit which was previously unknown and potentially useful. The information cannot be extracted using a query. Data mining is not querying the database. Human interaction is also an integral part of data mining. Data mining overlaps with the following:

- Machine learning
- Neural networks
- Genetic algorithms
- Clustering, segmentation and statistical techniques

The main objective of data mining is to discover the unknown patterns and present them in human comprehensible form. The issues in creating data warehouse are already discussed in Section 10.5. Data mining techniques are used when the data is large and may run into tera bytes. One of the essential requirements of data mining algorithms is efficiency and scalability. Data mining algorithms are semi-automatic in nature. The objective of a data mining algorithm could be the following:

Discover association rules: One of the popular terms used is market-basket analysis to discover associations and the following are a few sales data described:

- Milk, bread, juice
- Milk, juice
- Milk, eggs
- Bread, biscuits, coffee

The association rules mining would attempt to discover patterns and associations in sales. One option is to build all possible combinations of two items, three items, etc. and find out if some of these combinations are bought more frequently, and frequently enough to make us conclude that these items are actually bought together. In the above sample data, one can discover that milk and juice are bought together. The organization may use this information to offer a special discount or place these items in the store strategically. There are parameters such as confidence and support to discard rare patterns and discover frequent patters.

Build classification hierarchies: As an example, a computer company wants to find out the characteristics of customers who are likely to buy a computer. The company has the past sales data. They can now use a classification algorithm to divide the sales data into non-overlapping classes of customers based on their characteristics. The algorithm will start by dividing customers into classes based on some characteristic and check if the classes created are acceptable. The algorithm learns as it progresses to arrive at an acceptable classification hierarchy. Many statistical and information theory concepts are used to evolve the hierarchy. The company can then use the characteristics of the customers for preparing their marketing strategy.

Discover sequential patterns: Data mining can also help in discovering sequential patterns hidden in the data. For example, someone buys a camera, followed by an extra lens and then a memory card. These patterns once discovered can help the organization to decide their marketing strategy. E-commerce sites use this knowledge to make recommendations and send recommendation e-mails. The pattern associated with single item can also be discovered such as performance of a stock or market trends for a company. This knowledge can be used to make stock purchase decisions or forecast the demand.

There are many other techniques to analyse data and discover interesting patterns in the data. The discussion of data mining techniques is not exhaustive. Efficiency and scalability are the two main concerns of data mining algorithm. A new set of algorithms are being developed which analyse the data when it is generated, such as network traffic without storing the data. These algorithms are known as data streaming algorithms. Data mining is a relatively a new field and is developing fast. Business Intelligence (BI) is the latest field that aims to analyse the data for making business decisions.

CONCLUSION

In this chapter, some of the technologies related to ERP systems are learnt. An ERP system holds the organizational and transactional data. The related technologies help the organization to integrate customers using CRM and suppliers using SCM. ERP, SCM and CRM together are referred to as ERP-II. The available data is a rich source of information. There are techniques for analysing data to improve decision-making process. Data warehouse is the technology that transforms the transactional data into the form that is used for analysis. The analysis technology and techniques together are referred to a as data mining.

EXERCISES

Check Your Understanding

1. What is electronic data interchange?
2. What role does supply chain management (SCM) play in an organization? Explain SCM. How does SCM integrate with ERP?
3. What is customer relationship management (CRM)? Who are the users of a CRM system?
4. Explain data warehouse. What are the challenges in creating a data warehouse? What is the usage of a data warehouse?
5. Briefly describe data mining. What are various kinds of analysis done by data mining algorithms?

Apply Your Understanding

1. Find out how an organization shares data with another organization? Is it electronic data interchange or other mechanism? You may conduct a survey and do a web search.
2. Find out the commercial supply chain management (SCM) software. Does your organization use a SCM package?
3. Customer relationship management (CRM) is still a new technology. Do a survey to locate some companies that use CRM? What are the commercial CRM packages?
4. Visit some departmental stores to observe the purchase patterns of the customers. Do they seem to buy some items together? Are these items placed close by in the store?

ENDNOTE

1. W. H. Inmon, 'What is a Data Warehouse?' in *Prism*, 1(1), (1995).

chapter 11

Introduction to Commercial ERP Softwares

LEARNING OBJECTIVES

After reading this chapter, you will be able to understand the key features of following commercial ERP solutions:

- SAP ERP
- Oracle, Peoplesoft, JD EDWARDS
- MS Dynamics NAV/ Axapta
- BAAN
- RAMCO
- QAD

11.1 INTRODUCTION

We have already learnt that ERP solutions are semi-finished products that need to be configured. These products implement business processes and provide a backend database to support these business processes. The processes and the database reflects the industry for which ERP system has been built. For example, an ERP system meant for automotive industry will have different database fields than the one that is built for beverage industry. The processes will also be different for different industries. The ERP solutions for educational institutes will also be different from manufacturing and beverage industry. There are certain ERP softwares that cater to a particular functional unit of an organization, such as human resource management (HRM). These solutions provide complete functionality for HRM. The industries for which ERP solutions are available are shown in Table 11.1. Almost all the industries are supported by, and require an ERP solutions.

Depending on the requirements, a company will pick appropriate ERP solution. We have already learnt about the selection processes and selection team in Chapter 8. The selection team identifies various parameters that are important for their company and one important parameter is always functionality required by the organization. The selection team compares the functionality required by the company and the functionality provided by the ERP solution to pick an appropriate ERP solution. In this chapter, we will highlight features and functionality of major ERP softwares. It is not possible to cover all available ERP solution. Some of the products that we discuss in this chapter are market leaders and some are the representative industry solution. The information provided is mostly obtained

Table 11.1 Industry-specific ERP Solutions

Manufacturing	Service Industry
▪ Automotive	▪ Banking, Financial Services and Insurance (BFSI)
▪ Consumer goods	▪ Travel and transportation
▪ Chemicals	▪ Retail
▪ High technology	▪ Media and entertainment
▪ Industrial manufacturing	▪ Healthcare
▪ Oil and gas	▪ Communications
▪ Mining	▪ Aviation
	▪ Education and research
	▪ Engineering and construction
	▪ Fashion and apparel
	▪ Food and beverages

from the Web sites of the solution providers that may change over a period of time. A vendor may provide ERP solutions for multiple industries or may just specialize in a particular industry. SAP is a vendor that has ERP solution for automotive industry as well as for oil and gas industry, whereas Campus Dimensions provides ERP solution only for educational institutes. An ERP solution consists of a database, business processes, configuration tools and reporting tools. They provide graphical user interface (GUI) for conducting transactions. Let us first look at the Indian ERP market and then key features of major ERP solutions.

11.2 INDIAN MARKET

There are over 200 ERP solutions available in the market across the world. Market share in terms of revenue for the major players is shown in Figure 11.1. SAP is the largest ERP vendor with revenue of US$16 billion in year 2012.[1] SAP has close to 1,00,000 customers, Oracle and Microsoft are just right behind with 80,000 and 70,000 customers. These numbers are indicative only as each vendor has multiple product offerings and there are no reliable source of information. ERP market is growing and is expected to grow at the rate of 10–20 percent.[2,3] As shown in Figure 12.1, five major vendors have a share of 80 per cent and the remaining vendors have 20 per cent market share. SAP is the market leader in India and has a market share of about 50 per cent. Ramco is the largest Indian player among small enterprises that has a turnover of US$40 million, and market share of 10 per cent. Indian ERP market is also growing at the same rate as the global market. The total Indian ERP market is estimated to be about US$250 million. Since it is not possible to cover all the vendors and their ERP products in this chapter, we will cover only major ERP vendors and their products.

Companies in India are now investing heavily in IT and ERP solutions. Till date, ERP was considered a solution fit for large organizations but now small- and medium-sized enterprises are also investing in ERP systems. ERP market has grown from ₹ 1,495 crore in 2010 to ₹ 1,625 in 2011, at a rate of 9 per cent. Market share of SAP is 42 per cent, Oracle 16 per cent, Microsoft 12 per cent, and 31 per cent of others. SAP continues to be the leader in India. SAP and Oracle are popular with large organization. The Business By Design on cloud by SAP is popular among mid-size organizations. Microsoft products are popular with small to medium organizations.

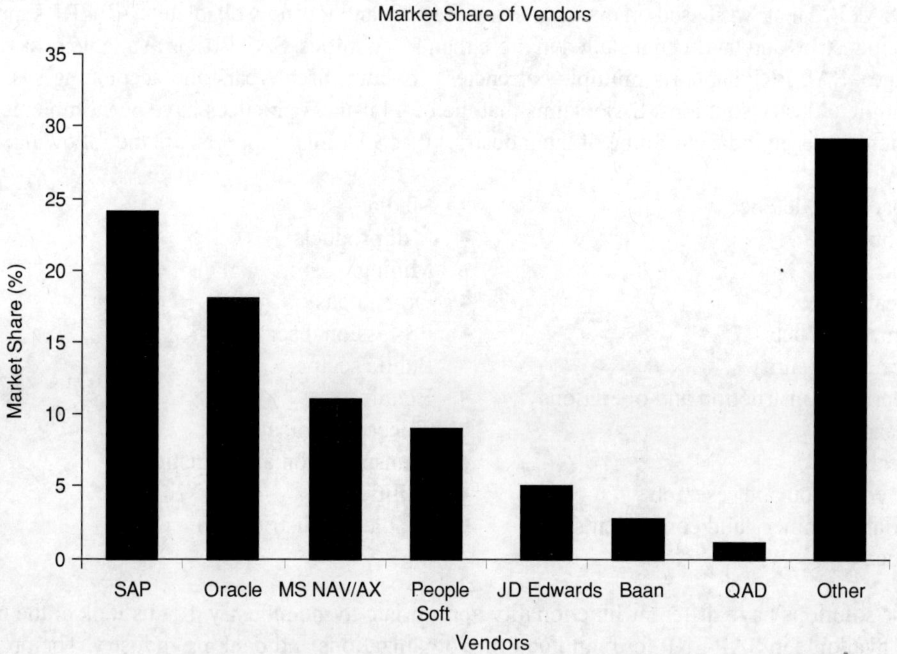

Figure 11.1 Market Share of Leading ERP Vendors

Indian government is supporting and promoting e-governance program in India which has also enhanced sales of ERP solutions. In 2001, reports contained a very dismal picture of ERP projects in India. The cost overrun and time overrun were reported close to 200 per cent. We discussed some of the reasons for ERP implementation failures in Chapter 1. The success rate of ERP implementations has gone up considerably since then. The percentage of ERP projects is 17 per cent of the all the IT projects in 2012 which was nine per cent in 2011.

11.3 SAP

SAP AG[4] is the world leader in enterprise software and software-related services in terms of revenue. Its headquarter is in Walldorf, Germany, with locations in more than 130 countries including India and the USA. SAP AG was founded in Germany in 1972. SAP AG has three ERP products:

- *SAP R/3* for large organizations. SAP is an acronym for Systems, Applications, and Products in data processing. This product has now been renamed to SAP ERP.
- *Business By Design* for small and medium enterprises.
- *Business One* for small and micro businesses.

Our discussion is focused on SAP ERP, as this is the flagship ERP product of the company. It supports multi-languages, currencies, financial calendars, financial reporting and tax laws. The present SAP ERP solution is based on client-server architecture (explained in Section 1.6, Chapter 1). Earlier version of the product was SAP R/2 that was based on mainframe architecture and it is now obsolete. SAP ERP supports more than 25 industries and has been installed in more than 50 countries. SAP ERP is available in as many as 25 languages. SAP ERP supports multiple currencies, tax-laws, fiscal years and accounting systems. SAP has multiple industry solutions. SAP claims that the best business practices have been implemented in their solutions for each industry. Some of the industries that SAP ERP supports, are the following:

- Aerospace and defence
- Automotive
- Banking
- Chemicals
- Consumer products
- Defence and security
- Engineering, construction and operations
- Healthcare
- High tech
- Higher education and research
- Industrial machinery and components
- Insurance
- Media
- Mill products
- Mining
- Oil and gas
- Professional services
- Public sector
- Retail
- Telecommunications
- Transportation and logistics
- Utilities
- Wholesale distribution

Each of these solutions have different functionality appropriate to the industry. Let us look at the modules that are available in SAP ERP for manufacturing organizations and banking industry. The product SAP ERP for a manufacturing organization has the following modules:

- **Logistics execution processes:** These processes support physical flow of materials. These processes are divided and supported by the following modules:
  - Material management (MM)
  - Sales and distribution (SD)
  - Production planning (PP)
  - Quality management (QM)
  - Plant maintenance (PM)
  - Service management (SM)
- Accounting and finance
  - Financial accounting (FI)
  - Controlling (CO)
  - Enterprise controlling (EC)
  - Fixed asset management (AM)
  - Project systems (PS)
- Human resource management
  - Human resource

The 12 modules listed above contain sub-modules to provide complete functionality. For example, FI module has the following sub-modules: General Ledger (GL), Accounts Receivable (AR), Accounts Payable (AP), Legal consolidation (LC) and accounting information system.

These modules provide complete framework for defining accounting system of an organization and carry out transactions. Similarly, other modules also have sub-modules. There are 72 sub-modules in SAP ERP, and there are close to 20,000 tables in SAP ERP to define the data requirements of an organization. SAP ERP can work with Oracle, SQL server, Ingress or Sybase. SAP AG has recently acquired Sybase that has now become preferred database server for SAP ERP. There are 1,000 standard business processes that have been documented and standardized for SAP ERP to reflect industry best practices. SAP ERP can support 2,000 other processes as well. SAP ERP provides login-based access. Every transaction is recorded and logged. Once a transaction has been saved, it cannot be deleted or modified. If a transaction is changed, a new copy is created leaving an audit trail behind. SAP ERP application server can be installed on Windows or Linux and their variants operating systems. SAP ERP application layer has been implemented in ABAP language that is proprietary language of SAP AG and is similar to PL/SQL language. According to each specific industry, the modules and sub-modules change. The modules for banking industry and automotive industry would be entirely different. The modules that we discussed above are core modules for a manufacturing industry. The product SAP ERP for a banking organization has the following modules and sub-modules:

- Financial performance management
- Risk and compliance management
- Sustainability
- Customer service contact centre
- Customer analytics
- Customer information management
- Marketing campaign management and customer segmentation
- Sales force management
- Charging and billing management
- Price optimization
- Loyalty management
- Lease management
- Corporate cash management
- Deposit management
- Loans management
- Collateral management
- Corporate loans
- Accounting and financial close for banking
- Real estate life cycle management
- Currency management and optimization
- Covered bonds
- Payment engine
- Rapid deployment solutions for banking

These modules are entirely different from the modules for a manufacturing organization. ERP is mostly associated with manufacturing because of its roots in manufacturing. But in last 15 years, scenario has completely changed. ERP solutions are available for every industry. You may visit Web site of SAP and look up the modules for different industries. We have listed modules for manufacturing and banking, two very diverse industries, above. It is not possible to go into details of each module. There are many dedicated books that explain SAP and its modules. You may recall that SAP ERP is a semi-finished product that has to be configured as per the functional requirements of the client organization. An organization may purchase license for a limited set of modules and get them configured.

Other systems such as CRM (customer relationship management), SCM (supply chain management), and business intelligence can be integrated to SAP ERP. SAP releases new versions of SAP ERP on a regular intervals to incorporate changes in the regulations and business practices.

Business By Design is a recent cloud-based offering from SAP for medium and small non-manufacturing organization who could be in retail or marketing etc. It is an integrated suite consisting of financials, human resources, sales, procurement, customer service, and supply chain. The modules that it offers are the following:

Financials

- Financial and management accounting
- Cash flow management

Customer relationship management

- Sales
- Service
- Marketing

Human resource management

- Organizational management
- Human resource
- Employee self service

Supply chain management

- Supply chain set up management
- Supply chain planning and control
- Manufacturing, warehousing and logistics

Supplier relationship management

- Sourcing
- Purchasing

Executive management support

- Business performance support

Project management

Compliance management

The discussion on SAP and its products should make it amply clear that a single company may have very diverse offerings in terms of functionality and architecture. One should carefully document requirements of the organization and then look for a matching ERP system.

11.3 ORACLE

Oracle[5] was founded in 1977 and was focused on providing relational database management system. In 1988, Oracle entered ERP market starting with accounting system and eventually building and releasing e-Business suite that consists of ERP, SCM and CRM. Turnover of Oracle Corporation is close to US$37 billion. Oracle, just like SAP offers industry-specific solutions. Oracle offers ERP solutions for more than 20 industries. These industries are listed below.

- Aerospace and defense
- Automotive
- Chemicals
- Communications
- Consumer goods
- Education and research
- Engineering and construction
- Healthcare
- Public sector
- Retail
- Travel and transportation
- Health sciences
- High technology
- Industrial manufacturing
- Life sciences
- Media and entertainment
- Natural resources
- Oil and gas
- Professional services
- Utilities
- Wholesale distribution
- Financial services

You will notice that Oracle supports almost all the industries that SAP supports except mining, media and insurance. ERP solution for manufacturing has the following modules and sub-modules.

Financials
- General Ledger
- Receivables
- Internet expenses
- Payables
- Assets
- iAssets
- Internet receivables
- Advanced collections
- E-Business tax
- Legal entity configurator
- Financial intelligence
- Web ADI
- Workflow
- Cash management

Distribution
- Procurement contracts
- Sourcing
- Purchasing
- iProcurement
- Landed cost management
- Services procurement
- iSupplier portal
- Procurement intelligence
- Advanced pricing
- Order management
- Shipping execution

Manufacturing and maintenance
- Engineering
- Collaborative planning
- Constraint based

Planning
- Service parts planning
- Bills of material
- Work in process
- Manufacturing execution

Projects
- Project costing
- Project billing
- Project management
- Project resource management
- Project collaboration

System for discrete manufacturing
- Project manufacturing
- Quality
- Cost management
- Inventory management
- Enterprise asset management

Sales and service
- Telesales
- Scripting
- Sales
- Quoting
- AR deductions and settlement
- Channel rebates and POS

Management
- Supplier ship and debit
- Service contracts
- Teleservice
- Universal work queue
- Install base

These offerings are close to what SAP ERP offers to manufacturing industry. These modules cover all function of a manufacturing organization. One can compare and contrast the modules and sub-modules of SAP and Oracle ERP with respect to their own requirements and then make a decision on what is more suitable. We have described selection process in Chapter 8. It is essential that an organization understands its requirements and selects the most appropriate ERP solution.

11.4 ORACLE PEOPLESOFT

Peoplesoft[5] was founded in 1987 with a focus on HRM. In 1995, it added solutions specific to academic institutions to its offerings. It also offers ERP solution for manufacturing organizations. But HRM and academic institutes solutions are its flagship solutions. In 2005, PeopleSoft was acquired by Oracle. PeopleSoft is also known for their educational ERP solution. Since we have already looked at modules offered by SAP and Oracle for manufacturing organizations, let us look at the modules of PeopleSoft for academics institutes:

- Academic advertisement
- Campus self service
- Contributors relations
- Hostel management system
- Financial aid
- Gradebook
- Recruiting and admissions
- Student administration
- Student financials
- Student records

PeopleSoft is not the only company providing solution for academic institutes. There are many more vendors such as Innovations Labs that has a solution for academic institutes called Campus Dimensions, Calibre Mindware Programming and eCampus etc. Oracle and SAP also have ERP solutions for universities and academic institutes. These solutions cover all aspects of an academic organization. We can clearly see that modules/functionality provided are industry specific.

11.5 JD EDWARDS

JD Edwards[5] (JDE) was founded in 1977 that was bought by PeopleSoft in 2002. PeopleSoft was then acquired by Oracle and hence JDE has become an Orcale company. The ERP product of JDE is EnterpriseOne and is for mid-size companies. JDE offers complete solution that consists of hardware, middleware, software and services unlike most other ERP solution providers who only sell the software and rely on implementation partner to select appropriate hardware, software and provide services. JDE claims that their ERP has low cost of ownership, requires less training and is a high return on investment (ROI) product.

JDE's ERP is available for the following industries: manufacturing, automotive, chemical, paper and packaging, food and beverages, fashion and apparels, home builders, oil and gas, commercial real estate.

Enterprise One offers the following modules and sub-modules for manufacturing sector:

Financial management
- Accounts payable and receivable
- Fixed asset accounting
- Advanced cost accounting
- Expense management
- Cash management

Capital asset management
- Resource assignment
- Equipment cost analysis
- Condition-based maintenance
- Preventive maintenance
- Work order management
- Real estate management
- Advanced real estate forecasting

Supply chain execution
- Transportation management
- Inventory management
- Warehouse management
- Advanced stock valuation
- Bulk stock inventory
- RFID processor
- EDI

Supply chain planner
- Supply chain business modeller
- Production distribution and planning
- Production scheduling
- Order promising
- Strategic network optimization

Manufacturing

- Manufacturing management
- Product data management
- Shop floor
- Requirements planning
- Quality management
- Engine to order

Mixed mode manufacturing

- Configure to order
- Engineer to order
- Manufacture to stock
- Manufacture to order
- Assembly to order

You can visit the Web site of JDE for further information and modules of other industry solutions. Web site of the vendor is a good source of information. The client list and their testimony also helps in making a decision. In order to get a clear idea if the product is suitable for you and fulfils your requirements, you will have to interact with implementation partners and consultants. Sometimes, multiple sessions may also be required.

11.6 MS DYNAMICS

Microsoft[6] was founded in 1975. Microsoft acquired Great Plains Software, Damgaard, Navision and Solomon Software between 2000–2002. Each of these companies had an ERP product. Microsoft renamed the products as follows:

- Dynamics AX (formerly Axapta)
- Dynamics NAV (formerly Navision)

These products have since evolved and multiple versions of each product have been released. All these product are for small and mid-size organizations. All these products provide the following functionality:

- Financial management
- Supply chain management
- Manufacturing
- Distribution
- Customer relationship management
- Sales and marketing
- Service management
- Human resource management
- Content resource management
- Shop floor control

Dynamics NAV is for small organizations who require at most 500 concurrent users. Dynamics AX is for larger organizations. AX can support as many as 3,500 concurrent users. NAV is very popular among small organizations and AX with middle-sized organizations. Both these solutions are for manufacturing organizations.

11.7 BAAN

The company was founded in 1978 and got into ERP space in 1990s. Its product was known as BAAN[7] that was renamed as SSA ERP Ln when the BAAN got acquired by SSA Global Technologies. SSA got acquired by Infor Global Solutions in 2006 and the ERP solution got renamed to Infor LN. The books and syllabus still use BAAN to refer to Infor LN. Infor LN is for engineering-based industries, including automotive, industrial equipment and machinery, high tech and electronics and aerospace and defence. The modules of Infor LN are the following.

- Global financial management
- Customer relationship management
- Sales and configuration order management
- Enterprise and supply chain planning
- Manufacturing control
- Sourcing and procurement
- Project management
- Quality management
- Service management
- Engineering data management
- Dynamic enterprise modelling

These modules together provide the functionality required by a engineering-based manufacturing firm.

11.8 RAMCO

Ramco[8] was founded in 1999. Its ERP product is OnDemand ERP. Ramco has ERP solution for the following industries: aviation, banking, financial services, insurance (BFSI), energy and utilities, equipment rentals and services, government, infrastructure, logistics, manufacturing, mining, professional services, and trading

The modules in the ERP system of Ramco for manufacturing organizations are the following:

- Manufacturing
- Supply chain management (SCM)
- Customer relationship management (CRM)
- Project management
- Analytics
- Financial management
- Human capital management (HCM)
- Enterprise asset management (EAM)
- Process control
- Advanced planning and optimization

Ramco has a solution for aviation industry. Its modules are very different from the modules of manufacturing industry.

Let us take a look at the modules in the ERP solution for aviation industry for managing its resources:

- Maintenance planning
- Hangar, shop and engine maintenance
- Reliability and engineering
- Technical records
- Human capital management
- Purchasing
- Inventory
- Warranty
- Maintenance
- Financials
- Third party maintenance
- Sales.

11.9 QAD

QAD[9] was founded in 1979. QAD provides ERP solution for global manufacturing companies specializing in automotive, consumer products, high technology, food and beverage, industrial and life sciences products. The modules of QAD ERP are the following:

- Financials
- Customer management
- Manufacturing
- Supply chain
- Service and support
- Enterprise asset management
- Analytics

CONCLUSION

In this chapter, we learnt about Indian ERP market. We have briefly looked at some of the popular and well-known ERP solutions. SAP is the largest ERP vendor followed by Oracle. There are over 200 ERP vendors across the industries. Some vendors focus on specific industries while many vendors provide solutions for multiple industries. There are global vendors and there are Indian vendors. The important thing is to pick the most appropriate ERP solution.

ENDNOTES

1. www.marketwatch.com/
2. www.amr-research.com
3. www.dqindia.com
4. http://http://www54.sap.com
5. http://www.oracle.com
6. http://www.microsoft.in
7. http://www.infor.in
8. http://www.ramco.com/
9. http://www.qad.com

Appendix A

Implementations in India

In India, many major corporate houses as well as small and medium enterprises have implemented ERP system and many more are in the process of implementing or considering an ERP implementation. A small list of ERP implementations in India is mentioned below. The source is mainly the Web sites of the companies and ERP implementations partners/vendors.

- Oracle
  - Escorts Limited—Agri Machinery Group, Faridabad
  - Sony India Pvt. Ltd, Bangalore, Chennai, Delhi, Kolkata, Mumbai
  - Jindal Vijaynagar Steel Ltd, Mumbai
  - Maruti Udyog Ltd, Gurgaon
  - BPL Ltd, Bangalore
  - Kirloskar Oil Engines, Satara, Maharashtra
  - Punj Lloyd Ltd. (Engineering Products), Delhi
  - Indian Aluminium Co. Ltd., Kolkata
  - Usha Martin Telecom (now Hutchison), Kolkata
  - GE India, Bangalore
  - Bharati Cellular Ltd., Delhi
  - Hikal Ltd. (Pharmaceutical and Agrochemical Major), Mumbai
- Baan
  - Aditya Cement
  - HDFC Bank
  - JCT Ltd
  - Amtrex
  - Dr Reddys Labs
  - Jindal Iron and Steel Ltd
  - Indian Aluminium Company Limited
  - Coats India
  - Escotel Mobile Communications Ltd.
  - TEI Technologies
- SAP
  - Goodlass Nerolac Paints
  - Apollo Tyres, 140 sales and distribution office in India SAP implementation
  - Bharat Forge—Essar Steel
  - Siemens
  - Arvind Mills
  - Mahindra and Mahindra
  - Samsung
  - Modi Alcatel
  - Oil and Natural Gas Commission (ONGC), India
  - Mohan Breweries and Distilleries
  - Gujarat Narmada Valley Fertilizers Company
  - Dr Reddy's Laboratories
  - GTN Textiles
  - Grauer & Well

- Eicher Tractors
- Nagarjuna Fertlizers and Chemicals Ltd
- ABB
- BPCL
- Numaligarh Refinery
- Cadbury India
- Colgate Palmolive India
- Siemens
- Volvo India
- Ranbaxy
- Times of India

■ MfgPro
- Emerson Network Power—Godrej

■ Orion (an ERP by ICICI Infotech)
- Pidilite

■ BPCS, an ERP from SSA Global Technologies (SSA GT)
- Monsanto which produces agricultural and biotechnological based products. The parent company in USA uses SAP.

■ ERsys of ISOF
- Ravissant Factory, (world's largest handmade silver manufacturer)
- ROULUNDS CODAN (India) Pvt. Ltd —Wisdom Pharma Pvt. Ltd
- Adhunik Yantra Pvt. Ltd
- Reed Medway, Ballabgarh

■ Ramco
- MMTC
- ICICI
- Bemis
- The Swatch Group
- Cisco
- Columbia Helicopters
- Schlumberger
- Hyundai
- Philips
- Numaligarh Refineries
- AP Government
- TTD, ICI
- Madura Industrial Textiles
- Jindal
- Northern Coal Fields
- Chennai Petroleum
- Amara Raja Batteries and Indian Airlines
- Shoppers Stop
- TVS Srichakra
- Steelage Industries Limited
- Jindal Iron and Steel Company Limited (JISCO)
- HDFC Bank
- Indian Airlines
- AFL Express
- Amara Raja Batteries Limited
- BSES
- Reebok India Company
- CavinKare
- Madras Cements
- MMTC Limited, New Delhi
- Philips Innovation Campus
- J.K. Ansell Limited (Aurangabad and Mumbai)
- Madras Cements Limited (MCL)
- Moser Baer Limited
- Fosroc Chemicals
- Gharda Chemicals Ltd
- Hyundai Motors
- Escotel Mobile Communication
- Cement Customer References
- East India Hotels—Oberoi
- Numaligarh Refineries
- Madura Coats
- ICICI
- Chennai Petroleum
- Florind Shoes
- ICICI Banking Corporation Limited
- ITC Limited (Greeting Cards Division)
- Government of Andhra Pradesh
- Tirupati Devasthanam
- Citigroup
- Group 4 Securicor
- Aditya Cement
- HDFC Bank
- JCT Ltd, Amtrex
- Dr. Reddys Labs
- Jindal Iron and Steel Ltd
- Indian Aluminium Company Limited
- Coats India
- Escotel Mobile Communications Ltd

Appendix B

Articles and Cases

When the work on this text book started, it was thought that the Indian scenario would be very different from the western scenario. After conducting multiple surveys, visiting many companies and interviewing many people, it soon became clear that the difference is not significant if at all it is there. RetailS has been used as the company throughout the book. Here is a list of cases that are widely used for class discussions.

1. Thomas H. Davenport, 'Putting the Enterprise into the Enterprise System', in *Harvard Business Review*, July-August, 1998.

   This article is now available in public domain. You can download it from the following URL: http://members.home.nl/c.schalkx/Papers\%20ARP/Davenport\%20(1998).pdf

   The article touches on all issues faced during an ERP implementation and provides illustrative examples. The instructor can use this article for class discussion after ERP systems have been introduced.
2. Nestle's Enterprise Resource Planning (ERP) Odyssey

   This case is available in public domain at the following URL:

   http://www.cio.com/article/31066/Nestl_eacute_s_Enterprise_Resource_Planning_ERP_Odyssey

   When you read this case, look for the signs and manifestations of resistance by the employees. Identify the mistakes that management made initially, and the steps they took to address the employees issues.
3. SAP Customer Success Story Consumer Products—Apparel and Footwear, Madura Garments

   This case reveals the objective set by the organization and how it was achieved. This case is available in public domain from the following URL: http://www.scribd.com/doc/42352262/CS-Madura-Garments

4. Vandelay Industries

   This is a case published by Harvard Business School. It has been written by Andrew McAfee under the supervision of Professor David Upton.

5. Darryl Romanow and Mark Keil, Prof. F. Warren McFarlan, 'Timberjack Parts: Packaged Software Selection Project', in *Harvard Business School*, Feb, 1998

   This is a very comprehensive case to illustrate ERP selection process in a multi-continental company. When you read this case, you will be able to identify with the techniques and issues discussed in Chapter 8.

6. Michael Hammer, 'Reengineering Work: Don't Automate, Obliterate', in *Harvard Business Review,* July-August, 1990

   This is an introductory article on re-engneering. You learn what is involved in re-engineering and its principles. The case brings out various challenges that a company faces during an ERP implementation; specifically change management, training, cultural changes, team etc.

   You may contact Harvard Business School for the cases 4–6. Teachers can register by going to their website and can access the case.

7. ERP implementation at BPCL

   The case examines in detail the ERP implementation exercise at BPCL. It focuses on the IT infrastructure put in place and BPCL's IT initiatives before the ERP implementation. One can buy this case for a nominal charge from http://www.icmrindia.org, case number ITSY005, 2002.

Index